For Reference

Not to be taken from this room

Aggression and Conflict

A Cross-Cultural Encyclopedia

ENCYCLOPEDIAS OF THE HUMAN EXPERIENCE

David Levinson, Series Editor

Aggression and Conflict

A Cross-Cultural Encyclopedia

David Levinson

ABC-CLIO
Santa Barbara, California
Denver, Colorado
Oxford, England

Library of Congress Cataloging-in-Publication Data

Levinson, David, 1947–
Aggression and conflict : a cross-cultural encyclopedia / David Levinson
p. cm. — (Encyclopedias of the human experience)
Includes bibliographical references and index.
1. Social conflict—Cross-cultural studies—Encyclopedias. 2. Aggressiveness (Psychology)—Cross-cultural studies—Encyclopedias. 3. Ethnic relations—Cross-cultural studies—Encyclopedias. I. Title. II. Series.
HM136.L46 1994 303.6—dc20 94-38978

ISBN 0-87436-728-X (alk. paper)

01 00 99 98 97 96 95 94 10 9 8 7 6 5 4 3 2 1 (hc)

ABC-CLIO, Inc.
130 Cremona Drive, P.O. Box 1911
Santa Barbara, California 93116-1911

This book is printed on acid-free paper ∞.
Manufactured in the United States of America

Contents

Preface

This volume is about the ways people hurt each other and about the ways people have learned to live peacefully together. The subject matter is defined broadly to include topics that fall within those general categories of human behavior called aggression, harm, conflict, war, peace, conflict management, and conflict resolution. I have defined each of these subjects very broadly so as to be able to cover as wide a range of topics as possible. *Aggression* is defined as an action by one person or group designed to harm another person or group. Various forms of physical (violent), verbal, and nonverbal aggression are covered. *Harm* is defined to include emotional harm such as embarrassment or humiliation, social harm such as isolation or exclusion, economic harm such as infliction of fines, and physical harm ranging from pain caused by a slap to death. *Conflict* is defined as a dispute between two or more individuals or groups over access to or control of resources. These resources might be economic in the form of food, land, or wealth; political in the form of leadership or power; social in the form of prestige or status; or personal in the form of self-esteem. *War* is defined as armed combat between different political communities and includes war between different societies, between different groups within a society, raiding, and feuding. *Peace* is defined as the absence of violent conflict between different political communities. *Conflict management* is defined as the process and mechanisms used to prevent conflict from developing. *Conflict resolution* is defined as the processes and mechanisms used to end conflict.

Within these general categories, this volume describes many more specific forms of human behavior and customs. My goal is to provide a broad survey of aggression and conflict around the world. Thus, many behaviors and customs such as homicide, capital punishment, and ethnic conflict that are found in the contemporary United States are included as are many others such as song duels, feuding, fissioning, that are found mainly among non-Western cultures. Each behavior or custom is defined, its variant forms in cultures around the world described, its distribution (if this information is available) marked, and possible explanations for its occurrence or distribution discussed. Examples are provided from cultures around the world for each of the topics covered.

The information in this volume comes mostly from two major bodies of information. First are worldwide cross-cultural surveys that attempt to measure, describe, and explain human behavior and culture through the analysis and comparison of information collected on samples of cultures around the world. In these surveys the number of cultures sampled ranges from a few dozen to several hundred, with the cultures being a representative sample of the 3,000 or so cultures known to have existed in the last 200 years. The second information source is the "ethnographic record." That is, reports based on the anthropological research called ethnography, which describes the ways of life of cultures around the world. Some 100 cross-cultural surveys and several hundred ethnographies on about 100 cultures were consulted in compiling this volume. Specific sources used for each entry are cited at the end of the entry as are other sources that will provide the reader with additional information.

The focus of this volume and this series is cross-cultural. That is, the topics covered, the behaviors and customs described, and the cultures used as examples in the entries are mainly ones that developed and continue to exist to some extent beyond the bounds of Western Civilization. These cultures are ones that are often referred to as "primitive," "nonliterate," "preliterate," "traditional," "small-scale," "simple," "native," "indigenous," or "non-Western." Out of personal preference, I generally refer to them as either indigenous, native, or non-Western societies, cultures, and peoples. "Society," "culture," and "people" are used as equivalents to mean a group of people who are commonly recognized to be culturally distinct. Usually this group occupies a distinct territory, has its own language different from that of its neighbors, and the members of the culture believe that their culture is different from the cultures of other people. It is estimated that there are about 1,500 non-Western cultures around the world maintaining some aspects of their traditional culture and another 1,000 or so whose traditional culture has largely disappeared. These cultures are the primary focus of this volume and this series. For the most part, I have focused on customs that are still practiced in some cultures, although some that have disappeared, such as human sacrifice and head-hunting, are also covered in an attempt to be comprehensive.

In some ways, the articles in this volume are disheartening as they can be read as a lengthy list of the different ways people hurt each other. However, the articles also give us reason to be hopeful about the human condition as they show that not all cultures are violent and ridden by conflict, that peace can be the basis for a stable way of life, and that there are numerous ways to manage and resolve conflicts without resorting to violence.

Aggression and Conflict

A Cross-Cultural Encyclopedia

Advisors

Advisors are individuals who attempt to resolve disputes by giving both sides their advice and opinion. Advisors are similar to mediators, with the major differences being that with advising the process is less formal and the advisor's opinion is less binding on the parties. Although all societies use advisors to some extent, they are of considerable importance in dispute settlement in only about 10 percent of cultures. These cultures are ones that are small and kin-based and that lack leaders or a government with the authority to enforce its decisions. These decisions include those having to do with resolving disputes, so it is not surprising that in these cultures people rely heavily on self-help methods of conflict resolution, especially the use of physical coercion, both as the first response to conflict and when advising fails.

Advisors are usually adult men who are widely respected for their knowledge of basic skills such as hunting or fighting, are considered repositories of religious and cultural knowledge, and are effective public speakers. Their authority is a moral authority and derives from their own exemplary behavior, as well as from social prominence in the community, as they often are members or leaders of the dominant kin group. Because they enjoy both moral and social authority, their advice is often taken by the disputants, although there is no requirement that it be followed and no formal means the advisor can use to force them to do so. Status as an advisor is often only temporary, and an advisor will no longer be consulted when the basic skills on which his reputation is based decline or he is believed by other members of the community to have become too authoritarian, making him ill suited for the advisor role.

The Ona of Tierra del Fuego and the San of Botswana, two traditional hunter/gatherer cultures, rely on advisors to help settle disputes within the community. For the Ona (a now-extinct culture in South America) it was the community leader who advised others involved in a dispute. In addition to advising, he also decided when to move the settlement, when to hunt, and when to unify the kin groups into a single community. His authority derived from this central role in cultural decision-making, his own exemplary behavior, and his additional role as guardian of cultural traditions. While his advice was not binding, it was often followed and he was able to convince both parties to follow his advice by pointing to the importance of settling the dispute so as to preserve their personal reputations and the reputations of their kin groups. For the San, the advisor is a man of broad experience derived through contact with the outside world and knowledge of the traditional San way of life. Because of this experience, he is frequently called upon to settle disputes in his own and other households in the community.

The advisory process is initiated by both parties asking the advisor to help settle the dispute. The advisor then hears both sides in an informal setting and gives his opinion, which often emphasizes adherence to rules of conduct acceptable to the group. The parties may then choose to settle the dispute by following his advice or to ignore the advice. A dispute is considered settled when the wronged party is satisfied.

See also SELF-HELP CONFLICT RESOLUTION; MEDIATION.

Guenther, Mathias G. (1979) *The Farm Bushmen of the Ghanzi District, Botswana.*

Gusinde, Martin. (1931) *The Fireland Indians. Vol. 1: The Selk'nam, On the Life and Thought of a Hunting People of the Great Island of Tierra del Fuego.*

Newman, Katherine S. (1983) *Law and Economic Organization: A Comparative Study of Preindustrial Societies.*

AGGRESSION BY WOMEN

It is a common belief that women are less aggressive and less violent than men. Much psychological research supports this belief as does Daly and Wilson's study of homicide, which demonstrates that in all places at all times in human history men have been far more likely to murder than have women, and that men have been far more likely to kill other men than women have been likely to kill other women. For example, in Oxford, England, from 1296 to 1398 there were 105 male-male homicides and only 1 female-female homicide; among the Tiv of Nigeria from 1931 to 1949 there were 96 male-male homicides and only 3 female-female homicides; and in Canada from 1974 to 1983 there were 2,965 male-male homicides and only 175 female-female homicides.

This does not mean, of course, that women do not act aggressively. An example of a culture in which women are violently aggressive is found on Margarita Island off the coast of Venezuela. Violent aggression is considered normal female behavior by Margariteño women, who pride themselves on being physically strong *(guapo)* and aggressive and on their ability to use violence to maintain their authority. Women routinely fight with one another and hit their husbands, who never hit them. Female aggression on Margarita seems to be the result of frequent absences by men, who often travel or periodically move from village to village when they have more than one wife. Thus, men are of little importance and have little power, with women bearing the full responsibility for themselves and their families. However, the Margariteños are an exception, and in most societies men act like Margarinteño women when it comes to aggression.

Anthropologist Victoria Burbank's recent survey of aggression initiated by women against other adults in the community provides an overview of the breadth and nature of aggressive behavior by women. In the sample of 317 societies, in 137 societies there were one or more reported instances of aggression by women. This suggests that female aggression occurs in only 43 percent of the world's cultures. This is probably an underestimate, as in many societies covered in the survey female aggression may have gone unreported. And, there are also societies where women regularly engage in socially approved aggression (a form of aggression not surveyed by Burbank) such as infanticide or aggression in reaction to the death of a loved one. Still, it is likely that there are societies where aggression by women rarely occurs. In the 137 societies, aggression by women takes a variety of forms. The types of aggression displayed by women and the percentage of societies where each type of aggression occurs is as follows:

Verbal (quarrels, insults, ridicule, etc.): 82%

Physical (hitting, pushing, striking, burning, etc.): 61%

Property (objects destroyed): 12%

Nonverbal (exposure of body parts, gestures): 7%

Nonperformance (nonperformance of duties or expected behaviors): 15%

Threatening (threats of physical harm): 7%

Locking out (keeping a person out of the house): 1.5%

Unspecified: 37%

The Bellonese of the Solomon Islands provide an example of the range of aggressive behaviors available to women in a given society. Bellonese women are dominated by their husbands, who may beat them at will. In response to mistreatment by their husbands, Bellonese women have been reported to attempt to kill or actually kill them, hire assassins to do the job, pull a husband's hair, displace their anger by hitting their children, commit suicide, shout at or insult their husband, complain about his behavior to others, laugh at him in public, compose mocking songs that are then sung by others in the village, or isolate herself. The last five options on the list are nonviolent expressions of aggression and are far more common than those that involve violence. For Bellonese men, however, the reverse is true, and they are most likely to quarrel or hit.

As regards the targets of female aggression across cultures, other women are the most frequent target of aggressive behavior. Other women are the target of female aggression in 91 percent of the societies studied, while men are the target in only 54 percent. Women are usually the target of direct verbal and physical aggression and are more likely to have their property destroyed than men, who more often are the target of less violent forms of aggression such as nonverbal and verbal insults, nonperformance, and threats, as among the Bellonese. Women aggressing against other women is especially common in societies with polygynous marriage (where a man may have two or more wives at the same time). As might be expected, the combatants are usually co-wives who quarrel with each other because of sexual jealousy, access to goods and services provided by their husband, his taking an additional wife, and the defense of their children's interests against the competing interests of the children of the other co-wives. For example, among the Mam of Guatemala polygynous households are a difficult arrangement that rarely lasts. First wives are jealous of the sexual attention the husband gives to the often younger, more attractive second wife and angry about having to share family resources with her and her children. Second wives resent the power held by the first wife and are threatened by the presence of her children. And, when both wives have sons, the wives then become rivals over their son's rights to inherit a share of the husband/father's property. Because cooperation is considered important, the co-wives coexist in cold silence when their husband is at home, but when he is away they quarrel and fight. Disputes among co-wives also can involve their children in societies with polygynous families, as among the Igbo of Nigeria. As one co-wife reported, "If I want to fight a woman, I send my child to hit her child. Then I know she will come, and we will fight."

In societies with monogamous marriage, the fights occur most frequently between women who are sexual rivals for a man and between a man's wife and the "other woman." Among male targets, husbands are the most common, with female aggression directed at husbands in 43 percent of the societies with female aggression. Often, the aggression is triggered by the husband's adultery or the wife's suspicion of adultery. For example, among the Tikopia of Polynesia a husband who stays out all night is greeted by his stick-wielding wife who beats him about the legs and pinches him to draw blood, punishment he must endure silently for fear of waking the other residents of the household. Besides co-wives, other women, and husbands, there are no other categories of individuals who are regular targets of female aggression in cultures around the world. It is unusual (less than 10 percent of societies) for women to fight with blood relatives such as brothers, sisters, or their parents or against in-laws such as their husband's sister or brother.

A variety of explanations have been offered to account for both why women act aggressively less often than men and to account for why women act aggressively at all. These explanations point to the role of factors such as hormonal differences between men and women, the reality that in many societies boys are raised to be aggressive and girls to be compliant, and resource competition. Competition for scarce goods and services (including husbands or men to mate with) seems to be the most plausible explanation, especially when one considers that female aggression is directed mainly against other women, takes place far more often among co-wives, and in societies with monogamous marriage is directed at adulterous husbands or potential female rivals.

When it comes to aggression against people from other communities or societies, female aggression is even rarer than in their own communities. Despite the myth of Amazon women warriors who went so far as to cut off a breast so they could more accurately aim their bow and arrows, women warriors are extremely rare. In a sample of 67 societies, women participated in warfare in only nine, but in only two of those societies did women regularly participate in war and in no society did the number of female warriors equal the number of male warriors. Additionally, in most societies women are routinely excluded from involvement in other activities related to warfare, such as making weapons, planning war tactics, or participating in ceremonies in preparation for war. They often do participate, however, in ceremonies following war, including ceremonies to celebrate a victory and to make peace with the enemy.

Women are rarely warriors for two reasons. First, warfare, being dangerous and far from home, is incompatible with childbearing and childrearing responsibilities; the first of these two tasks always falls to women and the second often does in most cultures. Second, in most societies around the world, when a woman marries she leaves her home community and moves to the community of her husband to live with him and his family or near his family. Since warfare often involves conflict between the community a woman is born into and the one she now lives in, she would be caught in a situation of conflicting loyalties if she participated in warfare. The problem of conflicting loyalties due to intermarriage is a key control on women fighting in wars, and in the nine societies where women are warriors, men either marry women only from the man's own community or the group engages in warfare only with other societies, not with other communities in their own society. These marriage and warfare patterns remove the possibility of conflicting loyalties and create a situation where it is possible for women to be warriors.

While women are rarely permitted to be warriors, they often play a central role as peacemakers, intervening to stop battles, acting as emissaries between warring communities, and arranging and participating in peace ceremonies. Here, their cross-cutting ties to the two communities that keep them out of war make them ideal diplomats who have contact with and are trusted in both communities.

See also AGGRESSION IN REACTION TO DEATH; DUELS; HUSBAND BEATING; INFANTICIDE; INSULTS; PEACEMAKING; SOCIALIZATION OF AGGRESSION; SEX DIFFERENCES IN AGGRESSION; SUICIDE.

Adams, David. (1983) "Why There Are So Few Women Warriors." *Behavior Science Research* 18: 196–212.

Brown, Donald E. (1991) *Human Universals.*

Burbank, Victoria K. (1987) "Female Aggression in Cross-Cultural Perspective." *Behavior Science Research* 21: 70–100.

Cook, H. B. Kimberley. (1992) "Matrifocality and Female Aggression in Margariteño Society." In *Of Mice and Women: Aspects of Female Aggression,* edited by Kaj Björkqvist and Pirkko Niemelä, pp. 149–162.

Daly, Martin, and Margo Wilson. (1988) *Homicide.*

D'Andrade, Roy G. (1974) "Sex Differences and Cultural Institutions." In *Culture and Personality: Contemporary Readings,* edited by Robert LeVine.

Firth, Raymond W. (1936) *We, the Tikopia: A Sociological Study of Kinship in Primitive Polynesia.*

Henderson, Richard N., and Helen K. Henderson. (1966) *An Outline of Traditional Onitsha Ibo Socialization.*

Kuschel, Rolf. (1992) "'Women Are Women and Men Are Men': How Bellonese Women Get Even." In *Of Mice and Women: Aspects of Female Aggression,* edited by Kaj Björkqvist and Pirkko Niemelä, 173–185.

Levinson, David. (1989) *Family Violence in Cross-Cultural Perspective.*

Wagley, Charles. (1949) *The Social and Religious Life of a Guatemalan Village.*

Aggression in Folktales

Virtually all societies have folktales and in many societies the interaction between characters in the tales is often aggressive, not uncommonly resulting in injury or death to one of the characters. Folktales are an element of what anthropologists call the expressive domain of culture. Folktales are expressive in two ways. First, as fictitious stories they are a product of the creativity of storytellers. Second, they express indirectly various desires, wishes, fears, and anxieties shared by the members of the culture. Thus, from the point of view of the expression of aggression, folktales are a means of indirectly expressing aggressive wishes or fears that are too difficult to express directly in daily life.

Displacement and projection are the two psychological mechanisms at work in the expression of aggression in folktales. Displacement means that an individual transfers his or her aggressive feelings from the appropriate target of that aggression to a safer, more distant target. Characters in folktales are one such displaced target. Projection is the attribution to others of one's own feelings, wishes, or fears. In projection an individual often believes that other people will react to him as he reacts or believes he will react to them. For example, in projection a person who gets angry and wants to get even when others reject him will believe that if he rejects someone else they will get angry and want to reject him. Characters in folktales can be one such object of projection.

Folktales, although told and enjoyed by individuals, are a cultural phenomenon, as the underlying themes and motifs are understood by and have deep emotional meaning for all or most members of the cultural group. They rarely have the same meaning for outsiders, who nonetheless can appreciate their aesthetic qualities. Cultures vary from one another in the degree to which aggressive social interaction is a theme in their folktales. A survey of 187 folktales from 19 cultures indicates that in 63 percent of the cultures a majority of the social interaction portrayed in folktales is aggressive in nature. The following short tale of the Yanomamö displays the aggressive interaction portrayed in some folktales (Wilbert 1963: 233):

> The sun is a man and the moon is also a man. The two regard each other as enemies because of the occurrence which I shall relate.
>
> One day the moon told a man to go and look for firewood. The man went off to look for it. When he brought it, he did not please the moon, who wanted a great deal more. Again it sent him into the forest. The man realized that what the moon wanted was to eat him. Then the man fled. He ran to the sun in search of asylum and protection. The sun hid him. When the moon arrived in search of him, the sun said that it had not seen the man. The moon, angered, insisted and even wanted to search the sun's house. Then the sun burned its surface and from that came the scars which show on its face.
>
> The moon went to the other side of the world, and, while the sun sealed its friendship with man, the moon was his irreconcilable enemy. When the moon appears rose-colored, it is because it, along with its family, is eating men. The sun also has a family, but does not eat human flesh. Sometimes the moon hides in its house in order to plan a new campaign. During that time women are very much afraid and, in order to protect themselves, paint a likeness of the sun on their cheeks; they also commonly paint it on large stones which they find on the path.

If it is true that folktales like this one indirectly express fears or wishes about acting aggressively that cannot be expressed directly, cultures with aggressive themes in folktales should differ in some ways from cultures with nonaggressive themes in folktales. And they do seem to differ in two ways. First, cultures with aggressive themes are ones whose people often experience severe food shortages caused by droughts, storms, and other natural disasters. Reflecting their anxiety about not having enough to eat and their need to move about in search of food, these cultures have folktales where there is much unpredictable and capricious aggression and where the object of the aggression either flees or submits. In these cultures, aggressive folktales can be interpreted as a projection of the people's everyday fears about the harsh and uncertain nature of their environment and their lack of control over it. Second, in cultures with much aggression in folktales parents socialize their children to be nonaggressive by severely punishing all aggressive behavior such as fighting, disobedience, and disrespect. Here, both projection and displacement seem to play a role, with aggression in folktales acting as a "safety valve" for the expression of pent-up aggressive feelings that cannot be expressed against other people because of childhood experiences that inhibit aggressive behavior.

See also Humor; Supernatural Aggression.

Cohen, Alex. (1990) "A Cross-Cultural Study of the Effects of Environmental Unpredictability on Aggression in Folktales." *American Anthropologist* 92: 474–480.

Wilbert, Johannes. (1963) "Los Sanema [The Sanema]." In *Indios de la Región Orinococ-Ventuari* 11–20, 177–236.

Wright, George O. (1954) "Projection and Displacement: A Cross-Cultural Study of Folk-Tale Aggression." *Journal of Abnormal and Social Psychology* 49: 523–528.

Aggression in Reaction to Death

Aggressive behavior and feelings of anger and hostility are common reactions by survivors to the death of a loved one in many cultures around the world. A survey of 78 cultures indicates that anger is experienced and aggression is shown by survivors in 76 percent of cultures, and the percentage may be even higher since in some cultures such as the United States such emotional displays are hidden from public view. Anger and aggression as a reaction to the death of a loved one and as a normal component of the bereavement process result from the survivor being deprived of something he or she wants, such as the love, economic support, comfort, security, and companionship provided by the deceased and the uncertain future the survivor now faces. The basis of the anger survivors feel in many cultures is summed up in a mourning hymn of the Jivaro Indians of Ecuador:

My dear one,
my dear little husband,
why have you left me,
why have you abandoned me?
What will it become of me?

Aggressive behavior associated with death and grief and mourning cannot be directed at the object of the anger behind the aggression—the deceased—so instead it must be directed elsewhere, either at oneself or at another person or at an object. Rather than serving as alternative ways of expressing anger, these two patterns of expressing anger (at oneself or at others or objects) usually occur together. That is, if people in a culture customarily express anger in one of these ways, they will express it in the other way as well. This suggests that cultures differ, with some allowing the open display of aggression in reaction to death while others inhibit or control it.

The most common form of self-directed aggression is body mutilation. Ifugao women in the Philippines scratch their faces, Amhara women in Ethiopia also scratch themselves and may also hit themselves with rocks, and Abkhazian women in the former Soviet Union scratch their bodies, tear out their hair, and beat their heads against the ground. Self-mutilation is attempted in about a third of societies and achieved in about another third. As the above examples suggest, women more often mutilate themselves than do men, perhaps because women are more generally expressive; women also cry and wail more following a death than do men. Another form of self-directed aggression is prohibitions placed on the survivors that restrict their activities and inconvenience and generally inhibit the quality of their life. For example, Jewish law has been interpreted as requiring "Three days for weeping, seven days for eulogy, thirty days for pressing garments and haircutting." During the first seven days the mourner must stay at home and must not study the Bible, greet another person, bathe, shave, cut his hair, conduct business, or engage in marital sex. Over the thirty days he may not shave or wear new clothes, and for a year he must refrain from participating in entertaining activities.

Aggression directed at others or objects can take the form of seeking revenge on the person who caused the death (either directly or through supernatural means such as witchcraft), attacking others, sacrificing animals, and destroying property such as a dwelling, fields, or possessions of the deceased. Since in many cultures all or most deaths are believed to be caused by others (often through witchcraft or sorcery), actions taken to identity the murderer are a frequent response to death by the family of the victim. Identifying the murderer both gives the survivors some comfort and allows them to seek revenge.

Since the possibility of aggression as a reaction to death is so common around the world, it is reasonable to assume that in many cultures there are societal mechanisms at work that prevent such aggression from being expressed or control its expression so that others are not harmed. These mechanisms can work by either suppressing the anger and aggression or channeling it so that it is not disruptive or harmful to others. Ritual specialists play an important role in some societies in suppressing aggression. They seem most effective in complex societies with large settled communities where the overt acting-out of aggression is already suppressed to some degree. Ritual specialists are individuals who play a formal role in funeral rites and include sorcerers and diviners, both of whom help the bereaved identify the cause of death, religious leaders who officiate at the funeral, and funeral directors who arrange for the disposal of the corpse. Evidently, by advising the mourners, taking care of some of their emotional needs, giving them something to do, and helping them define their feelings as something other than anger, ritual specialists help prevent anger from being expressed.

Channeling aggression involves directing the aggression at socially acceptable targets. The target may be the mourner him- or herself (although in most cultures the person is stopped before causing permanent harm), outsiders, the killer of the deceased, animals, or spirits. In cultures where all or most deaths are believed to be caused by others, much attention is given to identifying the killer and seeking revenge. Often a diviner, sorcerer, or witch is employed for this purpose. However, channeling aggression poses a threat to others in the community, so in some cultures efforts are taken to minimize these threats. In many cultures, the mourners are isolated for a period of time from the community, perhaps by being confined to their home where others can visit them. In other cultures, mourners are sometimes marked by wearing special clothing or hairstyles or by the absence of jewelry.

Death also brings with it another possible source of aggression—aggression by the spirit, soul, or ghost of the deceased directed at the living. Since in nearly all cultures people believe that the spirits of the dead can cause harm to the living, steps are often taken to prevent this from happening. For example, the Aymara of Peru retain a diviner to determine if the ghost is still present, and they stay awake all night, remaining in the house, never alone for fear of the ghost. Children are made to wear rosaries, crucifixes, or medals of saints to ward off the ghost. Fear of ghosts is also reflected in linguistic behavior in some cultures. For example, the Mescalero Apache try to avoid using the name of the deceased at all and in the past even re-

Reactions to death vary across cultures. Public rituals such as this observance of the Day of the Dead in Mexico are ways of dealing with emotions in reaction to the death of a close one.

named the children in the deceased person's family. Other common mechanisms include burying the corpse away from the village, staying away from places where the ghost or spirit is thought to roam, and handling the body in ways that will prevent the ghost from findings its way back to the dwelling where the person died.

See also SUPERNATURAL AGGRESSION; SUTTEE.

Karsten, Rafael. (1935) *The Head-Hunters of Western Amazonas: The Life and Culture of the Jibaro Indians of Eastern Ecuador and Peru.*

Opler, Morris E. (1946) "Reaction to Death among the Mescalero Apache." *Southwestern Journal of Anthropology* 2: 454–467.

Rosenblatt, Paul C., R. Patricia Walsh, and Douglas A. Jackson. (1976) *Grief and Mourning in Cross-Cultural Perspective.*

Tschopik, Harry, Jr. (1951) *The Aymara of Chucuito, Peru. Vol. 1: Magic.* Anthropological Papers of the American Museum of Natural History, 44: 133–308.

Werblowsky, R. J. Zwi, and Geoffrey Wigoder, eds. (1965) *The Encyclopedia of the Jewish Religion.*

ALLIANCES

Within the context of war, an alliance is an agreement between two or more political communities to support or fight with each other against another political community or alliance of political communities. Although an alliance can have substantial advantages in size, mobility, and resources over an enemy that is a single community or a small alliance, alliances are not especially common in warfare. In a sample of 40 societies, only 25 percent fought alliance wars, with seven often involved in alliances in internal wars, two in external wars, and one in both forms of war. Allies provide each other with support in combat, intelligence on the size and movement of the enemy, safe passage through each other's territory, supplies, and a place of refuge. Allies also help each other by not allying with the enemy, thereby denying it these types of cooperation and assistance and weakening it. Thus, alliances can have a major impact on the outcome of a war and may help determine if the communities fight at all (a group facing a powerful alliance may choose not to fight, to withdraw, or even to join the alliance), who wins, and the frequency, intensity, and spread of hostilities. In general, the presence of alliances in external wars seems to be associated with wars for land or political subjugation and less often with wars for prestige or plunder. External alliance wars also tend less often to be settled by peacemaking and instead are not resolved until one side is driven off or defeated. This seems to be the case because a political community will enter into an alliance in an external war only when the alliance is likely to produce clear benefits for it, such as additional territory or driving off a troublesome enemy.

The importance of alliances and the advantages they provide the members of the alliance are shown in the following account of wars involving the Fox and Sauk Indians in the early years of the European settlement of the Midwest (Forsyth 1912: 183–184):

> The Sauk and Fox Indians have been at war formerly with the Iroquois, and Wyandotts, who drove the Sauks up the St. Lawrence to the lakes, and the Foxes up the Grand River, and at Green Bay they formed a coalition and renewed their former relations to each other, since then (in alliance with the Chippewas, Ottawas, and Pottawatimies), they have been engaged in a war with the Illinois Indians; which ended in their final extermination: afterwards the Sauks and Foxes in alliance with other nations of Indians, made war against the Osage Indians, and on

> settlement of their differences they allied themselves to the Osage Indians, against the Pawnee Indians, with whom in alliance with the Osages they had a severe fight in 1814 on the head waters of the Arkansas River, where the Sauks lost the Blue Chief who was then celebrated among them.

Alliances may involve either horizontal relations or vertical relations between political communities. Horizontal alliances are ones between political communities of the same type, such as two or more bands, villages, clans, or nations. Vertical alliances are ones between political communities of different types, such as between a clan and a tribe or a tribe and a nation. For example, the Pashtun of Afghanistan form both horizontal and vertical alliances, involving subclans, tribes, and the nation. At the horizontal level, at least ideally, specific subclans, clans, and tribes will ally with each other against other specific subclans, clans, and tribes. At the vertical level, specific clans expect the support of specific tribes, while specific tribes expect the support of tribal coalitions, and these coalitions, in turn, expect the support of the Afghan government. For example, the Inay-atullah clan allies with the Muhasil tribe against the Anmir clan and Barzewan tribe. The Inay-atullah–Muhasil alliance then allies with the Chaknawar Mullah tribal coalition against the Anmir-Barzewan alliance, who ally with the Babra Mullah coalition. At the national level during the period of British control, a political community affiliated with the British expected support from the British in India, while their enemies allied with the Afghan state.

Alliances can also be thought of as either balanced or unbalanced. A balanced alliance is one where all members of the alliance are at peace with each other and alliances fight against other alliances. Possibly the most successful balanced alliance was the Iroquois Confederation of five (later six) nations in New York State. Formed partly to end warfare between the five member nations, the alliance lasted for several hundred years and was successful in driving off and taking the territory of neighboring groups such as the Sauk (mentioned above) in Ohio, Pennsylvania, Ontario, and the Midwest. An unbalanced alliance is one where political communities form three-group alliances with each political community a member of several alliances. When two communities are at war, each seeks the support of the third member of the alliance. The Yanomamö of Brazil have an unbalanced alliance system involving villages, with continual fissioning and combining of villages as wars begin and alliances shift.

Alliances are mostly unstable and often dissolve after the war ends. An alliance might dissolve because (1) it is part of an unbalanced alliance system, (2) the enemy is defeated and it is no longer needed, (3) a weaker member of the alliance seeks to displace a stronger member, (4) one member of the winning alliance leaves to ally with the losing alliance, (5) a member of one alliance secretly assists the enemy and helps it win, and (6) the alliance is defeated. In general, alliances formed by local groups (lineages, clans, villages) to fight internal wars are more stable than those formed by more diffuse groups to fight external wars. This is evidently the case because alliances between local groups are an outgrowth of existing ties between the groups or their leaders involving friendship, marriage, trade, and reciprocal ceremonial obligations. For example, the Tausug of the southern Philippines have two forms of alliance. Minimal alliances involve men who have ties of friendship or kinship and who usually live in the same or neighboring communities. These alliances are essentially permanent, and the men will support each other militarily, with the size of the alliance group dependent on the circumstances of the raid or war. Maximal alliances are much larger groupings of men based on the linkages between the leaders of different minimal alliances. These are, of course, much larger, but they are extremely unstable, with the alliances often dissolving and the component minimal alliances fighting on different sides in future wars.

See also FISSIONING; INTERNAL CONFLICT; WAR; PEACEMAKING.

Ahmed, Akbar S. (1980) *Pukhtun Economy and Society: Traditional Structure and Economic Development in a Tribal Society.*

Berndt, Ronald. (1962) *Excess and Restraint.*

Chagnon, Napoleon A. (1968) *Yanomamö: The Fierce People.*

Ferguson, R. Brian. (1990) "Explaining War." In *The Anthropology of War.*

Forsyth, Thomas. (1912) "An Account of the Manners and Customs of the Sauk and Fox Nations of Indians Tradition." In *The Indian Tribes of the Upper Mississippi Valley and Region of the Great Lakes,* edited by Emma H. Blair, 183–245.

Kiefer, Thomas M. (1968) "Institutionalized Friendship and Warfare among the Tausug of Jolo." *Ethnology* 7: 225–244.

Otterbein, Keith F. (1989) *The Evolution of War.* 3rd edition.

APOLOGY

Apology is an important and commonly used method of dispute settlement in some cultures. Apology as a mechanism for resolving disputes is defined as a formal, public act in which one person, the offender, asks for forgiveness from a second person, the offended, who grants forgiveness. Apology, so defined, is a ritualized set of expectations and behaviors designed to resolve a dispute between individuals and to maintain social order in the community. Thus, apology often involves not just the two parties but also a third person (such as an elder in the community or a community leader) who brings the parties together, apology in a public place, and the giving of a gift to the offended person. Also, the offender will often try to escape blame by attributing his behavior to uncontrollable circumstances, some third party (including supernatural intervention), or even suggesting that the offended person misunderstood the offender's words or actions.

Cross-culturally, formal apology as the major means of dispute resolution in a culture occurs relatively infrequently. In a study of 56 societies, only 14 percent commonly used formal apology, while 66 percent relied more on other mechanisms to resolve disputes. However, among the societies of the world where apology is important are such major ones as Japan, Korea, Taiwan, Iran, and Fiji. Societies that favor apology to resolve disputes tend to be ones with a rigidly ordered social system with both social status and political leadership closely tied to the differential status of different kinship groups. In these societies some kinship groups are more powerful than others and the leaders of those groups become leaders of larger political units such as the village or county and even the entire society. Additionally, the power or superior status of these groups is often thought of as divinely inspired and leadership is inherited. In this type of society apology reflects the general social order where subordinates ask for and are granted forgiveness by superiors, reinforces the authority of the superior through the public ritual, and mitigates the anger of the offended and, thus, helps the offender avoid serious punishment.

In cultures where apology is an important means of resolving conflict, apology is often a multidimensional custom, with specific forms of apology required for specific types of wrongs. The Rotumans of the Republic of Fiji rely heavily on apology and have five different types: (1) verbal apology in private for an accidental wrong; (2) verbal apology in public with an admission of responsibility; (3) formal presentation of a cooked pig with required speeches; (4) formal presentation of the pig, *kava* (a ceremonial drink), and a woven mat; and (5) formal presentation of the above gifts plus the offender wears a special wreath around his neck. In all situations, if the ritual is performed properly, the wronged party is under strong social pressure to forgive the wrongdoer.

The key features of formal apology in many cultures are displayed by the use of apology by the Tikopia of Oceania. Apology is used in a variety of contexts by the Tikopia. One common and required use is to resolve disputes involving "disturbances of the chief's peace." Such disturbances include waking a sleeping chief, ignoring his orders, or using property such as his canoe without his permission. Such disruptions of the social order are resolved by righting the wrong (for example, returning the canoe used without permission) and then by the offender making a formal apology to the chief, accompanied by the presentation of a gift *(malai)* such as wooden bowl, a fish hook, or prepared food. The offender is then forgiven.

It should also be noted that failure to apologize when such behavior is expected can lead to grave consequences. For example, in 1929 in the Korean city of Koshu a Japanese student insulted a Korean student and refused to make the requested public apology. (For context, note that during this time, Korea was under Japanese control and both cultures use apology.) The Korean students responded by going on strike. Japanese and Korean students fought one another, and a number of the latter were arrested. Rumors of Korean deaths spread throughout Korea and led to nationwide student strikes and demonstrations that were supported by the general population and resulted in the imprisonment of many demonstrators.

See also Rituals of Reconciliation.

Firth, Raymond. (1959) *Social Change in Tikopia.*

Grajdanzev, Andrew J. (1944) *Modern Korea.*

Hickson, Letitia. (1986) "The Social Contexts of Apology on Dispute Settlement: A Cross-Cultural Study." *Ethnology* 25: 283–294.

Howard, Alan. (1990) "Dispute Management in Rotuma." *Journal of Anthropological Research* 46: 263–292.

Assault

Assault is the use of physical force to harm another person. Assault is the most common form of physical aggression, occurring in every culture in the world. However, cultures vary widely in the frequency in which people assault each other, in the degree to which assault is considered acceptable, and in the degree to which assault is institutionalized as a mechanism of conflict resolution. As a formal mechanism of conflict resolution, assault takes the form of physical duels, combative sports, physical punishment of children, corporal punishment of criminals, and capital punishment. As an informal method of self-help conflict resolution, assault takes the form of fighting between the disputants, with the stronger or more agile person usually winning. In most cultures, fighting as a means of self-help conflict resolution is usually controlled by other members of the community, who will intervene to prevent a participant from being seriously injured or killed.

While some people fight with others in all cultures, cultures do vary in the frequency with which assaults take place. A survey of 111 cultures shows that in 46 percent people usually do not fight with each other, in 32 percent they fight sometimes, and in 22 percent they fight often. In another survey of 90 cultures, in 54 percent quarrels between men rarely turned violent, in 35 percent quarrels were sometimes violent and sometimes not, and in 11 percent they were usually violent. Among women, fighting occurs in only 31 percent of cultures and does not occur or occurs only rarely in the other 69 percent. For the most part, fighting between women takes place in polygynous families where women are in competition for access to the husband they share and to the resources he controls.

As a form of self-help conflict resolution, fighting is used most commonly in small, hunter-gatherer cultures where there is no central authority to adjudicate disputes. For example, the Mbuti Pygmies of Zaire settle disputes by fighting, with the fighting governed by a clear set of rules: hitting with a piece of wood is permitted but blood may not be drawn nor may a person be hit on the forehead. As the fight escalates, an older man or woman will separate the combatants who will then turn to verbal abuse. The abuse will turn into humor or one party will sulk, ending the dispute; peaceful relations can then resume. However, not all hunter-gatherer cultures rely on fighting to settle disputes as some, such as the Semai, repress anger and do not fight.

In many cultures, fighting occurs mainly when alcohol is being consumed, often during weekly or seasonal festivals or community gatherings. One survey of 90 cultures shows that in 42 percent of cultures fighting occurs mainly in association with alcohol use. For example, among the San of Botswana, often described as one of the most peaceful cultures in the world, alcohol consumption is not uncommonly followed by men threatening and fighting with each other, behavior that is quite rare when they are not drinking. It is generally assumed that drunken fighting is motivated less by a desire to settle a dispute than by the need to release anger or tension that has built up during the week or season proceeding the drinking party.

See also Aggression by Women; Capital Punishment; Combative Sports; Crime; Drunken Brawling; Physical Punishment of Children; Physical Duels; Self-Help Conflict Resolution.

Dentan, Robert K. (1965) *Some Senoi Semai Dietary Restrictions: A Study of Food Behavior in a Malayan Hill Tribe.*

Ember, Carol R., and Melvin Ember. (1992) "Warfare, Aggression, and Resource Problems: Cross-Cultural Codes." *Behavior Science Research* 26: 169–226.

Levinson, David. (1989) *Family Violence in Cross-Cultural Perspective.*

Tanaka, Jiro. (1980) *The San Hunter-Gatherers of the Kalahari: A Study in Ecological Anthropology.*

Turnbull, Colin M. (1965) *Wayward Servants: The Two Worlds of the African Pygmies.*

Avoidance and Withdrawal

Avoidance and withdrawal are similar nonconfrontational conflict management techniques. Avoidance means avoiding a person or a situation that is likely to led to conflict. Avoidance as a response to a potential conflict situation needs to be distinguished from kin avoidance customs in which institutionalized avoidance behavior is required between certain categories of relatives. Withdrawal means leaving a situation or the presence of another person where the threat of conflict has already occurred or in a situation that calls for an aggressive response by the individual.

Both avoidance and withdrawal are commonly used in day-to-day interaction by individuals in cultures where conflict and violence are discouraged and unusual. Avoidance and withdrawal at the group level comes in the form of shunning and fissioning, while banishment can be conceptualized as a form of coerced withdrawal.

Avoidance and withdrawal are used often by individuals in cultures where emotions in general are expected to be controlled and where violence is prohibited. The Javanese use *satru* to manage quarrels. *Satru* is a publicly recognized and respected form of behavior in which individuals stop speaking to one another, usually when one individual feels that he or she has been wronged by the other. All types of wrongs, from insults to failure to repay a debt, are subject to *satru*. Depending on the relationship between the individuals and the seriousness of the quarrel, the *satru* may last days, weeks, years, or even a lifetime. Similarly, in Japanese villages individuals who quarrel might stop speaking to each other or "fail to see" one other, although greetings will be exchanged if a meeting cannot be avoided. If this avoidance behavior does not end on its own, a mediator will often intervene to reestablish relations between the two individuals. And, among the Papago, avoidance is used to deal with all but the most serious crimes. At the same time, the Papago express great fear—some describe it as terror—of the dead and of animals. In fact, they fear these more than they fear actual situations that might cause physical harm. This fear of the dead and animals has been interpreted as the displaced expression of anger and aggression in a way that allows the release of the anger but shifts the target of the anger from the living to safer targets, such as the dead and animals. The Papago are an example of a culture where group survival traditionally depended on close cooperation among family and community members, making the overt expression of aggression a threat to the group; therefore, hostile feelings had to be tightly controlled. Avoidance and withdrawal are common responses to being wronged in this type of culture.

One of the central questions about avoidance and withdrawal is whether they are "healthy" ways of dealing with feelings of anger and aggression or whether they are manifestations of repressed anger and therefore are "unhealthy." They may be unhealthy in that they inhibit the expression of feelings that are then expressed in other ways that may be psychologically or physically harmful to the individual. Evidence for the "unhealthy" viewpoint is provided by rural Jamaicans. Although they believe that aggression should be expressed, the actual expression of aggression at the appropriate target (the individual who made the person angry) is prohibited and people are overtly friendly to one another, even when they are angry. At the same time, anger and aggression are often expressed in a variety of indirect ways. First, rural Jamaicans withdraw from situations where they believe they have been wronged. For example, if someone does not repay a favor, that person will not be asked to perform another favor. Jamaicans will also avoid a person who has offended them by responding to the offending comment with complete silence. Jamaicans also "quarrel with oneself" as they talk vigorously and out loud to themselves about what they should have done to someone who angered them. Finally, Jamaicans avoid conflict by trying not act in any way that will offend someone and provoke anger and by following the laws religiously. All of these techniques of avoidance and withdrawal suggest that rural Jamaican society might be free of anger and conflict. In fact, the opposite is the case: Jamaican parents routinely beat their children to control them, with the beatings escalating in harshness as the children grow older; women suffer from frequent migraine headaches; people gossip about each other viciously and often about those they are friendly with; they have great difficulty accepting criticism; and they are prone to blame their problems on others. All of this suggests that avoidance and withdrawal, while effectively controlling violence among community members, causes considerable damage to individuals by preventing the expression of anger and aggression.

An example of a culture where avoidance and withdrawal seem "healthy" is the Central Thai. Key values of Central Thai culture include individuality, personal autonomy, and the avoidance of all face-to-face conflict. The physical organization of communities and the composition of families reflect these values. Communities are composed of from several hundred to several thousand individuals who live in dispersed houses located in the midst of rice fields, with houses often connected to each other and to the central village only by waterways. Residential families are a nuclear family with additional relatives or friends sometimes living there also. A person is a member of the family so long as he or she contributes to the work of the family; failure to work or conflict always results in someone moving out. Arguments in the community end with one person walking away—"We had a few words and he left. That's all." People who feel wronged rarely retaliate and are unassertive in having their rights restored through the courts or by other means. Individuals and families stay out of disputes involving others and when a rare dispute becomes violent, all residents become deeply worried and hope that it ends quickly and is as quickly forgotten. Although virtually all social control is based on self-control and, especially, on avoidance and withdrawal and the nonexpression of anger, the Central Thai seem to suffer little for their self-control. Perhaps it is the mesh of cultural values, community organization, and individual behavior that nearly always produces harmony within the community while also being free of harmful effects to individuals.

Related to avoidance and withdrawal are silence and denial as mechanisms for managing conflict. As noted above, rural Jamaicans use silence to express anger, and silence is a component of avoidance and withdrawal in all cultures. Silence also serves to control disputes by helping individuals deal with uncertainty in social relations. For example, the Western Apache of Arizona remain silent or "give up on words" in a number of uncertain situations, such as when meeting strangers, in the early stages of courting, when a child returns from boarding school, when being loudly insulted, and when sad. These are all uncertain social situations because the relative statuses and roles of the individuals is unclear. Silence allows the participants to sort out the ambiguities of the situation and to clarify their status and roles and then act accordingly.

Denial is another technique used by individuals in cultures where the expression of hostile feelings is prohibited or restricted. Denial is usually manifested in a person denying that he or she feels angry with someone, even though that person has done something that one would expect would make him or her angry. The Zapotec of Mexico, for example, use denial, and it evidently helps maintain social order by perpetuating the image of respectful, conflict-free relations between people and preventing the start of arguments that might escalate into violence.

See also Fissioning; Kin Avoidance; Nonconfrontational Conflict Management; Nonviolent Communities; Shunning.

Basso, Keith H. (1970) "'To Give Up on Words': Silence in Western Apache Culture." *Southwestern Journal of Anthropology* 26: 213–230.

Cohen, Yehudi A. (1966) *A Study of Interpersonal Relations in a Jamaican Community.*

Geertz, Hildred. (1961) *The Javanese Family.*

Joseph, Alice, Rosamond B. Spicer, and Jane Chesky. (1949) *The Desert People: A Study of the Papago Indians.*

Norbeck, Edward. (1954) *Takashima: A Japanese Fishing Community.*

O'Nell, Carl W. (1986) "Primary and Secondary Effects of Violence Control among the Nonviolent Zapotec." *Anthropological Quarterly* 59: 184–190.

Phillips, Herbert P. (1966) *Thai Peasant Personality: The Patterning of Interpersonal Behavior in the Village of Bang Chan.*

Banditry

The term banditry covers a variety of practices, all of which have in common the robbing of others (usually members of other cultural groups or communities) of their valuables and perhaps also injuring or killing them. Bandits have come in many forms: criminal organizations such as the mafia in Sicily, gangs of robbers in the employ of barons in Medieval Europe, professional highwaymen such as the Hole in the Wall Gang in the American West, Bedouin caravan raiders in Arabia; Thugs and Dacoits in India, confidence men, pirates, and social bandits. With the exception of social bandits, all bandits are basically individuals or groups who make their livelihood by robbing or collecting money or valuables from others. For some, like the Thugs of India, banditry is their primary source of income, for others such as Bedouin caravan raiders, it is only one source among several.

The Thugs of India were perhaps the most highly institutionalized of all types of bandits known throughout human history. Thugs, who date to A.D. 1290, were an occupational group who engaged in the traditional occupation of *thugee.* The English word, thug, is derived from the Sanskrit word *thag,* meaning cheat or robber. Thugs were groups of professional highwaymen who befriended and then strangled, robbed, and buried wealthy travelers until the practice was ended by the British in about 1848. Thugee was a considered a profession and the men who engaged in it paid taxes and worshipped Kali, thc Hindu goddess of destruction. At its height, thugee involved a confederacy of gangs numbering from 10 to 200 mcn each. These gangs operated in secret, supported each other, and even spoke their own argot. Thugee survives in very isolated areas of India today in the form *dacoity,* which involves armed bands of five or more men, called Dacoits, who rob travelers in remote regions. Both Dacoits and Thugs were subject to punishment by hanging or banishment, although those who converted to Christianity during the British colonial era might escape severe punishment.

Unlike banditry for economic gain, social banditry, the most common form of banditry around the world, is a form of protest and rebellion that has occurred throughout human history, mainly in peasant societies. Peasant societies are ones in which a majority of the population lives in rural areas; they produce their own food and often a surplus through agricultural or livestock raising and are under the political domination of local or regional landowners, who in turn are governed by a monarchy or dictatorship. Peasant societies are often socially stratified, with a wealthy ruling elite, classes for the military, clergy, craftsmen, and merchants, and peasants, the lowest class. Serfs in Medieval Europe were peasants, as were many mestizo farmers in Central and South America. Social bandits were regarded by the rulers as outlaws, while they were seen by the peasants as heroes and fighters for justice. Men who became bandits came from the peasant community, lived in it, and were supported by it. They were

Robin Hood, a social bandit who robs from the rich and gives to the poor.

generally seen by the peasants as helping the community, although there were also situations when they were hired to repress peasant uprisings.

Although largely a practice of the past (social bandits now exist only on Sardinia and parts of South America and Africa), social banditry was quite common from the fifteenth century to the early twentieth century in Europe and other regions of the world. The only region without social banditry was North America, which lacked a peasantry, although some argue that outlaw gangs on the Western frontier were social bandits. Because they lack peasants and social classes, banditry does not occur in hunter-gatherer and tribal-level societies such as those ruled by a hereditary chief. Social banditry is also thought not to occur in modern, industrialized societies, again because of the absence of peasants, although it does occur in frontier regions such as rural Australia, where wealthy developers seek the land of poor settlers, and it did occur in Africa in indigenous states and more recently in frontier zones.

While they are sometimes thought of as revolutionaries, this was not often the case, although some became involved in peasant rebellions and revolts. Perhaps the best-known situation of this type was the role Pancho Villa played in the Mexican revolution. The portrayal of bandits as revolutionaries is often part of the mythology that develops around certain individual bandits in literature and song. Robin Hood, who may not have ever actually existed, is a classic example of the romanticization of the bandit and social banditry. Today, in the developing world, groups called guerrillas or revolutionaries or freedom fighters are a modern form of the Medieval social bandit.

Although bandit gangs were common, the actual number of bandits was few and many were killed by the government within a few years of embarking on their career. Those who survived for longer periods often managed to do so by allying themselves with the rulers and thus actually working against rather in the interests of the peasants or by operating in locales such as inaccessible mountain ranges that were of little interest to the ruling class. Bandits were almost always young men who came from peasant communities in rural areas. They were often marginal men such as deserters, ex-soldiers, farmers with little land to work, or rebels.

Historian E. J. Hobsbawm's world survey of banditry suggests that there were three types of social bandits. First is the "noble robber," who is ". . . the champion, the righter of wrongs, the bringer of justice and social equality." The Robin Hood figure is the classic noble robber who "robs from the rich and gives to the poor," is a victim of injustice himself, is supported and adored by his peasant followers, and is a hated enemy of the local ruling class but an ally of the national monarch. While few, if any, actual bandits lived up to this image, what is most important is that their peasant supporters saw them in this way and they thus served as a vehicle of social protest.

Second are what Hobsbawm calls "avengers." Avengers use frequent and cruel violence (which other bandits do not) to get revenge on the powerful and to show that even the poorest can act. Avengers have been relatively rare, appearing mainly in times of major social upheaval and coming primarily from the most repressed groups in the society. For example, the banditry of Joaquin Murieta in California was in reaction to white rule over Mexican Californians, and Montenegrin banditry of this type in the Balkans followed the disruptions of World War I.

Third are *"Haiduks"* (resistance fighters) of southeastern Europe who began appearing in the fifteenth century in reaction to the wealthy Christian landowners and the Turkish invaders. In Russia they were called *"Cossaks,"* in Greece *"klephts,"* in the Ukraine *"haidamaks,"* and in Hungary and the Balkans *"Haiduks."* They were bands (brigands) of peasant political resisters who mainly robbed and raided the Turks. Unlike other types of social banditry, men often joined for economic reasons, operated as tightly knit groups, kept apart from the local communities, and tended to persist over time.

As noted above, social banditry has now largely disappeared in regions of the world where it was once common, although the romanticized image of the social bandit (Robin Hood and Pancho Villa, among others) and other types of bandits (Butch Cassidy and the Sundance Kid) lives on in literature, song, and film. In the contemporary world, groups that might once have been considered bandits are classified as revolutionaries or guerrillas and are seen as integral actors in social protest and independence movements around the world.

See also RAIDING; WAR.

Blok, Anton. (1972) "The Peasant and the Brigand: Social Banditry Reconsidered." *Comparative Studies in Society and History* 14: 494–503.

Bowen, Ralph H., and Pierre Bettez Gravel. (1992) "Peasants and Pirates in the Aegean: An Instance of 'Social Banditry'?" *Studies in Third World Societies* 48, part 2: 159–170.

Crummey, Donald, ed. (1986) *Banditry, Rebellion and Social Protest in Africa.*

Hobsbawm, E. J. (1969) *Bandits.*

Hockings, Paul. (1992) "Thug." In *Encyclopedia of World Cultures. Volume 3. South Asia,* edited by Paul Hockings, 294.

Moss, David. (1979) "Bandits and Boundaries in Sardinia." *Man* 14: 477–496.

O'Malley, Pat. (1979) "Social Banditry, Modern Capitalism and the Traditional Peasantry: A Critique of Hobsbawm." *The Journal of Peasant Studies* 6: 489–501.

BANISHMENT

Banishment, ostracism, and exile are the removal of an individual from a community or society as punishment. Banishment has a long history in the Western world and was used by the Greeks and Romans; later, various colonial powers, most notably the British, banished criminals to their colonies. Most recently, exile was used extensively by the Russians under the Tsar and in the Soviet Union as a punishment for both political offenses and crimes. These individuals were deported and forced to remain in Siberia, where their presence also had the effect of adding to the Russian presence in a territory previously occupied mainly by indigenous peoples. In the developed world today, imprisonment has mostly replaced banishment as a punishment.

In non-Western cultures, as in Western ones, banishment is used mainly for serious offenses.

However, while in many Western cultures those banished might often survive, total banishment in non-Western cultures is often the equivalent of capital punishment, as it is unlikely that a banished person can survive alone as he will likely die of starvation or an accident, or be killed by a hostile neighboring group. For example, for the most serious offenses, the Huron would either execute or banish a criminal from the longhouse, with banishment being the equivalent of execution. And, among the Mbuti Pygmies, those found guilty of incest—a particularly heinous crime—were left to die in the forest.

The threat of banishment is an especially effective mechanism of social control in small, tightly knit communities where removal from the group means both social and physical death. For example, the Abkhazians of the Caucasus region of the former Soviet Union discipline juvenile delinquents by having elders threaten them with banishment at meetings of the extended family. The combination of the possibility of banishment, criticism by respected elders, and the public nature of the criticism is usually enough to end the delinquent behavior.

Banishment can also take less severe forms. For example, the San of Botswana make an uncooperative member of the band feel unwelcome by ignoring his requests for assistance, disregarding his suggestions, and generally making him feel uncomfortable, all designed to force him to leave and join another band. Similarly, the Goodenough Islanders force those who cause very serious disruptions to leave the community. Again, social pressures such as gossip, harangues, or placement of a curse will be used to force the person to leave, usually temporarily. In cultures where banishment is used, it is used much like capital punishment as a punishment for serious crimes and to remove from the community those who threaten the survival of the group.

See also Capital Punishment; Harangue; Shunning.

Garb, Paula. (1993) "Abkhazians: Growing in Age and Wisdom." In *Ethnographic Profiles,* edited by Melvin Ember, Carol R. Ember, and David Levinson.

Grünhut, Max. (1972) *Penal Reform: A Comparative Study.*

Otterbein, Keith F. (1986) *The Ultimate Coercive Sanction: A Cross-Cultural Study of Capital Punishment.*

Silberbauer, George B. (1981) *Hunter and Habitat in the Central Kalahari Desert.*

Young, Michael. (1971) *Fighting with Food.*

Blood Money

Blood money is the custom of paying compensation to the family or kin group of a murder victim. Blood money is related to blood feuding in that blood money is a way of resolving a feud without further violence. Instead of the kin group getting revenge and restoring its honor by killing the murderer, they receive instead compensation in the form of money, valuable property such as cattle or camels, or even the exchange of a person to take the place of the victim. The factor that motivates people to seek blood money is the belief that a lost life must be paid for. Among the Bedouin peoples of north Africa, this belief extends not just to lives lost through murder, but also lives lost by accident or even through the carelessness of the deceased, and to freedom lost through imprisonment. The questions of who must pay the money and how much is to be paid are the subject of intense negotiation in cultures like the Bedouin where blood money payments are a primary means of settling disputes between kinship and other groups.

Early evolutionary theorists believed that blood money was a more "advanced" means of settling conflicts than feuding (blood revenge), and thus was thought to be characteristic of more "civilized" cultures. Subsequent research has failed to support this claim, and in fact both customs can and do occur in the same culture. However, it is clear that blood money compensation often does require more sophisticated negotiations, a clear set of rules, and greater mutual understanding and expectations between the groups than does revenge. As a mechanism of conflict resolution, blood money has drawn considerably less attention from social scientists than have other mechanisms such as feuding, mediation, and litigation, in part because in many parts of the world it has been replaced by formal judicial proceedings.

The complexities and dynamics of blood revenge exist in full-blown form among the Somali, the dominant ethnic group in Somalia. The Somali believe strongly in a "life for a life," the basic premise behind both feuding and blood money. Brothers are expected to revenge the killing of a brother to reclaim the family honor. In practice, however, killings are more often revenged through the payment of blood money. How much is paid and how the payment is arranged depends on the types of social units involved, their relative social status in the community or society, the status of the murdered man, and the cost to a group of pursuing blood revenge. For example, when maintenance of friendly relations with the other group is crucial, no revenge will be pursued and no money sought, and murdered low-class men will bring a lower payment than the standard 100 camels or their equivalent. This suggests that the basic principle of a "life for a life" is often balanced against real life concerns such as the cost of that death (the value of the dead man to the group) and the cost of revenging the death (disruption of normally peaceful relations with other groups). From this perspective of costs and benefits, blood money compensation is a rational choice when the cost of blood revenge is too high a price to pay.

In addition to the cost-benefit economic nature of blood money, it is also a social and political transaction. For example, much of the activity regarding blood money in Somalia involves clans—unified groups whose members live mostly in one region and who all trace their lineages to a common ancestor. In blood money negotiations clan members band together to both receive and make the payments. Blood money is paid for murder, physical injury, and moral injury. There is a scale of payments (100 camels for a male death, 50 for a female death, 50 for the loss of an eye, 20 for a broken leg, etc.), although there is always room for negotiation.

See also FEUDING.

Erickson, Karen P., and Heather Horton. (1992) "Blood Feuds: Cross-Cultural Variations in Kin Group Vengeance." *Behavior Science Research* 26:57–86.

Kennett, Austin. (1925) *Bedouin Justice: Laws and Customs among the Egyptian Bedouin.*

Lewis, Ioan M. (1955) *Peoples of the Horn of Africa.*

BRIDE THEFT AND RAIDING

Bride theft is the term used for a number of related practices that share in common the forcible abduction of a woman by a man for the purpose of marriage. Bride theft is characterized by a man abducting a woman from a community from which a marriage partner would typically come, failure of the man to obtain permission from the woman or her parents or kin, and rape shortly after the abduction. A woman taken in bride theft is always known to the man and in some cases she is abducted because she has rejected his expression of interest in her.

Bride raiding differs from bride theft in that the woman comes from a more distant community and is not known to the man. Limited bride raiding is quite rare, although more general raiding for women from another community or culture, some of whom may be then taken as wives, is not.

Both theft and raiding are aggressive acts directed against a woman, her father, and her kin group. Additionally, raiding often takes place within the context of hostile relations between different societies. Both theft and raiding are generally disapproved of when they occur and the man might be subject to punishment, especially for bride theft. More commonly, however, in bride theft situations the matter is settled through negotiations between the two kin groups or between the man and his father-in-law. In bride raiding, because of the lack of ongoing ties between the kin groups or communities, no settlement is considered and hostility may last for years. Other names used for theft and raiding are bride capture, wife kidnapping, wife stealing, bride abduction, and marriage-by-capture.

Either bride theft or bride raiding occur in about 50 percent of societies, although in those societies where they do occur, only a minority of men acquire wives in this way. A survey of 53 cultures identified 30 percent of the cultures as having raiding and 23 percent as having theft, with cultures that have one not having the other. A few other cultures have the related practices of mock bride theft and ceremonial bride capture; these differ from actual bride theft in that the woman is a willing participant. In most cultures, both theft and raiding account for only a very few marriages, and mostly serve as alternatives to the typical ways of forming a marriage. Bride theft is usually carried out by a man acting alone who abducts a woman and rapes her. Sometimes, he may be assisted by friends or kin. Bride raiding generally involves groups of men who capture women from another community either as part of a raid for that purpose or as part of a more general raid. The woman is then married by the man who captured her or another man and becomes a member of the culture. Related to raiding for wives is the capture of women during warfare and the subsequent marrying-off of the women to men in the victorious society.

Studies of bride theft in a number of cultures around the world, such as the Pokot in East Africa, Yoruk in Turkey, and Tzeltal in Mexico, provide a fairly consistent portrait of the type of culture where bride theft occurs, although the particular motivations a man has for abducting a woman for marriage might differ from man to man. Among the basic features of societies where bride theft occurs are (1) a requirement that men marry in order to reach adult status and (2) various social forces that reduce the number of marriageable women available to these men. Among these forces are polygyny where one man has more than one wife at a time, rules restricting marriage to persons of the same community, broad extension of the incest taboo which eliminates distantly related kin as potential marriage partners, delay of marriage by women, and personal characteristics of a man that make him undesirable. Within this framework of marital choice customs and options are two other sets of key factors: economic transfers at marriage from the husband's to the wife's family and male dominance in the family. Most bride theft cultures are ones where the husband's kin group is required to pay a bride-price to the wife's family or, alternatively, the husband must perform bride-service for his father-in-law and where the woman moves to the village of the husband's family at marriage. This means that women are, to some extent, an economic commodity and that their families must be compensated for the loss of their economic and procreative services by the husband's family who now has access to these services. A woman's value in this marriage marketplace is based on many factors, including her age, physical attractiveness, family wealth, family reputation, and, most importantly, her reputation as a virgin. A woman who is not a virgin is not desirable and her family can demand little in the way of a bride-price. This is the reason a woman is often raped when she is abducted, for now her family will have little incentive to prevent the marriage (she is no longer marketable to any man other than the abductor) and they will be in a weak negotiating position regarding the bride-price.

The final factor that encourages bride theft in combination with the other factors noted above is the father/husband's dominance in the family and the vulnerable position of wives. Life is difficult for wives—and especially young wives—in bride theft cultures as they are dominated by their husbands and the husband's kin, live apart from their family, can expect little support from their family who do not want to put the bride price in jeopardy, and are often beaten by their husbands. Additionally, marriages are often arranged by the couple's parents, although in some cases the couple's wishes may be considered. Thus, while it is not in their own self-interest to marry, women are under great family and societal pressure to marry at a young age. This means that bride theft is an affront to the woman's kin and to her father and it is these offenses that are considered more serious than the actual abduction and rape. Because her market value is now low, her father has little incentive to take her back and instead is usually willing to negotiate a bride price that both allows him to preserve the family honor and permits the marriage to take place.

The same factors operate to encourage bride raiding as well, although the relationship between the kin groups is of minor importance, as under normal circumstances men and women from the two groups would not marry one another. This is an important reason why raiding might be preferred over bride theft, as the husband is not likely to be troubled by his wife's kin. However, it is not always that simple; among the Shona of Zimbabwe a husband might attribute misfortune to his wife's spirit, who is angry because a bride price was never paid. To set matters straight, he must then meet his obligations to her father.

In summary, both theft and raiding are relatively uncommon means of obtaining wives that take place in cultures where a combination of social, economic, and personal considerations create a shortage of marriageable women.

See also RAIDING FOR SLAVES.

Ayres, Barbara. (1974) "Bride Theft and Raiding for Wives in Cross-Cultural Perspective." *Anthropological Quarterly* 47: 238–252.

Bullock, Charles. (1950) *The Mashona and the Matabele.*

Cannibalism

Cannibalism, or anthropophagy as it is technically known, is the consumption of human flesh, organs, or bones by other humans. Thus, in some sense, cannibalism is the ultimate form of human aggression, as it is the physical internalization of one human being by another. Because it is both repulsive and fascinating (or, perhaps, because it is fascinating because it is repulsive), cannibalism has drawn considerable attention in the popular media and from nonscientific observers of other cultures, although it has been somewhat ignored by anthropologists until quite recently. Reports of early explorers, missionaries, and government officials in the New World, Oceania, and Africa often described cannibalism among the native peoples of those regions. This image persists, as evidenced by cartoons that depict native peoples boiling pith-helmeted Westerners in large pots. This image does not reflect reality, and, in fact, there is some question as to whether cannibalism as a regular practice has ever existed in any society.

Anthropological interest in cannibalism among non-Western peoples grew following the publication of Arens's 1979 survey, which led him to conclude that it is very unlikely that cannibalism ever existed in any culture. Other experts have subsequently taken a less firm view about its nonexistence, although the consensus now is that the past wisdom about its wide distribution and frequency were gross exaggerations. The evidence supporting the view that cannibalism never existed as a regularly practiced custom in any society is considerable. It can be summarized as follows.

1. Most of the evidence for cannibalism comes from the reports of early European explorers, missionaries, and government agents. These individuals likely embarked on their voyages already believing that the people they would encounter were cannibals. This idea that the inhabitants of unexplored regions of the world were cannibals was an established part of classical writings and was also reported by Columbus, who claimed that the Carib people in the Caribbean were cannibals, although they were not. The word *cannibal* is probably derived from the name of the Carib people, their name being misspelled as Canib by Columbus's party. Thus, these early arrivals in the New World and Africa reported what they expected to find, whether or not the practice actually existed.
2. Westerners who established contact with indigenous peoples often had an interest in describing these cultures as uncivilized—they often coveted indigenous peoples' land, labor, natural resources, and souls. Defining people and cultures as less than human has long been used as a justification for killing them, enslaving them, or taking their land.
3. These early reporters of cannibalism were not trained, objective observers and many did not speak the native language.

4. Early reports were often contradictory in their descriptions of how often cannibalism occurred, who was eaten, how the body was prepared, etc.
5. Most reports of cannibalism by trained ethnographers refer to the past and do not claim that cannibalism existed when the ethnographer was there. This is known as "memory ethnography" and is a less trustworthy method of collecting information than reporting what one actually observes.
6. People the world over are often quite willing to claim that others are cannibals. Just as Europeans believed that non-Europeans were cannibals, some native peoples claimed the reverse and Koreans have accused the Chinese of cannibalism and vice versa. Often the people accused of being cannibals are enemies of the accuser or people who are already considered to be inferior, such as suspected witches, social misfits, religious minorities, and women in cultures where men consider women to be inferior.

Despite misgivings about the trustworthiness of reports about cannibalism, there have been two worldwide surveys of the practice, based on available information of questionable reliability. In one, a survey of 240 cultures, cannibalism was present in 25 percent of the cultures; in the other survey of 156 cultures, cannibalism was present in 34 percent. Both surveys counted only institutionalized cannibalism and ignored private cannibalism that was considered abnormal by people in the culture. Cannibalism comes in two primary forms—endocannibalism and exocannibalism. Endocannibalism is the eating of people from one's own culture. It is reported as usually occurring as part of funeral rites and apparently often symbolizes the continuity of the culture from one generation to the next by physically passing the flesh or organs of one generation to the next. Exocannibalism is the eating of people from other cultures and reportedly often takes the form of trophy cannibalism where the heart, brain, or other body part of an enemy warrior is eaten to denigrate the defeated warrior. Survival cannibalism—the eating of human flesh to survive during environmental disasters or famine—is fairly common throughout human history and is the one type of cannibalism reliably documented. With regard to the distribution of alleged cannibalism, it is most frequently reported for cultures in South America and Oceania, less frequently for Africa, and not at all for Europe, the Middle East, or Asia. However, if the Medieval blood libel of Jews, where they were accused of killing Christian children to use their blood in religious rituals, is considered to be an actual case of cannibalism, Europe then belongs on the list.

Whether or not cannibalism is actually practiced, the belief and associated symbolic rituals are an important component of many religious systems around the world. For example, the Communion rite in Roman Catholicism involving the symbolic consumption of the body and blood of Jesus Christ through the actual consumption of a wafer and wine is in part symbolic cannibalism. In contemporary American culture, cannibalistic ideation continues to exist in popular culture in the Dracula story, where the vampire must drink fresh human blood to survive, and in popular movies such as the *Night of the Living Dead,* where the dead return to eat the living. Ongoing interest in cannibalism in many cultures seem to reflect the various elements of the human experience symbolized by cannibalism, including the meaning of one's own existence, social order, and cultural continuity over time.

Two cultures have drawn special attention as purveyors of cannibalism: the Aztec Empire of pre-Columbian Mexico and the Fore of New Guinea. Aztec cannibalism, as described by the

Spanish conquistadors and writers who arrived shortly after the conquest, was closely tied to Aztec human sacrifice, which estimates place at anywhere from 20,000 to 250,000 persons per year. Scholars have suggested a variety of explanations for Aztec sacrifice and cannibalism, with the former considered the socially and religious more important of the two practices. Explanations focus on the possible need to obtain protein from human flesh due to a shortage of other foods, the central role played by the heart and blood in the Aztec conception of the universe, and sacrifice as an aspect of the social stratification system.

Alleged cannibalism by the Fore people came to the attention of outsiders because of its possible link to a infectious neurological disease called kuru, a slow infection of the central nervous system whose discovery and study won the Nobel Prize for Physiology/Medicine for Dr. D. Carelton Gajdusek in 1976. Kuru is a degenerative viral disease and reported cannibalism, in which women and children ate the brains of deceased relatives, was cited as one possible means of transmission. Reports of this Fore pattern of cannibalism all date to early contact times and mostly come from Fore men who themselves did not consume human flesh. More recent analysis of the information suggests that Fore cannibalism—if it actually existed—did not cause the transmission of kuru. Rather, it was likely transmitted to women and to children by women who handled the corpses and brains (which were extracted for ritual use) of persons who died from kuru.

See also HUMAN SACRIFICE; HEAD-HUNTING.

Arens, W. (1979) *The Man-Eating Myth: Anthropology and Anthropophagy.*

Brown, Paula, and Donald Tuzin, eds. (1983) *The Ethnography of Cannibalism.*

Harner, Michael. (1977) "The Ecological Basis for Aztec Sacrifice." *American Ethnologist* 4: 117–135.

Harris, Marvin. (1977) *Cannibals and Kings: The Origins of Cultures.*

Ortiz de Montellano, Bernard R., (1978) "Aztec Cannibalism: An Ecological Necessity?" *Science* 200: 611–617.

Price, Barbara. (1978) "Demystification, Enriddlement, and Aztec Cannibalism: A Materialistic Rejoinder to Harner." *American Ethnologist* 5: 98–115.

Sahlins, Marshall. (1979) "Cannibalism: An Exchange." *New York Review of Books* 26: 45–47.

Sanday, Peggy R. (1986) *Divine Hunger: Cannibalism as a Cultural System.*

Shankman, Paul. (1969) "Le Rôti et le Bouilli: Lévi-Strauss' Theory of Cannibalism." *American Anthropologist* 71: 54–69.

Steadman, Lyle B., and Charles F. Merbs. (1982) "Kuru and Cannibalism." *American Anthropologist* 84: 611–627.

CAPITAL PUNISHMENT

In his survey of capital punishment in 53 cultures, anthropologist Keith Otterbein defined capital punishment as "the appropriate killing of a person who has committed a crime within a political community." So defined, capital punishment is used in 51 of the 53 cultures surveyed, making it nearly culturally universal. Not only is capital punishment widely used, but it is also generally approved; people in 89 percent of the 53 cultures expected it to be used for certain crimes or approved of its use. In only two of the cultures where it occurs do people generally disapprove of its use. Although capital punishment is used or is permitted in nearly all cultures, there is considerable variation across cultures in the crimes it is used for, who does the killing, how the criminal is executed, and the purpose people believe it serves. Whether or not capital punishment is an effective deterrent to further crime is unclear, although there is evidence among the nations of the world that capital punishment does not reduce the frequency of crime.

The crimes most often punished by capital punishment (those so punished in over 50 percent of cultures) are homicide, stealing, sacrilege such as witchcraft, and sex crimes such as rape, adultery, and incest. Traitors are subject to capital punishment in 27 percent of cultures, while offenses such as desertion in war, political assassination, arson, and kidnapping are cause for execution in only a few cultures. In most cultures, the crimes punished by execution are those that are most threatening to the culture and the well-being of the people, although cultures vary in what is meant by most "threatening" and "well-being."

In the majority of cultures it is the political leader, a council, or the community religious leader who rules that a person should be executed. In about 20 percent, it is the criminal's kin; in 18 percent, the community as a whole; and in 10 percent, the victim's kin. Most executions are carried out in public, but in some cultures they are private or even secret, with the criminal simply disappearing, never to be seen again. Although it is assumed that public executions such as those in Medieval Europe had the effect on others of deterring them from committing a similar crime, it is more likely that they served more as a form of public entertainment.

In about 50 percent of cultures, weapons such as swords or spears are used to execute the criminal. Hanging is used in a third, while other methods are, in order of frequency, burning, incapacitating the criminal and letting him die, drowning, poisoning, decapitation, stoning, and hurling from a height. Perhaps weapons and hanging are mostly used because they are the surest way of killing the person. In cultures where the perpetrators of serious crimes are banished, and where that banishment is likely to lead to their death through starvation, killing by an enemy group, or exposure to the elements, banishment can also be considered a method of capital punishment.

While not much is known about people's motivation for approving capital punishment or for expecting it to be used, one reason commonly given by people in different cultures is to remove the criminal so that he cannot commit the crime again. Other reasons are for revenge, to show the power of the king, or to wipe out an insult, as well as various combinations of these.

Cross-cultural research indicates that the reason why a culture uses capital punishment is somewhat more complex than the reasons given by members of the culture. Evidently, different types of cultures have different underlying reasons for killing those who commit serious crimes. In small, hunter-gatherer cultures, capital punishment is used to remove those who commit crimes so serious or whose behavior is so disruptive to others or the group as a whole that the survival of the group is threatened. In larger, kin-based cultures, capital punishment is used selectively to punish crimes depending on whether or not kin groups or councils are present and have the authority to punish crimes. Last, larger cultures with centralized political leadership vested in a chief or king use capital punishment as a social control mechanism to publicly demonstrate—and thereby reinforce—the power of the chief or king.

See also Banishment; Crime; Feuding.

Otterbein, Keith F. (1986) *The Ultimate Coercive Sanction: A Cross-Cultural Study of Capital Punishment.*

COMBATIVE SPORTS

Combative sports are amusements or recreational activities played by two or more opponents (individuals or teams) that involve direct or indirect (through a weapon or simulated weapon) physical contact or, in the absence of physical contact, are warlike in nature and require the use of real or substitute weapons. In American society, football, wrestling, ice hockey, hunting, and fencing are all combative sports. Noncombative sports include baseball, bowling, golf, and skiing. As the following list of some Olympic sports shows, both combative and noncombative sports are popular around the world.

Combative	**Noncombative**
Archery	Canoeing
Basketball	Cycling
Biathlon	Diving
Boxing	Equestrian
Fencing	Figure Skating
Field Hockey	Gymnastics
Ice Hockey	Skating
Judo	Skiing
Modern Pentathlon	Sledding
Soccer	Swimming
Shooting	Tennis
Volleyball	Track and Field
Water Polo	Weight Lifting
Wrestling	Yachting

The thousands of different games and sports played by people around the world fall into three general categories: chance, strategy, and physical skill. Combative sports always involve physical skill in determining the winner, with strategy and chance sometimes playing an important role as well.

Combative sports are of interest because of their possible links to other forms of aggression and, especially, to war. Some social scientists believe that combative sports provide an alternative to war as a means of expressing aggression and, thus, will be found most often in societies that are relatively peaceful. This is known as the *drive discharge* or *catharsis* model of aggression. An example of this is the manner in which soccer is played by contemporary Zulu men. The Zulu were a warlike people until defeated by the British, and they have long lived under the oppression of Dutch-imposed apartheid in South Africa. Under the restrictive government, they have been unable to express their frustrations and anger directly. Soccer provides a socially acceptable way of expressing hostility and matches are taken very seriously. Prematch activities include divination, rituals, use of herbal medicines, and various efforts to ward off the effects of sorcery and witchcraft. A victory is seen as the successful use of supernatural power.

Other social scientists disagree with the drive discharge model. Instead, they argue that the opposite is true: combative sports and warfare are part of a general cultural pattern that encourages aggressive behavior. This is called the *culture pattern* model and suggests that combative sports will be more common in societies that are warlike. An example of this type of culture was the Iroquois Confederacy prior to the American Revolution. The Iroquois were a confederation of five (later six) nations who, prior to European settlement, controlled most of what is today New York State and parts of Ohio, Pennsylvania, and Ontario Province in Canada. They acquired this large territory (the Iroquois probably numbered no more than 12,000 persons) by waging aggressive and often vicious warfare against neighboring tribes such as the Erie, Neutral, and Huron. Their favorite physical game was what Americans now call lacrosse. It involved two teams drawn from two nations, or from two villages or clans within nations. The men trained for the event and wore only a deerskin or cloth loincloth. The object was to move

Combative sports contests occur in many cultures, such as this wrestling contest in rural Moldova.

a wooden or deerskin ball down the field and through the goal by carrying it on a webbed-stick or passing it ahead to teammates. The competition for control of the ball was fierce and often led to injuries. The event was watched by a crowd who bet heavily on the outcome, further adding to the excitement. In many ways lacrosse resembled Iroquois warfare and called for the same fierce aggressiveness and desire to win that was expected of warriors in combat.

The distribution of combative sports in cultures around the world mainly supports the culture pattern model. Although it is not always the case, more often than not, cultures that wage war often are more likely also to have combative sports than are societies that are peaceful. The same seems to be true for the United States, where in the World War II and Korean War periods, attendance at football games and participation in hunting increased, while attendance at baseball games decreased. Why war and combative sports go together is not clear, although it may be that combative sports, especially when they involve boys, are a way of raising aggressive boys and of training them to be warriors.

See also SOCIALIZATION OF AGGRESSION; WAR.

Berglund, Axel-Ivar. (1976) *Zulu Thought-Patterns and Symbolism.*

Morgan, Lewis H. (1901) *League of the Ho-de-no-sau-nee or Iroquois.* Vol. 2. Edited and annotated by Herbert M. Lloyd.

Sipes, Richard G. (1973) "War, Sports and Aggression: An Empirical Test of Two Rival Theories." *American Anthropologist* 75: 64–86.

Worchel, Stephen. (1974) "Societal Restrictiveness and the Presence of Outlets for the Release of Aggression." *Journal of Cross-Cultural Psychology* 5: 109–123.

CONFLICT RESOLUTION

Conflicts between individuals or groups occur in all societies, with the intensity, frequency, reasons for, and expression of conflict varying widely from one society to another. All societies also have means to resolve conflicts among members of the group; again, there is considerable variation among societies. In modern nations like the United States a variety of mechanisms are available, with the choice depending on considerations such as the source of the conflict, the level of the damage incurred by one or both of the disputants, and the relationship between the parties. For example, one divorcing couple might be able to settle disputes about the division of joint property between themselves. But another couple may not be able to settle the matter through direct negotiation and turns instead to a mediator such as a clergyperson to help them resolve the conflict. And a third couple may not agree at all and both hire attorneys who litigate their clients' case in a court before a judge using witnesses and evidence.

In some non-Western societies, conflict resolution is less complicated and the choices available to disputants are more restricted. Scholars have suggested different classification systems to account for the various types of conflict resolution mechanisms found around the world. Probably the broadest and most inclusive is that developed by Katherine Newman through an analysis of legal systems in 60 societies. She lists eight types of legal systems:

1. **Self-help** or self-redress, in which the two disputants settle the conflict themselves, either peacefully or violently. Often, in self-help systems one party is able to simply impose his or her solution on the other party.
2. **Advisor** systems, in which a third party may give advice to the disputants, but they need not seek or follow the advice. The advisor is usually a respected person in the community who has moral authority to advise on the matter under dispute.
3. **Mediation,** in which a third party is expected to intercede to work out a compromise. Although their recommendations are not binding, mediators and go-betweens are often successful because of community pressure on the disputants to settle the matter.
4. **Elders' Council** systems, in which the disputants must use a third party who adjudicates and issues a decision that is binding. The third party is a respected person or group of persons such as elders, community leaders, or family heads.
5. **Restricted Council** systems, in which the disputants must use a third party who adjudicates and issues a decision that is binding. Here, the third party is a council composed of the community elite—the wealthy, the landowners, the political leaders—who have considerable decision-making power.
6. **Chieftainship,** in which the dispute is settled by the community or society leader who has the power to settle disputes and the means of enforcing his decisions.
7. **Paramount Chieftainship,** in which the society leader, who is usually a member of the royal family, is the ultimate authority. There are also sublevels of appeal and jurisdiction, with many disputes settled by local or regional officials appointed by the paramount chief.
8. **State Level systems,** in which there is centralized political leadership, a widespread cadre of government officials, and a uniform legal code. Courts with different areas and levels of jurisdiction are a major arena for dispute settlement.

The particular systems of conflict resolution found in a society are largely a function of the level of cultural complexity of the society. Cultural complexity means the relative number of different types of social, political, legal, and economic institutions found in a society and the interrelationships among those institutions. Some key markers of a high level of cultural complexity are an economy based on agriculture; the presence of social classes; large, permanent settlements; and a system of writing. The more complex a society, the more types of conflict resolution techniques will be available to individuals or groups in the society. Thus, a highly complex society like the United States uses all eight types, while in a less complex hunter-gatherer society, only self-help, advisors, and sometimes mediation are likely to be used. These cultures traditionally lacked formal mechanisms of conflict resolution that required the presence of a strong centralized political authority such as a king, chief, or judge to enforce the decision. One of the major effects of Western contact with and domination of many non-Western societies has been the imposition of complex Western legal systems, which eventually tend to displace the less formal native systems. It is often the case, however, that for some time both systems operate, with the indigenous people making heavy use of their traditional mechanisms in order to settle disputes locally and not involve colonial officials.

See also Advisors; Apology; Avoidance and Withdrawal; Blood Money; Councils; Feuding; Mediation; Self-Help Conflict Resolution; Oaths; Ordeals.

Koch, Klaus, and J. A. Sodergren. (1976) "Political Correlates of Conflict Management: A Cross-Cultural Study." *Law and Society Review* 10: 443–466.

Newman, Katherine S. (1983) *Law and Economic Organization: A Comparative Study of Preindustrial Societies.*

Schwartz, Richard D., and James C. Miller. (1964) "Legal Evolution and Societal Complexity." *American Journal of Sociology* 70: 159–169.

Sheils, Dean. (1986) "Cultural Evolution and Conflict Resolution." *Wisconsin Sociologist* 23: 4–14.

Wimberly, Howard. (1973) "Legal Evolution: One Further Step." *American Journal of Sociology* 79: 78–83.

Councils

A council is any group of limited membership that convenes to discuss or adjudicate certain issues, following a set of written or unwritten rules and procedures. Councils come in a broad range of forms and deal with a wide variety of matters in cultures around the world. Here we are concerned with only those types of councils whose role at least in part is to adjudicate disputes. About 15 percent of cultures rely on councils as the primary means to settle disputes among individuals or groups in the community or society. Other cultures also use councils, although they rely more heavily on other types of conflict resolution. Compared to conflict resolution mechanisms such as apology, retaliation, and mediation, councils are a more complex legal institution. They are more complex because the membership of the council is somewhat fixed, it operates in a structured manner, and the disputants are required to bring their dispute before the council, which has the authority to render a binding judgment. However, councils still have one key feature of informality: in many societies, a council has no means of enforcing its decision. This does not mean that the decision is meaningless; rather it is usually adhered to because the disputant's respect the status of the council members and because the community often supports the council's decision, not because the council has the authority to enforce it. In more complex legal institutions such as courts and chieftainships, the judicial authorities do have the means to enforce their decisions, often by means of an organized police force.

Councils that adjudicate disputes come in the form of either elder's councils or restricted councils, with the former more common. Elder's councils are composed of men (very few cultures permit women to serve on councils) who are selected for membership on the basis of some criteria such as age, reputation, or status as the head of a specific subgroup (clan, village) in the culture. Elder's councils are relatively democratic, representative bodies whose members represent all major social groups in the culture. Depending on the culture, these social groups might be families, lineages, clans, villages, neighborhoods, etc. In many cultures, elder's councils operate at various levels of jurisdiction, with one adjudicating matters at the village level, another at the regional level, and perhaps a third at the societal level. The social groups represented on each council are different, as each level of council represents a larger and broader segment of the society.

Councils settle disputes by holding hearings to ascertain the facts. Usually both disputants are permitted to present their case through speeches, witnesses, and testimony from supporters. In some cultures, councils may also use other means to collect the facts or determine the truth, including oaths, ordeals, and diviners. The council members are often advised by trusted members of their constituencies, and many members of the community attend the hearing. The council then issues its decision, which is usually arrived at through consensus, and orders punishment, compensation, or corrective action.

The Tiv of Nigeria make extensive use of elder's councils. Tiv society is divided into districts, kindreds, and families. Family matters are settled by the household heads. The kindred councils consist of the heads of each lineage in the kindred. These are men who are selected because they are the dominant individual in the group, because they are elderly (which means that they are closer to the ancestors), and because they are able public speakers. If this individual is not the oldest man in the lineage, he is then supported by the oldest man. The district council is composed of the members of the various kindred councils. Since for the Tiv the lineage rather than the individual is the basic social unit, the system is democratic and representative as each lineage is represented at both the kindred and district level.

Restricted councils are councils whose members are selected because they are prominent men in the community and represent prominent groups. The members might be a hereditary chief, the leader of a wealthy family, or a major landowner. In cultures with restricted councils, the council is a ruling elite whose decisions are usually adhered to because of the status of the council members in the community. For example, in traditional Samoan society, each village was ruled by a council composed of the hereditary chiefs, who convened each Monday morning. Disputes were settled through fact-finding by means of an oath-taking ritual. The Samoans also had a Great Council, composed of the chiefs of each village, that met only sporadically but served to unite the various island communities into a single society.

A third type of council is the chief's council, composed of men who advise the chief on various matters that come before him for a decision. However, it is the chief who makes the final decision and is seen as the final authority by the members of the culture. Thus, unlike the elder's and restricted types of council, an advisory council is not directly involved in conflict resolution.

See also ADVISORS; CONFLICT RESOLUTION; MEDIATION

Bohannan, Paul, and Laura Bohannan. (1958) "Three Sourcebooks in Tiv Ethnography."

Unpublished manuscript, Human Relations Area Files.

Mead, Margaret. (1930) *Social Organization of Manua.*

Newman, Katherine S. (1983) *Law and Economic Organization: A Comparative Study of Preindustrial Societies.*

Richards, Audrey, and Adam Kuper. (1971) *Councils in Action.*

COUNTING COUP

Counting coup is the name used for a set of customs related to public recognition of bravery in warfare characteristic of the Plains Indians of the central United States and southern Canada. Counting coup was part of the warfare complex of these groups that was a major feature of Plains culture in the eighteenth and nineteenth century. Warfare between the groups and then with the U.S. cavalry ended by 1890 when the Plains groups were either relocated or placed on reservations. Among major Plains groups are the Crow, Blackfoot, Comanche, Cheyenne, Arapaho, Pawnee, and Lakota.

The word "coup" is French for "blow" or "stroke." It was taken by the Plains Indians from French trappers and traders in Canada. For the Indians, coup meant touching an enemy warrior in a way that did not harm him, but also in a way that put one at great risk. Thus, coup was an act of bravery and for the Plains Indian warriors being brave and fearless was an important component of the cultural image of being a man. Counting coup was the practice of each warrior publicly telling about his brave deed or deeds after the battle. These stories were then retold at future community gatherings, especially those at which new coup were counted and added to a warrior's list of brave deeds. In this way, warriors accumulated coup throughout their lifetime, with their status as warriors depending on the amount of coup earned and their ability to lead successful missions. For example, Red Cloud, the celebrated Sioux chief, counted coup 80 times during his career.

While touching an enemy, usually with an object such as whip, lance, club, rifle, bow, stick, etc., constituted coup in all Plains groups, other acts also qualified. Among the Cheyenne, a warrior could count coup by saving a wounded comrade, having his horse shot out from under him, locating the enemy, charging the enemy alone, killing an enemy, or scalping an enemy. The Comanche counted coup for stealing horses, taking scalps, and killing an enemy, although in all situations coup depended more on the amount of risk at which the warrior placed himself rather than the actual act of killing an enemy warrior or stealing a horse. The Blackfoot counted coup for bravery at close quarters in combat, including riding over an enemy, killing at close range, riding fearlessly against the enemy, or capturing a valued object such as a war shirt, a war bonnet, a shield, or a bow.

As mentioned above, counting coup and the accumulation of coup symbolized bravery and was the way men earned public recognition as able and fearless warriors. For young warriors, counting their first coup was a major accomplishment, and all warriors remembered the day they counted their first coup. Coup was recounted frequently, and in ceremonies warriors wore coup shirts or carried coup sticks.

See also MILITARY GLORY; HEAD-HUNTING; HUMAN SACRIFICE; RAIDING; SCALPING.

Grinnell, George B. (1962) *Blackfoot Lodge Tales: The Story of a Prairie People.*

Hoebel, A. Adamson. (1960) *The Cheyennes: Indians of the Great Plains.*

CRIME

A crime is a violation of a law that requires that the criminal be punished. A crime differs from a violation of a norm (rule of behavior) or a custom or other offenses or wrongs in that there must be a formal process available for handling the criminal. Thus, crime is found only in cultures with a government powerful enough to define a behavior as a crime and to administer punishment to the criminal. This means that not all cultures have crime, for some (such as hunter/gatherer societies) lack leadership with judicial authority. However, all cultures have behaviors defined by the group as violations of norms that are subject to punishment, although the punishment will be inflicted by the victim, the victim's kin, or the entire group, rather than judicial authority.

Listed in the box below are only some of the broad range of behaviors that are considered to be crimes in some cultures, organized into the major categories of crime. Behaviors that are considered crimes or violations of norms in all or most cultures include incest, arson, theft, political assassination, nonpayment of debt, and treason.

Offenses against Life
abortion
blood feuds
cannibalism
death-hastening behavior
gerontocide
homicide
infanticide
suicide

Offenses against the Person
assault
battery
child abuse and neglect
kidnapping
elder abuse
evil eye
gossip
insults
libel
rape
slander
sorcery
spouse abuse and neglect
witchcraft

Sexual and Marital Offenses
bestiality
bride theft
coercive sex
desertion
extramarital sex
homosexuality
illegitimacy
incest
miscegenation
nonsupport
premarital sex
prostitution
seduction
sodomy

Property Offenses
arson
burglary
cruelty to animals
diverting water source
embezzlement
fraud
livestock rustling
malicious mischief
poaching
robbery
stealing
theft
trespass

Nonfulfillment of Obligations
breach of contract
malpractice
negligence
nonpayment of debts

Offenses against the State
assassination
banditry
bribery
conspiracy
contempt of court
counterfeiting
desertion
electoral fraud
espionage
falsification of documents
illegal entry
insubordination
mutiny
perjury
piracy
political malfeasance
sedition
slavery
smuggling
subornation
tax evasion
treason

Religious Offenses
black magic
blasphemy
grave robbing
impiety
possession of illegal charms
ritual offenses
sale of ceremonial objects
taboo violations
theft of ceremonial objects
violation of Sabbath
witchcraft

Social Offenses
breaches of etiquette
disorderly conduct
drug abuse
drunkenness
gambling
greed
laziness
loafing
lying
moonshining
noncooperation
quarrelsomeness

It is extremely difficult, if not impossible, to compare crime in different cultures. This is because of (1) the variation in definitions of crime and what behaviors are considered criminal; (2) the absence of information on the frequency of crime; and (3) when there are crime statistics, questions about how accurate and reliable that information is. One survey of from 50 to 117 cultures that broadly defined various categories of crime found that homicide is common in 10 percent of cultures, assault in 22 percent, theft in 20 percent, and trespass in 14 percent.

In all cultures except those where all people are equals (which are very few in number), different categories of individuals often have different sets of rules governing their behavior. These categories include the wealthy, leaders, warriors, religious practitioners, the young, the aged, and, in many cultures, men and women. The status of some of these categories exempts their members from punishment for offenses. For example, warriors are often not punished for aggressive behavior within the community, as they are expected to be aggressive. On the other hand, the special status of some other categories places greater burdens on their members. For example, religious practitioners are often expected to follow the laws and norms of behavior more closely than are other people and also often have to follow a special set of rules. Buddhist priests in Thailand, for instance, have eight sets of rules they must follow (Ingersoll 1969: 149). The first set is the most serious and prohibits:

1. Having sexual intercourse with any person or animal
2. Taking anything that is not given
3. Killing a person, or in any way causing a person's death
4. Deliberately lying or speaking deceitfully

Just as there are differing definitions of crime, there is a broad array of punishments for crime used in cultures around the world. In general, the more serious a crime is considered to be in a culture, the more serious the punishment, although, as discussed below, various mitigating circumstances often influence the defining of a specific criminal act as serious and the severity of the punishment. The major categories and types of punishments are:

Physical Punishments
Beating
Capital punishment
Flogging
Mutilation
Torture
Social Punishments
Gossip
Pillory
Ridicule
Social isolation
Property Punishments
Compensation
Confiscation
Destruction of property
Fines
Deprivation of Rights
Banishment
Enslavement
Imprisonment
Military service

In every culture for every crime there are always mitigating circumstances that might influence how serious a specific criminal act will be considered and how harshly the criminal punished. Thus, while cultures have a set of laws that define crimes and set punishments for them, these laws often represent the ideal and are not necessarily followed strictly in day-to-day life. Major mitigating circumstances are how much harm the crime caused, the motivation (purposeful or accidental) of the criminal, the relative statuses of the criminal and the victim, whether the criminal is a member of the society or a foreigner, and whether the criminal is insane. For example, if a Kalinga can prove immediately that he harmed someone by accident, he is immune from punishment. Or, among the Central Thai, thieves are likely to go uncaught unless they steal from a person wealthy enough to pay the police to investigate the matter. Thus, while the Central Thai classify stealing as a crime, in day-to-day life it is only a crime if one steals from a wealthy person.

Probably the most common mitigating circumstance is the status and personal characteristics of the criminal. In nearly all cultures with status distinctions based on either heredity or earned wealth, power, or education, those with higher status are less likely to be charged with crimes and less likely to be severely punished. In some cultures, rules governing the differential treatment of individuals on the basis of their social status are codified in law, while in others they are simply customary. The Amhara of Ethiopia, for example, have clear rules to assist judges in pronouncing sentence and punishment is expected to decline in severity in the following order (Messing 1957: 312):

The man who knows the law

The forgetful person (unstable personality)

The "balagär" (rustic peasant)

The poor and ignorant person (illiterates)

The stranger

The ignorant woman

The imbecile or invalid

The Ethiopian from a non-Amharic-speaking province

The child below age 12

The Amhara judge also considers the personality of the criminal and might adjust the punishment in consideration of whether the individual is known to be lawless, a bully, envious, careless, or proud, among other characteristics.

Despite the wide variety of types of crime and offenses committed in cultures around the world and the equally broad array of punishments for those crimes, little is known about the causes of crime in general across cultures, although there is fuller knowledge of the causes of some specific crimes such as homicide, suicide, and rape. We do know with some degree of confidence that personal crime (homicide and assault) is one component of a broader cultural pattern of violence. In cultures where there is much violent crime (committed in all cultures mostly by men), men often also fight in wars, derive personal glory from military successes, are expected to act aggressively, and as children are subjected to harsh disciplinary techniques that might make them mistrustful of and hostile toward other people. There is also some commonality across cultures as regards theft. Theft is a commonly committed crime in cultures where there are clear wealth differences between individuals and families and where children are raised in ways that stress obedience and self-reliance and therefore leave them feeling somewhat unloved. In this situation, theft may be an effort to replace the love missing in childhood through the acquisition of the possessions of others.

See also ASSAULT; BANISHMENT; BRIDE THEFT AND RAIDING; CAPITAL PUNISHMENT; CRUELTY TO ANIMALS; DEATH-HASTENING BEHAVIOR; GERONTOCIDE; HOMICIDE; INFANTICIDE; MACHOISM; RAPE; SHUNNING; SUICIDE; WITCHCRAFT.

Allen, Martin G. (1972) "A Cross-Cultural Study of Aggression and Crime." *Journal of Cross-Cultural Psychology* 3: 259–271.

Bacon, Margaret K., Irvin L. Child, and Herbert Barry III. (1963) "A Cross-Cultural Study of the Correlates of Crime." *Journal of Abnormal and Social Psychology* 66: 291–300.

Barton, R. F. (1949) *The Kalingas.*

Ember, Carol R., and Melvin Ember. (1992) "Warfare, Aggression, and Resource Problems:

Cross-Cultural Codes." *Behavior Science Research* 26: 169–226.

Ingersoll, Jasper C. (1969) *The Priest and the Path: An Analysis of the Priest Role in a Central Thai Village.*

Messing, Simon D. (1957) *The Highland-Plateau Amhara of Ethiopia.* Ph.D. Dissertation, University of Pennsylvania.

Murdock, George P., et al. (1987) *Outline of Cultural Materials.* 5th edition.

Russell, Elbert W. (1972) "Factors of Human Aggression: A Cross-Cultural Factor Analysis of Characteristics Related to Warfare and Crime." *Behavior Science Notes* 7: 275–312.

Seymour-Smith, Charlotte. (1986) *Dictionary of Anthropology.*

CRUELTY TO ANIMALS

Cruelty to animals is not a topic that has been subject to systematic cross-cultural study, although there are mentions in ethnographic reports of how animals are treated in some cultures. In probably all cultures there are some instances when some individuals treat animals cruelly. As regards cultural proscriptions about the treatment of animals, in 48 percent of cultures at least one type of animal (usually dogs) is routinely treated cruelly. Included in this group of cultures are at least 5 percent in which parents either encourage or allow their children to treat animals cruelly. This regular cruel treatment follows two patterns. In most of those cultures where animal cruelty is allowed, the targets are most often animals kept as pets who are regularly beaten, kicked, whipped, cursed, stoned, teased, or poorly fed. In a smaller number of cultures where animals are used as beasts of burden, horses, camels, and donkeys are regularly mistreated and expected to perform their work despite illness, injury, or malnourishment. In 24 percent of cultures there is no routine cruelty to animals, although some animals may often be treated cruelly. And in 28 percent of cultures cruelty to animals is unusual. Included in this last category are a number of cultures, such as the Blackfoot and Iroquois in North America, that prohibit cruelty to domestic animals.

The types of animals treated cruelly run the full breadth of animals used domestically or hunted, with dogs, cattle, horses, and chickens the most common targets. In some cultures it is domesticated animals who receive the harshest treatment, in others it is beasts of burden, and in still others it is animals taken in the hunt (who are often tortured as they are slaughtered).

Beyond cruelty to animals by isolated individuals, we find in some cultures institutionalized cruelty to animals, often in the form of sport or entertainment. Broadly defined, institutionalized cruelty encompasses a broad range of human activities, all of which cause harm to animals. These include hunting, fishing, or trapping for nonsubsistence reasons; raising animals under harsh conditions; use of animals in sports such as horse racing, dog racing, bullfighting, cockfighting, rodeo, etc.; confining and displaying animals in zoos and aquariums; the use of animals in scientific experiments or medical research; and the sacrifice of animals in religious rituals. While some individuals consider some or all of these as examples of cruelty to animals, only in a few cultures are all of these activities prohibited. Institutionalized cruelty can also be defined more narrowly to include culturally acceptable practices that center on the purposeful physical harm of animals for the noneconomic benefit of human beings. From this perspective, the most common form of institutional cruelty is animal sacrifice in religion, a common practice in many cultures, although animal sacrifice often has an economic purpose as it is performed to please the gods or spirits who will then assist the believers.

Beyond sacrifice, the two most common forms of animal cruelty around the world are bullfighting and cockfighting. Other types of cruelty—such as bear-, bull-, and dog-baiting, which were popular amusements in England in the seventeenth and eighteenth centuries—have now mostly disappeared.

Bullfighting is a spectator sport and public ritual in which a bull is fought by a matador and usually killed by being stabbed with a sword as part of an elaborate ritual. Bullfighting is popular in Spain, southern France, Portugal, and Mexico, where the fights take place in large public arenas and are witnessed by crowds that may number in the tens of thousands, depending on the size of the stadium. Bullfighting is a highly specialized and ritualized activity, with a number of highly trained participants, including the bulls, which are raised to be especially aggressive; the matador; horsemen; cape wavers; and other assistants. The participants wear specialized clothing, participate in a pre-event procession, and the actual fight and killing of the bull requires a sequence of highly stylized movements. The skill of the matador's performance is judged by the crowd as indicated by the level of applause and cheering; he is rewarded with one ear of the bull, both ears, or both ears and the tail. The aggressiveness of the bull and the matador's skill, bravery, and grace all enter into

Animal offerings, such as this Koryak dog sacrifice, are a key element of religion in some cultures, but would be categorized as cruelty in others.

the crowd's assessment of his performance. From a cultural perspective, bullfighting is a complex spectacle that is related to economic, political, religious, and social factors in the cultures where it is found. One view is that bullfighting is neither a game nor a contest (the bull has no chance of winning or even surviving) but instead a form of ritual sacrifice through which male identity and values are publicly displayed and acknowledged. Bullfighters have almost always been men with attempts by women to become bullfighters usually resisted.

Cockfighting is a popular sport in the Philippines, Indonesia, and Latin America, especially in Puerto Rico, Cuba, and Haiti. Cockfighting involves the breeding and training of game cocks for the purpose of pitting them against each other in fights. Cockfighting is a broadly popular activity in cultures where it occurs. Where legal, it is regularly scheduled in cockfighting pits; where illegal, it occurs on a more informal basis. Cockfighting is an exclusively male activity and involves the two men who pit their cocks against each other's and the large number of men and older boys who watch, bet on the fight, and join in its excitement. Gambling is a major component of the fight and men bet with each other at the start of the fight and throughout until one cock wins by killing or maiming the other. Injury is caused by sharpened natural spurs or sharp bone or metal spurs placed over the natural ones. A major feature of cockfighting is the cock owner's identification with his fighting cock and the male aggressiveness that the cock symbolizes. Thus, training and managing a cock or betting on a particular cock may have significant emotional and self-identity content for the men involved. Compared to bullfighting, cockfighting is a more intensely personal and emotional activity. At the same time cockfighting, like bullfighting, is also a highly ritualized activity enmeshed in the economic, political, and social order of the society or community.

A final form of cruelty to animals is the harming or killing of animals owned by an enemy in order to exact revenge. In England, for example, horse maiming and killing has occurred in the countryside during periods of economic strife and has, in the past, also been carried out, in a form called "hamstringing," by villagers to annoy local squires.

Some observers have suggested that cruelty to animals is a form of displaced aggression that allows individuals to express anger without precipitating a conflict with the appropriate human target of that anger. As regards individual behavior, this is no doubt true in some situations; however, there is no evidence that cruelty to animals serves as an institutionalized means of indirectly expressing anger in cultures around the world.

Conrad, Barnaby. (1961) *Encyclopedia of Bullfighting.*

Geertz, Clifford. (1973) *The Interpretation of Cultures.*

Pitt-Rivers, Julian. (1993) "The Spanish Bull-Fight and Kindred Activities." *Anthropology Today* 9: 11–15.

Rivera, Generoso F., and Robert T. McMillan. (1952) *The Rural Philippines.*

Steward, Julian H., et al. (1956) *The People of Puerto Rico: A Study in Social Anthropology.*

Death-Hastening Behavior

Death-hastening behavior is action or inaction by members of a society that directly leads to the death of another member of the society. Death-hastening behavior can take any one of three forms: (1) failing to support the material needs of an individual, (2) abandoning an individual, or (3) killing an individual. Death-hastening behavior differs from homicide in that death-hastening is socially acceptable, and it differs from capital punishment or death through blood revenge in that the person killed or allowed to die is not accused or being punished for committing a crime.

Death-hastening actions are taken primarily against individuals who have become a burden to the group and threaten its survival. These are usually the elderly, although death-hastening may also be used with infants (infanticide) and the disabled. As regards the elderly, death-hastening behavior occurs in about 40 percent of the world's non-Western societies. Death-hastening behavior is one of three ways people treat the aged in cultures around the world. The first way is to support them by supplying them with food and shelter, helping to transport them, affording them respect, and involving them in community activities. The second way is to not support them by forcing them to live alone, insulting them, taking property from them, and treating them as witches. These nonsupportive activities, while lowering the quality of a person's life, do not necessarily lead to death. The third way is to hasten their death. In most societies, elderly people are treated in all three ways, with different aged people treated differently.

The major determinant of whether or not an aged person is the object of death-hastening behavior is whether that person is considered by others to be either intact or decrepit. In nearly all cultures, a person is considered intact when he or she is productive. A person is considered decrepit when he or she is a social or economic liability; that is, the individual requires the support of others to survive, support that would otherwise go to others who are productive or might put the person providing the support at risk. Of course, societies vary widely in how they define productivity and liability. In most societies, an aged person is considered productive until a change in his or her health or a change in the society's circumstances causes others to redefine the person as decrepit. Once an individual is classified as decrepit, they are far more likely to be the object of death-hastening behavior. When an individual is considered productive, he or she is more likely to be supported or the object of nonsupportive, but not death-hastening, treatment.

Thus, the image of old people floating off into the sea on an ice flow is an oversimplification. While in about 36 percent of non-Western societies some aged are left to die, it is usually only those considered decrepit who are the socially acceptable objects of death-hastening behaviors. For example, among the Yanomamö of northwestern Brazil, only the aged, who are unable to participate in migrations, and the seriously ill, who cannot be cured, are killed either by beating with a stick or abandonment in a cave. The Saami (Lapps) of northern Europe in the past killed only the decrepit aged who, like the Yanomamö decrepit aged, could not migrate, in this case in pursuit of reindeer herds. These people were either drowned through a hole in the ice or pushed off a cliff. The latter custom was called *saalekeskoute*, meaning "blessed journey." It is usually family members who kill or abandon their decrepit relatives. While such actions bring personal grief to the participants, they also realize that using extraordinary efforts to keep the person alive will likely drain resources such as food, shelter, energy, and time from others and may put the survival of the entire group at risk.

Despite the acceptance of death-hastening behavior in some societies and the role played by decrepitude in deciding who dies, it is also important to note that in some societies adult children kill their parents for other reasons. Perhaps the most common reason is that sons desire resources such as money, land, status, or power controlled by their fathers. Killing their father may be the quickest means to obtaining these resources for adult sons who no longer want to wait. This situation occurred in peasant communities in Europe in the past where fathers controlled the family farmland and, therefore, the lives of their adult sons. When fathers passed the land on to their sons before they died, they often did so only with written assurance that the sons would provide them with specified amounts of food each year.

See also GERONTOCIDE; INFANTICIDE; HOMICIDE.

Daly, Martin, and Margo Wilson. (1988) *Homicide.*

Glascock, Anthony P. (1984) "Decrepitude and Death-Hastening: The Nature of Old Age in Third World Societies." *Studies in Third World Societies* 22: 43–67.

Sokolovsky, Jay, ed. (1990) *Culture, Aging, and Society.*

DEINDIVIDUATION

Deindividuation is the psychological state in which an individual loses a sense of his or her own identity and instead feels anonymous and unconnected. Psychological experiments show that individuals in a deindividuized state can be easily led to behave more aggressively than they would under normal circumstances. This is because when people feel anonymous they are less likely to be concerned with controlling behaviors that might be negatively evaluated by others. In psychological experiments the participants were deindividuized by masking them, immersing them in an all-consuming social group, or making them dress alike. When deindividuized in these ways, they behaved more aggressively toward others than did participants in the experiments who were not deindividuized.

Cross-culturally, the concept of deindividuation has been applied to violent behavior in warfare in a survey of 27 cultures. In cultures where warriors kill, torture, or mutilate the enemy, these warriors prepare for battle by deindividuizing themselves by altering their physical appearance. Presumably, by changing their physical appearance they temporarily lose their own personal identity and are now free to act more aggressively than they would normally. For example, Blackfoot Indian warriors of the Great Plains wore medicine feathers, necklaces, face and body paint, carried decorated shields, and applied paint to their horses. The Masai of Kenya, who in pre- and early-colonial times fought with neighboring groups, went to even greater lengths. Warriors combed their hair into pigtails, and wore long necklaces, a feathered cap, a helmet decorated with ostrich feathers, ornamental leggings, and body oil.

These examples suggest that deindividuation may be one psychological component of the military glory complex, found in many cultures around the world, where men achieve status and power through their exploits in war. Deindividuation frees them to act more aggressively and therefore become more successful warriors than they would otherwise. Of course, unique dress and body ornamentation, both in these two cultures and others, serves purposes beyond deindividuation, such as creating group uniformity and distinguishing comrades from the enemy in battle and warriors from non-warriors in their own culture.

See also COUNTING COUP; MILITARY GLORY; SCALPING.

Ewers, John C. (1955) *The Horse in Blackfoot Indian Culture with Comparative Material from other Western Tribes.* U.S. Bureau of American Ethnology, Bulletin 159.

Merker, Meritz. (1910) *The Masai: Ethnographic Monograph of an East African Semite People.*

Watson, Robert J. (1973) "Investigation into Deindividuation Using a Cross-Cultural Survey Technique." *Journal of Personality and Social Psychology* 25: 342–345.

Uniforms are a means of deindividuation; here a Cossack squad chief assists two cadets with their new uniforms.

DRUNKEN BRAWLING

People react to alcoholic beverages in different ways. Some become silly, others flirtatious, still others quiet, and some become angry and hostile, sometimes to the point of acting violently. Of course, it is not only the alcohol that makes people behave in a certain way, but also their expectations about what alcohol will do to them, the place where they drink, and the people they drink with. For example, fights are rare in quiet wine bars frequented by couples on a Saturday evening, but common in country-western bars frequented by groups of young men on Friday nights. Just as with individuals, cultures around the world vary in the types of behaviors typically displayed by members of the culture when drinking.

One form of drinking behavior that occurs with some frequency around the world is drunken brawling. Drunken brawling is the regular occurrence of physical assault among people in a community while they are intoxicated. Drunken brawling mostly involves men; it may involve women, but usually as the victims of beatings administered by their husbands after their husbands return home. The drinking and fighting takes place as part of drinking bouts involving groups of men or as part of a community festival during which large quantities of alcoholic beverages are consumed. During the festivities some individuals become angry and verbally abusive and provoke fights with others. These fights are expected to occur with other members of the community watching and intervening only if the violence becomes too severe. For example, festivals of the Highland Quechua of Ecuador consist of eating, drinking, dancing, and singing. People are expected to get drunk, and it is the individual who refuses to drink who is seen as unfriendly and is punished, perhaps by being whipped. Those who do not want to drink find it best to avoid the festival altogether. When drunk, normal rules of behavior are abandoned and people insult each other. Sons might fight with their fathers or godfathers, and a brother with his brother, behaviors that are unheard of in daily life. The behavior is excused completely because the individuals are drunk, and no hard feelings remain after the festival ends and the participants sober up.

This pattern of drunken brawling, while occurring in about 42 percent of cultures, is especially common in Native cultures in North America (16 percent) and South America (12 percent). In fact, of the cultures where drunken brawling occurs, two-thirds are in the New World. Why drunken brawling is more common in indigenous New World cultures is not clear, although one key factor is that Native Americans learned how to behave when drinking from those who first introduced them to distilled spirits. These were often traders and trappers who drank heavily and acted violently themselves. An explanation for drunken brawling and heavy drinking in general emphasizes the role drunken brawling plays in reducing stress and anxiety in the community. Drunken brawling often acts as a safety valve that allows people to express anger and act aggressively in a context that allows them to escape any punishment for their behavior and also prevents the violence from going too far. The safety valve function of drunken brawling seems strongest in communities with strong leaders. Perhaps in these communities people cannot openly express aggression for fear of punishment, and drunken brawling provides a safe outlet for its expression. On the other hand, in communities with weak leadership, drunken brawling does not seem to be a safety valve but instead is part of a general pattern of frequent interpersonal violence, including wife-beating and fear of supernatural aggression.

Marshall, Mac, ed. (1979) *Beliefs, Behaviors, and Alcoholic Beverages: A Cross-Cultural Survey.*

Parsons, Elsie W. C. (1945) *Peguche, Canton of Otavalo, Province of Imbabura: A Study of Andean Indians.*

Schaefer, James M. (1973) *A Hologeistic Study of Family Structure and Sentiment, Supernatural Beliefs, and Drunkenness.*

DUELS

Duels are a form of conflict resolution usually engaged in to settle a quarrel or to defend one's honor. As a form of conflict resolution, duels are less about settling the disagreement through the impartial consideration of the facts and more about venting aggressive emotions through direct competition between the two parties. The most common forms of duels are the following:

1. Physical duels such as wrestling and boxing matches, chest-pounding duels, head-butting, and buffeting
2. Duels with weapons such as swords, clubs, spears, and arrows
3. Word duels involving the ritualized exchange of spoken insults
4. Song duels involving the ritualized exchange of sung insults

All types of duels are institutionalized, ritualized mechanisms of conflict resolution. They differ from day-to-day expressions of aggression in that the duel is governed by a set of rules that determine which conflicts are subject to settlement through dueling, who may participate, what dueling behaviors are permissible, and how one party wins. Additionally, duels are conducted in public and the winner is usually determined by the judgment of the observers.

See also PHYSICAL DUELS; SONG DUELS; WORD DUELS.

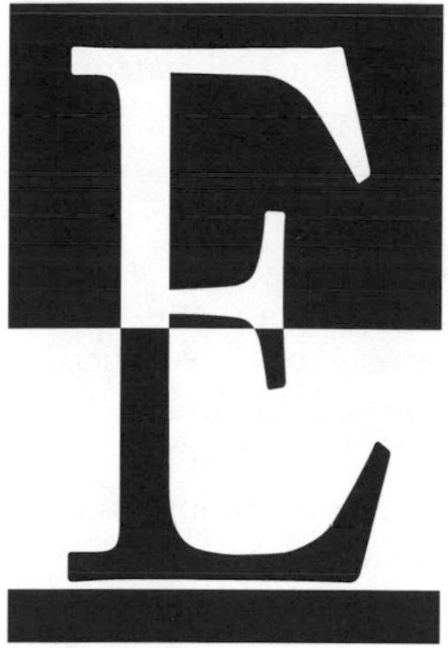

Ethnic Conflict

Ethnic conflict means violent conflict between or among groups who differ from each other in terms of culture, religion, physical features, or language. Ethnic conflict has been for the last several years and continues to be the most common form of collective violence in the world. In 1988, the majority of the 111 violent conflicts in the world involved minority and majority groups within nations. As of July 1993, there were no fewer than 25 ethnic conflicts that involved the regular use of violence—mass killings, executions, terrorist bombings, assassinations, looting, rapes, forced expulsion, and other acts of violence—by one or both groups to achieve their aims. In addition, there are several dozen other conflicts that are mostly nonviolent and hundreds of situations of political/economic/cultural repression that may eventually erupt into open conflict and violence.

Although attention is always drawn to the bloodiest and most protracted of ethnic conflicts—Catholics and Protestants in Northern Ireland; Serbs, Bosnian Muslims, and Croats in the Balkans; Sri Lankan Tamils and Sinhalese in Sri Lanka; Kurds in the Middle East; Armenians and Azerbaijani in Nagorno-Karabakh—the many nonviolent conflicts should not be ignored as they are the seedbeds of the violent conflicts of the future. Nonviolent ethnic conflict often takes the form of political, economic, or cultural repression of ethnic minorities and includes restrictions on voting, burdensome taxes, exclusion from certain professions, residential isolation, educational quotas, prohibitions on the use of the ethnic language, and restrictions on religious worship. A 1989 survey lists 261 minority groups (many of which are ethnic groups) in 99 of 126 nations as the victims of such oppression, suggesting a long and troubled future for ethnic relations around the world.

Another form of ethnic conflict is legal conflict, which is occurring with some frequency in North America, Australia, and elsewhere where native peoples (Indians, Inuit/Eskimos and Aleuts in North America; aboriginal peoples in Australia; Maori in New Zealand; and Saami in Nordic nations, among others) are seeking to reestablish their legal, economic, political, cultural, and religious rights through petitions to the state and national governments and legal actions. These actions have the goals of restoring to them ownership of their ancestral lands or payment of compensation for the lands that are nearly always now owned by nonindigenous people, official recognition as a distinct political entity, freedom from state and some federal laws, religious freedom, and the right to self-determination and self-government.

Ethnic conflict often involves more than just conflict between the groups, as there is often conflict between factions within each group, and other nations and peoples often become involved. In Sri Lanka, for example, the conflict between the Sinhalese and Sri Lankan Tamils has been accompanied by assassinations, bombings, and riots between political factions in both groups and violence directed at Muslims in Sri Lanka. Similar situations have occurred in Northern Ireland, Azerbaijan, and elsewhere as political rivals and their followers battle for influence and power. Often the key policy distinction between the factions is their support for peaceful accommodation resolutions to the conflict versus violent conquest resolutions.

At the international level, ethnic conflicts usually also involve nations and citizens of nations who are not direct combatants in the conflict. Ethnic conflicts are a major source of refugees and displaced persons who seek safety in noninvolved nations or nations that are supportive of their interests, or nations with large ethnic confederate populations. These large refugee populations put heavy economic, social, and political stress on the host nation and may lead to ethnic conflict within that nation, as in Germany, and give the nation a stake in seeing the external conflict quickly resolved. While those forced to flee are usually members of the warring groups, other noncombatants may be affected as well. For example, in Sri Lanka hundreds of thousands of Muslims not involved in the conflict fled from the eastern Tamil region to safety in the western region in addition to the Tamils who fled north and east and out of the country and the Sinhalese who fled south.

In addition to accepting refugees, nations with an interest in the conflict or ties to one of the groups may choose to become directly involved by assisting one ethnic group, as with the British in Northern Ireland, Turkey and Greece in Cyprus, and India in Sri Lanka, among others. Additionally, even if a government remains officially neutral or uninvolved, its citizens will often support members of their ethnic group in another nation as in Jewish support for Israel and Irish-American support for Irish Catholics in Northern Ireland. For many people, mother country sentiments remain powerful and feelings of ethnic solidarity quickly convert into political and economic support when the security of the homeland is threatened.

Types of Ethnic Conflict

Although students of ethnic conflict often lump all such conflicts together as a single type of human conflict, ethnic conflict actually takes a variety of forms. One key distinction is between conflicts that occur in unranked situations versus those in ranked situations. In an unranked situation the ethnic groups are relatively equal in power or perceive themselves to be so. This is the case in some postcolonial African nations such as Nigeria, Kenya, and South Africa where different ethnic groups compete for political and economic power. In a ranked situation, the ethnic groups in a nation are ordered in a hierarchy of power. Conventional wisdom holds that ethnic conflicts will be more common and less amenable to control in unranked situations where the groups are in competition for wealth and power and where one group is not powerful enough to repress the other groups. This was the situation in the former Soviet Union where Russian domination kept ethnic conflicts under control.

Another distinction related to this first one is between conflicts in the developing world and those in the industrialized world. The former often center on competition between ethnic groups for political dominance while the latter often involve separatist movements by ethnic minorities and repression by the government.

A third distinction can be made among different types of violent ethnic conflict on the basis of the goals of the participants in the conflict. From this perspective, violent conflicts in the world today fall into five categories:

1. **Separatist Movements.** Violence occurs as part of an effort by an ethnic group to become politically independent or as part of an effort by a nation to prevent the group

from doing so. Such conflicts are quite common and most often involve minority groups seeking to establish an independent nation in their ancestral homeland, which is now controlled by the nation within which they live.

2. **Internal Rivalry for Autonomy, Political Power, or Territorial Control.** Violence occurs as part of a conflict between ethnic groups in one nation or between an ethnic group and the government over access to and control of economic resources, political power, territory, or political autonomy within the nation. When the goals of the group seeking autonomy within the nation or more power or wealth seem unattainable, they may shift their goal to separatism. Such conflicts are especially common in former colonies, and to a large degree result from colonial policies that purposefully created rivalries between indigenous peoples and also afforded more education, status, and government or business access to one group. Upon independence, these multiethnic nations are often faced with ethnic competition for political power that pits those who enjoyed more power under colonial rule with those now seeking power. Because of the link to colonial policies, such conflicts are most common in former colonized nations in South Asia and Africa.
3. **Conquest.** Violence occurs as part of a war involving two or more nations where ethnic differences between or among groups is a major factor in their mutual animosity. The objective of the war might be the conquest of the other ethnic group or its removal from all or some of its territory. Such conflicts are now quite rare.
4. **Survival.** Violence occurs as part of an attempt by a national government to forcibly assimilate, harm, remove, or drive out an ethnic minority or deprive it of the social, religious, political, or economic rights granted to other residents of the nation. While most such conflicts in the world today are mainly nonviolent, although political rioting is not uncommon, these conflict situations have the potential to explode into violence in many nations around the world.
5. **Irredentist.** Violence occurs as part of an attempt by an ethnic group(s) or nation(s) to regain or retain territory on the basis of an alleged ancestral or historical right to the territory. Often the territory is controlled by another nation, but it is located adjacent to, and the population is mainly of, the ethnic group dominant in the nation seeking ownership of the territory. Irredentist conflicts, which are very common today, are often the result of national boundaries established during colonial times, or in eastern Europe during the era of Soviet dominance, with these boundaries often ignoring already existing ethnic boundaries and claims by local groups to what they considered their ethnic homeland.

The table on page 52 lists the major ethnic conflicts around the world as of January 1994—the ethnic groups involved, the nations where they are occurring, and the type of conflict, based on this five-type typology. Some conflicts, of course, are of more than one type, because the motivations of the conflicting groups are different or because political factions within one group may have different goals. For the most part, this list omits the mainly nonviolent survival conflicts involving issues of minority rights. A full list of these may be found in the publications by Gurr cited below.

Religious Conflict

Closely related and sometimes indistinguishable from ethnic conflict is religious conflict—

Ethnic Conflicts in 1994

Ethnic Group(s)	Nation	Conflict Type
Abkahzians, Georgians	Georgia	Separatist
Albanians, Serbs	Serbia	Survival, Irredentist
Armenians, Azerbaijani Turks	Azerbaijan	Irredentist
Assamese	India	Separatist, Survival
Baha'i	Iran	Survival
Basques	Spain	Separatist
Bodo	India	Survival
Bosnians, Serbs	Bosnia, Serbia	Survival, Conquest, Irredentist
Catalans	Spain	Survival
Catholics, Protestants	Northern Ireland	Separatist, Irredentist
Chakma	Bangladesh	Survival
Chechen-Ingush	Russia	Separatist
Copts	Egypt	Survival
Croats, Serbs	Croatia	Separatist, Conquest, Survival
Cypriots	Cyprus	Separatist
Indo-Fijians, Fijians	Fiji	Survival
Foreigners in Germany	Germany	Survival
French Canadians	Canada	Separatist, Internal
Gypsies and Travelers	Europe	Survival
Hausa, Yoruba, Igbo	Nigeria	Internal
Hindus, Muslims	India	Survival, Internal
Hungarians	Romania	Survival, Irredentist
Hutu, Tutsi	Burundi, Rwanda	Survival, Internal
Israelis, Palestinians	Middle East	Survival, Separatist, Irredentist
Jakun, Tiv	Nigeria	Survival
Kachin, Karen, Mon	Myanmar	Survival, Internal
Kashmiri	India	Separatist, Irredentist
Kurds	Iran, Iraq	Separatist
Kurds	Turkey	Survival, Irredentist
Luo, Kalejin	Kenya	Internal
Nagas	India	Separatist
Nepalese	Bhutan	Survival
Ossetes	Georgia	Separatist
Russians	Former Soviet Republics	Survival, Internal
Russians and Ukrainians	Moldova	Separatist
Shi'ite Muslims (Marsh Arabs)	Iraq	Survival
Sikhs	India	Separatist, Survival, Internal
Tamils, Sinhalese	Sri Lanka	Internal, Separatist
Tibetans	China	Survival, Separatist
Timorese	Indonesia	Survival
Vietnamese	Cambodia	Survival

conflict between two groups who adhere to different religions. Since the religion of conflicting groups is often the most visible symbol of group differences to outsiders, many conflicts between ethnic groups are often assumed to be religious in nature. However, this is often only a perception of outsiders who are unaware of long-standing hostility and competing territorial claims between the groups and does not mean that all ethnic conflicts result from religious differences between the combatants nor that all religious conflict is ethnic conflict. Some ethnic conflicts, such as those involving the Kurds in the Middle East and the Basques in Spain, involve groups of the same religion (Islam and Catholicism, respectively), although there are other cultural differences between the groups. In other conflicts, religious differences are present, such as between the Protestant and Catholic Northern Irish, but other factors such as economic conditions and political repression are more basic causes of the conflict. And in other conflicts, such as between the Israelis and Palestinians, religious differences are a major barrier to peaceful relations but are not the only cause of the conflict. Finally, there are some conflicts, such as between Muslims and Hindus in India, that are essentially religious in nature, although in this case the two groups are actually quite similar culturally.

Perhaps the most common form of ethnic conflict is the persecution of religious minorities. Today, groups suffering from persecution that is mainly caused by religious differences (although issues of economic and political competition are rarely absent altogether) include Copts in Egypt, Baha'i in Iran, and Shi'ite Muslims called Marsh Arabs in southern Iraq.

One special form of religious conflict is that of religious fundamentalist movements that often involve efforts by fundamentalist leaders and their followers to replace secular rule with religious rule. While Christian, Hindu, Jewish, and other fundamentalist movements can be found around the world, it is the Islamic fundamentalist movement that draws the most attention.

Islam is one of the major world religions, with more than 950 million adherents worldwide in 1993, slightly fewer than one-half the number of Christians in the world. A follower of Islam is called a *Muslim* in English, which is now preferred to *Moslem,* the term conventionally used until about 20 years ago. Islam was founded by Mohammed in what is now Saudi Arabia between 610 and 632 A.D. The sacred book of Islam is the Qur'an (Koran), which is held to be the one true statement of God's word, and in the view of Muslims, supersedes divine revelation as set forth in the Jewish and Christian bibles. The Five Pillars of Islam followed by Muslims are: (1) accepting and testifying that there is no god except Allah and that Mohammed is his true prophet; (2) praying five times daily, in the direction of Mecca; (3) fasting during the month of Ramadan; (4) giving alms to the poor; and (5) making a pilgrimage to Mecca, the holy land. Beyond a system of belief and worship, Islam is also a prescription for daily living and Muslims live their lives in a manner consistent with Islamic requirements. Thus, like Judaism, Islamic practice is filled with rules and prescriptions for daily life that go beyond religious practice. The two main branches of Islam are Sunni and Shi'ite Islam, with each and especially Shi'ite having a number of distinct subsects.

Although its origins are in the Middle East, Islam spread through trade, conquest, migrations, and conversion over the centuries to north Africa, northwest Africa, Central Asia, South Asia, and Southeast Asia. Today, the four nations with the largest Muslim populations are not in the Middle East but in Asia—Indonesia, Bangladesh, Pakistan, and India. Of these, Pakistan, along with Iran in the Middle East and the Sudan in Africa, are Islamic rather than secular nations. All other nations with majority Islamic populations are secular.

Although the nations with the largest Islamic populations are outside the Middle East and North Africa, Islamic fundamentalism is centered in the Middle East where Islamic and Arab identity are closely interrelated and are contrasted with Christian and Western identity. At the same time, however, Islamic fundamentalism is global in that some Muslims in many nations adhere to the political agenda of the movement and in addition, whether fundamentalism is directly involved or not, Muslims are involved in ethnic conflict situations in Bosnia, Serbia (Albanian Muslims), Cyprus (Turkish Muslims), Georgia, Azerbaijan, the Philippines (Muslim separatists on the island of Mindanao), India (Muslims in general and in Kashmir in particular), Sri Lanka, Israel, France, and Nigeria. And in the United States, the bombing of the World Trade Center in New York City in 1993 produced a rise in anti-Muslim and anti-Arab feelings among the general population.

The fundamentalist movement in the Middle East centers on efforts by fundamentalists to replace secular governments in a number of (if not all) nations with Islamic governments or governments that adhere to Islamic values. To achieve this end, Islamic organizations have sought power through elections and have resorted to violence, including assassinations, terrorism, riots, strikes, and the persecution of non-Muslim minorities. Fundamentalists have also mounted what are called "cultural offenses" in such nations as Egypt to replace secular principles with Islamic ones. For example, efforts have been made to ban Western art and literature, to change the school curriculum, and to require women and girls to wear veils. In the affected nations, the responses to the perceived threat have varied—Tunisia, Algeria, and Egypt have reacted by forcibly repressing fundamentalist organizations. Jordan has allowed them political participation and fundamentalists hold the majority in the Jordanian parliament, while Saudi Arabia has sought to placate them while the royal family maintains absolute control. Outside the region, where in many nations fundamentalism is seen as a possible threat to order and secular rule, some ethnic conflicts are motivated at least in part by a desire to limit Muslim power.

The roots of the current Islamic fundamentalist movement go back 1,400 years to the founding of Islam and the ensuing and never-resolved conflict with the values of Western civilization and Christianity and the frequent military battles between the Islamic world, nations, or civilizations and the West. For the past 300 years Europe has had the upper hand, to the point that the political map of the modern Middle East is a product of European colonialism and Western customs and products are found throughout the Middle East. The fundamentalist movement is in large part a reaction against Western domination through the creation of independent Islamic nations and a unified Arab polity based on Islam, as existed in the past. Thus, the rhetoric of the movement stresses anti-Western, anticolonial, and anti-imperialism themes and targets governments, institutions, and individuals believed to be loyal to or examples of these themes. And, in accord with Islamic belief, the movement is to many if not all participants a Holy War or struggle involving a battle of Good versus Evil, with an Islamic victory and the conversion of others to Islam a triumph by Good.

Causes of Ethnic Conflict

As yet there is no complete answer to this question, and given the different types of ethnic conflict and the different situations in which they occur, the question may ultimately require several, perhaps related, answers. In attempting to explain ethnic conflict in general as well as specific conflicts, one must consider the basic nature and strength of ethnic ties, situational factors that may encourage the development of ethnic solidarity and ethnic-based competition, and the actual motives articulated by the groups. As regards ethnicity, political scientist Donald Horowitz reminds us that ethnic solidarity is "powerful, permeative, passionate, and pervasive." Additionally, some biologically oriented researchers suggest that strong feelings of ethnic solidarity and ethnic conflict have their roots in human biological evolution and thus, it is not surprising that ethnic groups will fight to dominate other groups or to protect their own interests. Another, though not necessarily contradictory, line of thought is that in many nations over the last several decades, ethnic groups have emerged or reemerged as interest groups whose members coalesce as a means of gaining political and economic power. Recently, a number of situational factors have drawn special attention as causes of ethnic conflict including the end of centralized rule in former Communist nations; the end of colonial or colonial-style rule in Africa and Asia; the ideal of democracy, which places groups in direct competition; and economic inequalities between ethnic groups both within and across nations.

In a recent attempt to explain rebellions by minority groups, political scientist Ted Gurr has suggested a complex theory that incorporates many factors that may be related to ethnic conflict in general. These factors include, in the most general sense:

1. The minority group's history and current status, which includes the group's degree of disadvantage relative to other groups in the nation, the strength of the group's self-identity, the extent of group cohesion and its capacity to mobilize its resources, and the extent of repression by the dominant group

Ethnic Hutus flee southern Rwanda to escape the advancing Tutsi-led Rwandan Patriotic Front, July 1994.

2. The opportunities available to the groups for political action including the control exercised by the ruling regime, the group leader's strategy and tactics, and shifts in state power that provide the opportunity for rebellion
3. Global processes that intensify grievances such as the modern state system that stresses nationalism and centralized control and the global economy that has led to the economic exploitation of some groups
4. The international scope of conflict, which can involve the same group in a number of nations, such as the Kurds, or the spread of conflict across nations from one group to other groups
5. The effects of state power on political action, such as the form of government, which may lead the government to try to resolve the minority group's grievance or alternatively to repress it

Managing and Resolving Ethnic Conflicts

Many experts now believe that most ethnic conflicts are uniquely resistant to resolution and that the international community and national governments would be wiser to invest their resources in trying to manage and control these conflicts rather than in trying to resolve them. Recent experience suggests that this is sound advice—while conflict resolution efforts do sometimes produce formal accords, they rarely yield long-term peace and harmony. Ethnic conflicts in Cyprus, Northern Ireland, Bosnia, and Sri Lanka and northwest India have all been "settled" by accords, but the conflicts quickly flared up anew and continue. In most situations, ethnic conflicts end only through the subjugation or expulsion of one group by the other, a resolution that is likely to leave the loser unsatisfied and ready to resume the conflict when the opportunity presents itself in the future, which can be several decades away.

Ethnic conflicts are resolution-resistant for a number of reasons. First, we need to remember Donald Horowitz's point that ethnic solidarity is "powerful, permeative, passionate, and pervasive." Second, the stakes in ethnic conflicts are or are often believed by the combatants to be very high—the survival of their group, their domination by another group, or their domination of the other group. These are the very issues that precipitate the strong ethnic solidarity described by Horowitz and are ones members of ethnic groups are willing to kill and die for. Third, ethnic conflicts are usually not just disputes about tangible objectives such as political control or access to employment, but also involve powerful xenophobic and ethnocentric feelings and symbols and the resulting scapegoating and stereotyping that tend to make such conflicts particularly impervious to rational resolution. Fourth, the international experience has so far produced few permanent alternatives to ethnic conflict in multiethnic nations and regions. The United States is perhaps the only nation that holds to the view that a nation will be stronger by assimilating all peoples into one national whole, although that goal has yet to be achieved. A few other nations adhere to a pluralism model with groups sharing power, but of these, Canada is burdened by the French-Canadian separatist movement and Switzerland by the Jura autonomy movement. While Belgium and the Mauritius seem free of protracted, violent conflict, they along with Switzerland are unique situations that do not provide a model for most other nations. Fifth, ethnic rights and ethnic conflict are neither legally recognized nor regulated at the international level and are still to a large extent treated as an internal matters, to be resolved by the nation itself. Unfortunately, in most situations the state itself is a party to the dispute or has a stake in the success of one group at the expense of another group. Thus, the state is often a self-interested and ineffective force for peaceful, long-term ethnic conflict resolution that leaves all parties satisfied. Additionally, because ethnic conflicts are defined as internal matters, United Nations and multination alliances have generally restricted their involvement to peacekeeping and rescue missions designed to limit the fighting and have played a lesser role in long-term resolution. Similarly, the activities of nongovernmental organizations are mostly geared to assisting refugees and displaced persons, and sheltering, feeding, and treating the victims.

Binder, David, and Barbara Crossette. (1992) "As Ethnic Wars Multiply, U.S. Strives for a Policy." *New York Times* (7 February 1992).

De Silva, K. M., and S. W. R. de A. Samarasinghe. (1993) *Peace Accords and Ethnic Conflict.*

Elmer, Glaister A., and Evelyn A. Elmer. (1988) *Ethnic Conflicts Abroad: Clues to America's Future?* AICF Monograph Series, no. 8.

Esposito, John L. (1984) *The Islamic Threat: Myth or Reality?*

Gurr, Ted R. (1993) *Minorities at Risk: A Global View of Ethnopolitical Conflicts.*

Gurr, Ted R., and James R. Scarritt. (1989) "Minority Rights at Risk: A Global Survey." *Human Rights Quarterly* 11: 375–405.

Horowitz, Donald L. (1985) *Ethnic Groups in Conflict.*

Levinson, David. (1993) "Ethnic Conflict and Refugees." *Refugees* 93 (August 1993): 4–9.

Lewis, Bernard. (1990) "The Roots of Muslim Rage." *Atlantic Monthly* (September 1990): 47–60.

Messina, Anthony M., et al., eds. (1992) *Ethnic and Racial Minorities in Advanced Industrial Democracies.*

Miller, Judith. (1992) "The Islamic Wave." *New York Times Magazine* (31 May 1992): 22–26, 38, 40, 42.

Minority Rights Group. (1990) *World Directory of Minorities.*

Rupesinghe, Kumar. (1987) "Theories of Conflict Resolution and Their Applicability to Protracted Ethnic Conflicts." *Bulletin of Peace Proposals* 18: 527–539.

Ryan, Stephen. (1990) *Ethnic Conflict and International Relations.*

Samarasinghe, S. W. R. de A., and Reed Coughlan, eds. (1991) *Economic Dimensions of Ethnic Conflict.*

Stavenhagen, Rodolfo. (1987) "Ethnic Conflict and Human Rights: Their Interrelationship." *Bulletin of Peace Proposals* 18: 507–514.

ETHNOCIDE

Ethnocide is a term coined by the French after World War II and means the extermination of a culture not involving the physical extermination of the individual members of the culture. The notion of ethnocide as something different from *genocide* was implied in Raphael Lemkin's 1944 definition of the latter term, which brought the issue of genocide to the forefront of world debate.

Throughout human history, one common form of ethnocide has been the forced conversion of religious minorities, although these often involve genocidal actions as well, especially the threat of death if one does not convert. However, in many situations, the ultimate goal of the adherents to the majority religion was the eradication of the minority religion, not the killing of all its followers. Examples of ethnocide for religious purposes include the forced conversion of Jews in Spain in 1492, the oppression of Old

Believers in Russia, the persecution of Huguenots, Anabaptists, and others in Europe, and more recently, the persecution of the followers of Baha'i in Iran. Although some adherents do convert and many are killed, the most common responses are for many to flee and seek residence in nations where they will not be persecuted and for those who stay to practice their religion in secret. In Spain, after 1492, for example, many Jews (called *conversos)* converted to Catholicism although they continued to practice Judaism in secret. And when some emigrated later to lands of greater tolerance such as Brazil, they resumed the open practice of their religion.

While ethnocide can be considered as a phenomenon distinct from genocide, behaviors and policies that fall within the rubric of one or the other often co-occur. This has been especially true in those regions of the world settled by Europeans in the last five centuries—the New World, southern Africa, and Australia. The indigenous cultures of these regions have been subjected to both genocidal and ethnocidal acts that have reduced the overall population from tens of millions or more to only a few million and the number of distinct cultures from several thousand to less than one thousand. Most of these losses have resulted directly from the killing of the indigenous peoples and from the spread of European-introduced diseases, but ethnocide has also played a role. In this context of settlement colonization, ethnocidal acts include:

1. Banning the use of the native language
2. Forced relocation from the traditional homeland to a distant and environmentally different place
3. Economic disruption of the traditional economy (economic genocide) including the deliberate destruction of fields and orchards, damming or diversion of rivers, destruction of natural resources such as wild game, use of the people as slave labor, and exploitation as low-paid wage laborers
4. Banning the practice of the indigenous religion and forced conversion to the religion of the settlers
5. Placement of the people on reservations or reserves
6. Mixing of peoples from different cultures on one reservation and defining them politically as a single group
7. Removing children from their own families and placing them in nonindigenous homes or schools
8. Instituting educational systems that ignore or denigrate the traditional culture and teach instead the language and culture of another society
9. Replacing traditional forms of government with ones modeled on the government of the dominant culture
10. Policies or actions that ignore the social, cultural, economic, and health needs of the victims of ethnocide or genocide
11. Denial of the right of cultural and political self-determination

Beyond the means used and the results of those means, a major difference between genocide and ethnocide is how the dominant group defines the victims. In genocide, the victims are usually defined as being subhuman or somehow so different from the perpetrators that the genocide can be excused as not involving human beings. In ethnocide, the victims are not seen as subhuman or nonhuman, but rather as culturally, economically, or religiously inferior and the ethnocidal acts are often justified as an effort to aid or civilize these inferior peoples. This reasoning has been a major justification for various relocation, reservation, boarding school, and missionary programs in the United States carried out by the dominant white culture for the supposed benefit of the American Indian population, from the white culture's earliest contacts with American Indians through the 1990s. However, despite the good intentions of some individuals, these ethnocidal acts are almost always motivated by a desire to gain control of land or other resources controlled by native peoples.

See also Genocide; Pacification.

Cooper, Roger. (1982) *The Baha'is of Iran.*

Davis, Shelton. (1977) *Victims of the Miracle: Development and the Indians of Brazil.*

Girodet, Jean. (1981) *Dictionnaire du Bon Français.*

Jonassohn, Kurt, and Frank Chalk. (1987) "A Typology of Genocide and Some Implications for the Human Rights Agenda." In *Genocide and the Modern Age,* edited by Isidor Wallimann and Michael N. Dobkowski. 3–20.

Lemkin, Raphael. (1944) *Axis Rule in Occupied Europe.*

Stannard, David E. (1992) *American Holocaust.*

Evil Eye

The "evil eye" is the belief that a person can cause harm to another person or their property by simply looking at that person or his/her property. This harm may come in the form of sickness, an accident, or destruction of property such as breaking a valuable pot, burning a house, or killing livestock or crops. A survey of 186 cultures indicates that the belief is present in 36 percent of cultures, although not all people in these cultures believe in the evil eye and believers vary in the intensity of their beliefs. The geographical distribution of the belief is striking. Virtually every culture in India, the Near East, the Middle East, North Africa, much of East Africa, and Europe has or had an evil eye belief. It also occurs in much of Mexico and a similar belief of "bad air" is found in the Philippines. In regions bordering these regions it occurs only sporadically, and elsewhere in the world it is essentially nonexistent. In North America, the belief is found only among members of immigrant groups from the Old World; there was no such belief among American Indians. This distribution pattern has led some experts to suggest that the belief began in the Middle East or India and spread to other cultures from there. Others suggest that it may have developed independently in a number of places, although the presence of believers in Mexico and the Philippines is most likely due to the Spanish and Catholic influence on the native cultures of those regions. Wherever it began, the belief goes back at least 5,000 years and was incorporated into the three major world religions that developed in the Middle East—Judaism, Christianity, and Islam—although among many followers of these religions today it is considered a superstition.

Wherever people believe in the evil eye, it is almost always linked with envy. People who are wealthy or good-looking are often the targets and the destruction of valuable possessions is a widespread result of "casting the evil eye." Cross-culturally and throughout history, the evil eye belief is found mainly in cultures that produce social and physical goods that can be envied. Thus, it is likely that the evil eye belief emerged following the development of agriculture and settled communities about 7,000 years ago. In these communities, wealth distinctions became obvious and people could well envy the pottery, weaving, metal goods, money, cattle, pigs, sheep, and so forth, of others. Wealth distinctions were accompanied by status distinctions, meaning that there were also categories of people—royalty, upper classes, high castes, chiefs—who could also be envied. Another characteristic of evil eye cultures is a strong belief in a high God active in human affairs. This belief, of course, is a central element of Judaism, Christianity, and Islam.

In a survey of evil eye beliefs and practices in 12 nations, anthropologist Clarence Maloney identifies eight general features of the belief:

1. Power emanates from the eye and strikes a person or object
2. The object is something of value
3. The destruction or harm occurs quickly without warning
4. The one casting the evil eye may or may not know that he or she has the power to do so
5. The victim may or may not know who cast the evil eye
6. The belief is used to explain illness, accidents, and other misfortunes
7. It can be prevented or cured
8. Envy is involved

Within the context of these general patterns, there is much variation in beliefs and practices associated with the evil eye in cultures around the world. There is even considerable variation within cultures from family to family and individual to individual, especially in regard to measures one must take to prevent the power of the evil from affecting one or reversing its effects. As regards the source of the power, common beliefs are that it comes directly from the caster him or herself, from a certain category of people (the elderly, women, Jews), from a god or supernatural force, from the personal ritual impurity of the caster, from the Devil, or from an evil eye deity. In some cultures it is thought to be always present and always possible, in others it may also be always present and possible, but the consequences are not as serious.

In some cultures anyone is thought capable of casting the evil eye, in others, only certain categories of people, such those in low castes, strangers, outsiders, religious officials, witches, babies (also a frequent target), and even animals. Similarly, in many cultures, certain categories of people are more often the target, especially the wealthy and handsome, the dominant group in the community, women, babies, and the weak. Fruits and vegetables, livestock, crops, houses, and all sorts of material objects are frequent targets.

Given the widespread belief that the evil eye can strike anytime an individual admires something about you or something you possess, it is not surprising that thousands of preventive measures are taken to ward off its effects. Incantations are sung, chanted, recited, and spoken to ward off the evil. Amulets in the form of charms, necklaces, crosses, pins, and ribbons in thousands of varieties are worn on the body or attached to clothing. Often, the object must be a certain color. For example, Muslims believe that the color blue is most protective, while Jews and Christians prefer red. Formulae in the form of ritualized sayings and actions may also be used. And, precautions are taken to avoid an evil eye caster. For example, food is prepared in private, one eats in private, one always walks behind someone suspected of being a caster, and a child is called by a name given to the opposite sex to confuse the supernatural force behind the evil eye. Cures also include a wide array of incantations, amulets, and rituals. They also may require the intervention of a professional curer such as a sorcerer, exorcist, or priest.

A variety of explanations has been suggested for the evil eye belief. Most experts believe that any explanation must consider the role of envy since the presumption of envy underlies the belief in most cultures. Other factors that may play a causative role in some societies include a paranoid view of the world, unexpressed anger and hostility, a projection of one's own envy onto others (I am envious and want to destroy what they have, so I believe they are envious and want to destroy what I have), and childrearing practices that produce adults who need much emotional support from others. Some of these same factors may also explain individual variation in the intensity of the belief among people in the same culture. And in multicultural communities it is often those people who are socially and economically disadvantaged who have the strongest belief in the evil eye.

In many cultures around the world the evil eye belief is now weaker and has fewer strong believers than in the past. Belief in the evil eye lessens when a culture changes in a way that provides individuals with relatively equal opportunity for achievement. For example, the belief is now much weaker or gone altogether in the second- or third-generation descendants of European immigrants who came to the United States around 1900. The opportunity for economic success and the American value system that stresses individual responsibility and self-reliance contradict the beliefs that one's status in life can be attributed to the wishes of others and that one is incapable of achieving the same level of status or wealth as others.

Dundes, Alan, ed. (1981) *The Evil Eye: A Folklore Casebook.*

Maloney, Clarence, ed. (1976) *The Evil Eye.*

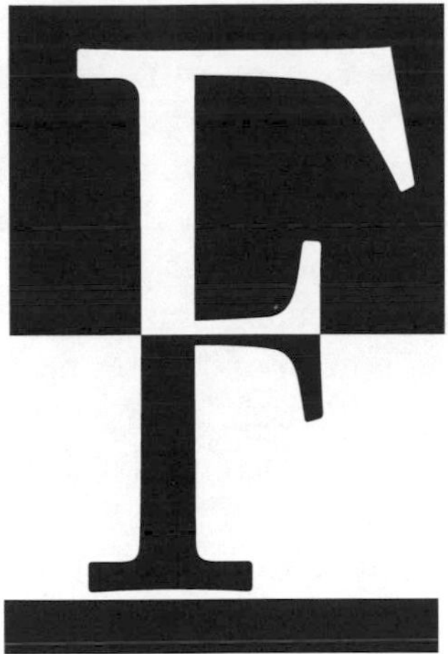

Family Violence

In Western cultures family violence usually refers to physical violence between members of the nuclear family household and other close kin, with violence directed at children, wives, and elders the three most common forms. Although violence directed at family members is usually defined as abuse, the term *abuse* has little meaning cross-culturally, as cultures vary widely from one another in behaviors that are culturally defined as abusive. For example, in some cultures it is considered abusive to hit a child who is not yet old enough to understand the consequences of his or her actions or to leave one's child in the care of a nonrelative, but it is not abusive to subject him or her to a painful genital mutilation at puberty. In other cultures, the definition of abuse is the reverse. Cultures also vary internally in their definitions of what is abusive and what is not. Depending on the relationship between the family members, age differences, the nature of the alleged misbehavior, and other economic and social factors, various forms of physical violence may be considered appropriate or inappropriate in different social circumstances.

Physical violence between family members is a fairly common occurrence in most cultures. In a survey of 95 cultures, in only 17 percent of cultures physical violence between family members rarely or never occurred. The most common forms of family violence are wife beating and physical punishment of children; with wife beating the most violent in terms of the likelihood of the physical injury or death to the victim. Aside from wife beating and husband beating, there is little patterning cross-culturally in the types of family violence likely to be found in any given culture. Cultures that are mostly free of family violence are usually ones where marital relationships are characterized by social and economic equality, sharing, cooperation, and a commitment to the family unit.

See also Death-Hastening Behavior; Footbinding; Genital Mutilation; Gerontocide, Homicide; Husband Beating; Infanticide; Painful Initiation Rites; Sibling Fighting; Socialization of Aggression; Wife Beating.

Levinson, David. (1989) *Family Violence in Cross-Cultural Perspective.*

Feuding

Feuding refers to an ongoing, potentially violent relationship between two groups who reside in the same political community. The groups are usually large kinship groups such as fraternal interest groups (groups of brothers who live in the same community), lineages, clans, or extended families. The key feature of a feuding relationship between the groups is blood revenge, where certain acts by members of one group against members of the other require the latter to seek revenge by killing a member of the former. The first group may then seek revenge by killing a member of the second, and the pattern of revenge killings may continue until peace is negotiated or both sides feel that revenge has been won. This does not mean that the two groups are in a constant state of open hostility, as blood revenge may occur only sporadically, and even then some members of the community, usually the women, may remain on cordial terms. Feuds are also referred to as blood revenge, blood feuds, vendettas, and kin group vengeance. Feuding differs from internal war, which is conflict between different political communities in the same society, and from external war, which is conflict between two different societies, although it is sometimes difficult to distinguish between feuding and internal war, especially when the political units are also localized kinship groups.

A study of feuding in 186 societies indicates six levels of feuding in cultures around the world (percentage of societies in parentheses):

1. Feuding is considered morally imperative (22 percent)
2. Feuding is considered the most appropriate response (8.9 percent)
3. Feuding occurs only in certain circumstances (10.7 percent)
4. Feuding is considered a last resort (11.9 percent)
5. Feuding occurs but is punished (37.5 percent)
6. Kin groups are not recognized as an avenging unit, so feuding does not occur (8.9 percent)

As these percentages show, feuding is permitted in 53.5 percent of societies. These figures apply to the situation in the early 1900s. Since World War I feuding has diminished or disappeared in many societies where it was common previously, evidently because these societies were incorporated into modern nations where the local, regional, or national police and legal systems were the primary mechanisms for settling serious disputes and they eventually replaced feuding. Feuding was especially common and vestiges remain in cultures near the Mediterranean Sea such as among Sicilians, Calabrians, Albanians, Serbs, Montenegrins, and Libyan Bedouins.

In the United States, the best known feud involved the Hatfield family of West Virginia and the McCoy family of Kentucky. The feud evidently began in 1882 when Tolbert McCoy stabbed and killed "Big Ellison" Hatfield in a successful effort at preventing him from voting in Kentucky instead of his home state of West Virginia. Hatfield family raids avenged the killing and were followed by McCoy raids into West Virginia, leading to a cycle of raids and murders that took 65 lives and involved nearly all the inhabitants of Pike County, Kentucky; Logan County, West Virginia; the governors of the two states; and the local militia. The feud finally ended in the early 1900s when a Hatfield boy married a McCoy girl, according to the legend. The Hatfield-McCoy feud was only one of many that occupied families in southern Appalachia from about 1865 to 1915. Other major feuds included the French-Eversole War, the Knott County War (between the Hays and Jones families), the Allen-Edwards Wars, and the White-Baker War. These and other feuds resulted in more than 1,000 deaths as well the burning of homes and the destruction of property during the 50 years. Most were the result of the split allegiance that characterized the region during the Civil War. After the War, hard feelings between families who fought with the Confederacy and those with the Union manifested themselves as feuds. Local political power conflicts after the War, as between the Hatfields and McCoys, were often the precipitating event. Feuding was also encouraged by the regional settlement pattern whereby large, extended families tended to live near one another in "hollows" and apart from other families. Once the feuding began, it lasted for years, with each family vigilant for any slight to its honor and then seeking immediate revenge. The feuds eventually ended (although the memory of them is still a factor in local elections) when the region was drawn into the regional and national economic and political systems.

In societies with feuding the offenses that require blood revenge are the murder of a kinsman by a member of another kinship group or an affront to the honor of a kinswoman by a male member of another kinship group. An affront to the honor of a kinswoman is the more frequent precipitator of violence and is a major cause of feuding in societies in the Mediterranean region because of the status of women in these societies and economic arrangements between families whose children marry one another. In many of these societies, when a woman marries she moves to the community of her husband's family. In addition, she often brings with her a substantial dowry and recognizes that her children will belong to her husband's kin group, not the group to which she was born. Thus, a woman and her family give up much at marriage. In turn, the husband's family makes little material contribution to the marriage, except to give its name and honor, which the wife gains upon marriage. Thus, it is important that kin groups maintain their good name and honor and any slight to that honor must be erased through revenge. And, since it is girls and young women who will marry out, slights to their honor, and especially their sexual purity, must be avenged. Since it is a family matter, it is often the brothers (fraternal interest groups) of the unmarried sisters who initiate the feuding.

The Sarakatsani, a Greek-speaking pastoral people of northern Greece, display the major features of feuding. Family honor is a vital matter to the Sarakatsani and comes into play when a male member of the family is physically or verbally attacked by an outsider, a kinswoman is the victim of sexual assault or insult, or a kinswoman is guilty of sexual misconduct. The notion of honor is much concerned with the concepts of manliness and sexual shame and serves as the basis for the social value of the family as judged by outsiders.

In accord with their conception of honor, the Sarakatsani seek revenge for two types of attacks on their honor—killing of a man and sexual assault of a woman. The killing of a man requires revenge by killing the murderer or driving him permanently away, with the former preferable. To the kill the murderer means "to take out the blood" of their murdered kinsmen, as the Sarakatsani believe that by taking the blood of their kinsmen, the murderer took strength from the family. The sexual behavior of daughters, sisters, and wives is of central concern, as the sexual behavior of women is controlled by the family. If a woman commits adultery, she and her lover are killed by her husband, to restore honor to the family. If a daughter loses her virginity before marriage, she and her lover are killed by her father or brothers. If a woman is raped or sexually dishonored such as by having the betrothal broken, only the man is killed.

All of this might suggest that the Sarakatsani are in constant state of feuding with a real possibility that the men may kill each other off completely. This does not happen, because insults that require blood revenge do not occur too often, the guilty man can flee and stay away permanently, the Greek police often intervene and arrest the guilty man, or the offended family might choose not to seek blood revenge because the cost of the revenge (the likely death of one of their own men) seems too high.

See also BLOOD MONEY; INTERNAL CONFLICT.

Campbell, J. K. (1964) *Honour, Family, and Patronage: A Study of Institutions and Moral Values in a Greek Mountain Community.*

Caudill, Harry M. (1963) *Night Comes to the Cumberlands.*

Erickson, Karen P., and Heather Horton. (1992) "'Blood Feuds': Cross-Cultural Variations in Kin Group Vengeance." *Behavior Science Research* 26: 57–86.

Otterbein, Keith F., and Charlotte S. Otterbein. (1965) "An Eye for an Eye, a Tooth for a Tooth: A Cross-Cultural Study of Feuding." *American Anthropologist* 67: 1470–1482.

FIGHTING WITH PROPERTY

In some cultures, one of the major results of pacification by Europeans was the replacement of violent means of settling disputes and acquiring status and prestige with nonviolent means. In some cultures this was brought about by involvement in a regional or national legal system, in others it was by the of witchcraft and sorcery to get even with enemies, and it was also achieved by practices known collectively as fighting with property. Fighting with property has been documented for a number of cultures in North America and Melanesia. Two of the best-described cases are the Kwakiutl of British Columbia who switched from "wars of blood" to "wars of property" and the Goodenough Islanders who now "fight with food." Among both the Kwakiutl and the Goodenough Islanders, fighting with property became the primary means of achieving status and controlling disputes that previously would have been settled violently. And in both cultures, the elaboration of this practice followed the cessation of warfare and raiding and clearly became a substitute for them.

A major theme in Kwakiutl culture is the pursuit of individual, family, and tribal prestige and status. Traditionally, prestige was achieved and rivals defeated or won over through either success in warfare or potlatching. Potlatching is the ceremonial giving away or destruction of wealth to increase one's status in the tribe. Traditional potlatching was relatively small-scale and involved mostly the disposal of blankets or coppers (scrolled copper sheets), slaves, and canoes.

Following the cessation of warfare in about 1849, potlatching replaced warfare as the primary means to achieve prestige and status. The Kwakiutl themselves recognized the transformation:

> We are the Koskimo [a Kwakiutl tribe], who have never been vanquished by any tribe, neither in wars of blood nor in wars of property. Of olden times the Kwakiutl ill treated my forefathers and fought them so that the blood ran over the ground. Now we fight with button blankets and other kinds of property, smiling at each other. Oh, how good is the new time. (Codere 1950: 118)

While potlatching was peaceful, it resembled traditional warfare in many ways: potlatches were carefully planned; the prestige of the individual who gave the potlatch, his extended family, and his tribe were all affected by the outcome; potlatches were called *p!Eas* meaning "to flatten," as in "to flatten under a pile of blankets"; the songs were war songs, and the ceremonial imagery was the imagery of war. The items given away to rivals in the post-1849 ceremonies were blankets, silver bracelets, calico, coppers, cooking utensils, and other items with the difference in pre- and post-warfare potlatching being the quantity and overall value of the items given away. Before 1849, the largest known potlatch involved the disposal of 320 blankets, 4 slaves, and 4 canoes. The largest after 1849 was in 1936 and involved 33,000 blankets and other items equal to the value of 25,000 more blankets. Being wealthy enough to give away vast quantities of these items (and having status and community support strong enough to get credit from others to acquire this quantity) gave the potlatch host prestige and won for him and his group one of the limited number of potlatch positions in the tribe. Rivals periodically sought to unseat one another by hosting a potlatch and giving away even more. The basic cause of the elaboration and expansion of potlatching and its continuation well into the twentieth century was the cessation of warfare and the need to find a replacement mechanism for earning prestige and competing with rivals. A decline in the Kwakiutl population due to disease and the economic success of the Kwakiutl made potlatching the ideal mechanism. The population decline meant that there were now less people to compete for the potlatching positions, making more people eager to compete. And money and goods such as blankets earned through employment in the European fishing and lumbering industries meant that the Kwakiutl could acquire much excess wealth to fight with.

Fighting with food or "food-giving-to-shame" is a form of self-punishment meant to punish an offense by the offended person giving property (usually food) to the person who wronged him. Food-giving-to-shame is a common mechanism of social control among the Goodenough Islanders and is used both informally and formally. The *abutu* ceremony in which an offended person, his kin group, and his supporters in the community seek to give more food to the offender and his supporters than the latter can give in return is the most elaborate form of food-giving-to-shame. Despite being elaborate and requiring the harvesting of much food, *abutu* is used both to settle disputes within and across villages, primarily involving adultery and divorce. The objective of *abutu* is to shame and insult your rival by giving more to him than he can give to you. The shame of losing is so great that Goodenough Islanders

A Sitka potlatch, 1901.

believe that it is better to bear the ridicule for not competing than to compete when you know you will lose. The foods given away are yams, taro, pigs, and bananas. The winner is the person who can give away the most, with separate calculations made for each type of food.

As with Kwakiutl potlatching, *abutu* existed in limited form before pacification and expanded both in frequency and the quantity of food used only after pacification. It also took on increased significance as a social control mechanism and now is used to resolve 35 percent of disputes both within and across villages. Goodenough Islanders recognize the growth of *abutu:*

> Now *abutu* is too big. Today many people have big gardens. Before, our fathers had big yams but small gardens. They didn't work every day because they did *lokano* properly. They looked after their food. They had one garden for *lokano* and one for eating, that's all. Now people are planting and planting, and eating and eating all the time. And they are always thinking about making *abutu.* (Young 1971: 224)

And, again, like potlatching, *abutu* centered on existing cultural themes including the pursuit of prestige and social control through shaming and self-punishment combined with newfound economic wealth. For the Goodenough Islanders the new wealth was achieved primarily through more efficient gardening with Western steel tools.

It should be noted that both potlatching and *abutu* are more than mechanisms for dispute resolution and the achievement of status; they are also important mechanisms of social integration within and across communities and a means by which wealth can be shared.

See also PACIFICATION; SELF-PUNISHMENT; WESTERN INFLUENCE ON INDIGENOUS WARFARE.

Barnett, Homer. (1959) "Peace and Progress in New Guinea." *American Anthropologist* 61: 1013–1019.

Codere, Helen. (1950) *Fighting with Property.*

Earle, Timothy. (1982) "The Ecology and Politics of Primitive Valuables." In *Eclectic Perspectives,* edited by John Kennedy and Robert Edgerton, 65–83.

Young, Michael W. (1971) *Fighting with Food: Leadership, Values and Social Control in a Massim Society.*

FISSIONING

Fissioning is the splitting of a community. Fissioning occurs when the groups that form a community separate completely or when one group moves away and forms a new community or joins another community. The opposite of fissioning is fusion, which is the formation of a community through the joining together of two or more previously independent groups or the expansion of a community through the arrival of a formerly separate group. It should be noted that fissioning does not refer to the moving away of groups who are segregated in some way from the community, such as Gypsies in Europe and elsewhere, whether or not they choose or are forced to move away.

Fissioning occurs in a number of cultures for a variety of reasons including better economic opportunities elsewhere, a population expansion that makes the group too large to survive on local resources, and disputes or the threat of disputes that disrupt social cohesion within the community. In non-Western cultures the groups who form a community (village or band) are kinship groups such as lineages or families who are often linked to one another politically, socially, and economically. Thus, fissioning is not just moving away, but might also involve severing ties between groups and establishing ties with new groups. However, fissioning does not always result in the severing of all ties and, in fact, in some cultures it can be a mechanism that creates cultural cohesion and greater cooperation between groups. For example, Tiv compounds often fission after the death of the compound head, especially when there are disputes about succession or the cause of death or when some families are dissatisfied with the new head. Sometimes, all the families will separate and settle elsewhere, although more often only one family leaves but the families continue to farm together, or as the Tiv say, they are "sitting separately" but use "one field." As regards cultural cohesion, fissioning is very common among the San bands of Botswana, with families continually leaving a band and joining a new one. While unresolved disputes are sometimes the reason for leaving, more often it is simply a desire to live elsewhere or the pursuit of more plentiful food. This continual movement of families creates ties among different San bands that help unite them together as a single culture.

As a form of conflict resolution, fissioning is quite common around the world, with at least some fissioning taking place after disputes in 78 percent of a sample of 64 cultures. It is usually the group who is unhappy with the outcome of the dispute that moves away. In general, fissioning occurs only in response to serious or ongoing disputes or disputes that threaten the survival of the community. The Mbuti Pygmies have both internal and external fissioning. In the internal form, families who are not wanted are isolated within the camp, as the other groups build their huts apart from the undesirable group. External fissioning generally occurs when disputes disrupt the cooperation needed in hunting and the community then splits into two separate groups or one group leaves and joins another band. Among the Yanomamö of Brazil it is a combination of group size and violent disputes or the likelihood of continual violence that leads to fissioning. The Yanomamö live in circular villages with men and women encouraged to marry others from the same village and new groups added through fusion. Large villages are preferred and important because some Yanomamö groups are in a continual state of war with other groups, and the larger the village the less likely it is that they will be attacked and the more successful they will be in attacks on other villages. However, when the village grows to between 100 and 150 residents, disputes and especially fights and club duels over women and extramarital affairs become so common that the internal order of the village is threatened and weakens the effectiveness of the men of the village as a military force. When the threat of internal disorder or actual disorder reaches this point, the village fissions. Sometimes the village will separate in half and each group will establish separate gardens near one another so they can support each other in raids by other villages. At other times, when the disruption is too great, one small faction will leave and establish a new or join another village.

Bohannan, Paul. (1957) *Tiv Farm and Settlement.*

Chagnon, Napoleon A. (1968) *Yanomamö: The Fierce People.*

Ross, Marc H. (1983) "Political Decision-Making and Conflict: Additional Cross-Cultural Codes." *Ethnology* 22: 169–192.

Tanaka, Jiro. (1980) *The San Hunter-Gatherers of the Kalahari.*

Turnbull, Colin M. (1965) *Wayward Servants: The Two Worlds of the African Pygmies.*

FOOTBINDING

Chinese footbinding was the practice of tightly binding girls' and women's feet to keep the feet small. It dates perhaps to as early as the tenth century A.D. and certainly was practiced by the 1300s during the Ming dynasty. It was finally banned after the Revolution of 1911 by the Chinese government following some 200 years of growing opposition both inside and outside China but continued in some isolated, rural communities into the 1940s.

Binding involved wrapping the feet of girls and women in cloth to prevent the bones and muscles from developing normally and curling the toes under. The result was small, deformed feet that prevented women from walking rapidly or for long distances and made it painful for them to stand. Binding began when the girl was between four and eight years of age and after several years the girl could decide to continue or not, although the choice not to continue meant social banishment, as women with large (normal) size feet were considered unattractive and their fathers could not sell them into concubinage or prostitution, let alone arrange a marriage for them. The initial binding period, in addition to deforming the feet, often also produced various harmful and painful side effects such as ulcers, gangrene necessitating amputation, and damage to the ankles and legs. The feet also remained tender and painful and fathers and husbands punished their daughters, or wives by pulling the binding tight, squeezing the feet, or whipping the unbound feet. Binding began among the upper class but quickly spread to all levels of Chinese society.

The stated reason for binding was that it made women's feet more attractive and was pleasurable for men, and sexual relations with a woman whose feet were deformed through binding was described by Chinese men as being as pleasurable for them as having relations with a virgin. Footbinding also became a symbol of Chinese autonomy and opposition to foreign rule, and thus outside efforts to end the practice were ineffective. The real reason for binding was to control the activities of women by keeping them at home and preventing them from traveling long distances alone, and making them dependent on their fathers and husbands. While the aesthetic and sexual purposes of binding were often emphasized, the gender inequality and male control purposes were recognized as well, and, in fact, sometimes openly acknowledged within Chinese society as the real reason. For example, in the *Nü Erh Ching*, a book about virtuous women, it is stated that, "Feet are bound, not to make them beautiful as a curved bow, but to restrain the women when they go outdoors."

Footbinding was able to develop as a practice unique to Chinese society because women rarely engaged in any agricultural work, and, thus, their activities could be restricted without any economic cost to the family or society in general. Only the poorest segment of society who needed to put daughters to work did not engage in binding. From this perspective, footbinding can be understood as one in a general class of cultural practices meant to restrict the activities of women in cultures where women are an economic and social commodity that is traded through arranged marriages between different kin groups. Since a woman's purity and willingness to obey her husband are often major determinants of the "price" she commands, her family must protect these. Other similar mechanisms used in other cultures toward the same end include genital operations, family control of women's sexual activities as a feature of feuding behavior, and bride theft. Just as the basic reason for binding was economic, the practice began to disappear in the 1700s at least in part as a result of the industrial revolution and its influence on the Chinese economy, which created a labor market that could be filled by women. Women now became more valuable economically as workers and more independent, rendering footbinding obsolete. However, because of the rural, peasant nature of the majority of the population who continued to subsist mainly through family farming, footbinding disappeared slowly and only in the twentieth century did the practice end entirely.

See also GENITAL MUTILATION.

Lang, Olga. (1946) *Chinese Family and Society.*

Levy, Howard S. (1966) *Chinese Footbinding: The History of a Curious Erotic Custom.*

Genital Mutilation

In his world survey of sexual behavior, Edgar Gregerson noted that "Whatever the reason, people in many different societies have felt and still feel that the genitals should be altered in one way or another by cutting, piercing, hacking, or slicing, or by inserting objects." Modification of genitals of one's children, relatives, and neighbors is culturally approved, and in many societies around the world, required behavior. Mutilation of the genitals of war captives, slaves, and other outsiders is also a fairly common aftermath of war and raiding. In Western and westernized societies, male circumcision is currently the only common genital modification, and it is usually performed in a medical setting when the infant is young. In traditional non-Western societies, genital operations were and are commonly performed in the community and often, for boys, the operations are part of a ceremony marking their entrance into adulthood.

Male genital mutilations come in three major forms.

Circumcision is the removal of the foreskin and is the most common genital modification. It is estimated that 50 percent of the men in the world today have been circumcised. It is required of Jews and customary for Muslims and circumcision of male babies is a routine medical procedure in some Western societies including the United States. In non-Western societies circumcision usually occurs later in life, commonly at puberty when boys are initiated into adult status. Some social scientists suggest the circumcision is found primarily in societies where boys develop a strong attachment to their mothers and a weak attachment to their fathers. Circumcision plus other stressful and traumatic activities as part of initiation rites presumably allow the boy to break his emotional ties to his mother and assume a male identity.

Superincision (supercision) is the slitting of the foreskin lengthwise, without removal. It occurs only in a few Polynesian societies.

Subincision is the slitting of the underside of the penis lengthwise to the urethra. It is found almost exclusively among a few aboriginal cultures in Australia. These are all cultures located in territories inhabited by kangaroos, the males of which have two-headed penises. It has been suggested, both by the people themselves and anthropologists, that subincision is an attempt to imitate kangaroos.

Other forms of male genital mutilation are bleeding the penis without permanent modification, removal of one testicle (hemicastration), complete castration, nipple excision, and inserting objects under the foreskin. All of these only occur under special circumstances and usually only for a select group of boys or men.

Female genital mutilations come in four major forms. Unlike male modifications, female mutilations are not regularly incorporated into initiation ceremonies and they are usually performed on girls before they reach marriageable age.

Ritualistic circumcision is the nicking of the clitoris and involves no gross mutilation.

An initiate immediately following circumcision.

Circumcision or Sunna, the Muslim name, is the removal of the clitoral precipice and less often the removal of the tip of the clitoris also.

Excision or Clitoridectomy is the removal of some or all of the clitoris and sometimes part of the labia minora.

Infibulation or Pharaonic Circumcision is the removal of all of the female genitalia and the sewing shut of the remaining edges of labia majora, leaving only a small opening for the passage of urine and menstrual fluid. At the time of marriage, the opening will be enlarged to allow sexual relations.

Female genital mutilations occur in 40 nations and many more cultures within these nations, primarily in Africa and the southern Middle East. Estimates place the number of African women who have experienced genital mutilation at nearly 100 million. Although current interest in these operations is focussed on African cultures and nations, such operations have been used elsewhere. For example, from about 1890 to the late 1930s clitoridectomies were surgically performed in the United States as a "cure" for masturbation. Unlike male modifications, female modifications often cause serious health and emotional problems. Girls may die from the operation or complications such as infection; women experience chronic health problems such as urinary infections and painful intercourse and childbirth, inability to experience orgasm, and menstrual pain, and the society often must bear additional health care costs.

The severity of the modifications and the resulting problems for women has led to a loud and ongoing debate about the legitimacy of such operations and efforts to end the practice. On one side of the debate are those who see the mutilations as motivated by sexual inequality and male control of women, a position supported by the use of these operations in cultures where women are considered to be inferior to men and where men control female sexuality. Advocates for the banning of female mutilations also see them as a violation of the human rights of girls and women. Efforts by both private and government groups have sought to end female mutilations in Africa through legislation, public pressure, and education, with mixed success. On the other side of the debate are those—usually men in the cultures with operations but also some women as well—who argue that the operations are a major symbol of ethnic identity and a matter of ethnic self-determination, and therefore not a matter subject to control by outsiders. The view of those who seek to end the operations is that change must come from within the cultures and nations themselves, through a combination of public attention, education, legislation, and the support of political leaders.

See also FOOTBINDING; PAINFUL INITIATION CEREMONIES.

Frayser, Suzanne. (1985) *Varieties of Sexual Experience.*

Gregerson, Edgar. (1982) *Sexual Practices: The Story of Human Sexuality.*

Hosken, Fran. (1982) *The Hosken Report: Genital and Sexual Mutilation of Females.*

Levinson, David. (1989) *Family Violence in Cross-Cultural Perspective.*

McLean, Scilla, and Stella Efua Graham, eds. (1983) *Female Circumcision, Excision, and Infibulation: The Facts and Proposals for Change.*

Slack, Alison T. (1988) "Female Circumcision: A Critical Appraisal." *Human Rights Quarterly* 10: 437–486.

GENOCIDE

The term *genocide* was coined in 1944 by the Polish-American scholar Raphael Lemkin and is from the Greek *genos* (race or kind) and *cide* (to cut, kill). The 1948 United Nations Convention on Genocide provides the most generally accepted definition, one that has now been ratified by over 100 nations:

> In the present Convention, genocide means any of the following acts committed with intent to destroy, in whole or part, a national, ethnic, racial or religious group, as such:
>
> (a) Killing members of the group;
>
> (b) Causing serious bodily or mental harm to members of the groups;
>
> (c) Deliberately inflicting on the group conditions of life calculated to bring about its physical destruction in whole or in part;
>
> (d) Imposing measures intended to prevent births within the group;
>
> (e) Forcibly transferring children of the group to another group.

To the types of groups covered in the UN Convention, some scholars add political and economic groups. By broadening the definition in this way, repression involving the killing or forced relocation of political opposition groups such as those carried out by the Soviet Union in World War II, the People's Republic of China during the Cultural Revolution, by the Indonesian government against Indonesian communists, and the El Salvador government against El Salvadoran Leftists, to name a few in this century, can be considered a form of genocide. Politicide is the label sometimes used instead of genocide when the victims are political groups. Such acts, however, are not subject to UN sanctions, although the UN has never directly intervened in any activity simply because it was considered genocide.

Various attempts have been made by social scientists to develop classification systems to help order and explain the numerous and various types of genocides that have occurred throughout human history. One classification scheme developed by Helen Fein differentiates between genocides that appeared before the rise of modern nation-states—(1) those to eliminate other faiths, and (2) those to eliminate rival tribes—from those carried out by nation-states: (3) mass killings to legitimize political power, (4) killings to destroy indigenous cultures, and (5) killings to destroy rebellious elements. Another typology distinguishes among four major types, on the basis of the purpose of the genocide: "(1) to eliminate the threat of a rival; (2) to acquire economic wealth; (3) to create terror and (4) to implement a belief, theory or an ideology" (Jonassohn and Chalk 1985: 12). The fourth type is further subdivided into four subtypes based on whether the group targeted for genocide and the accusations against it are true or false. A third typology developed by Barbara Harff lists four types on the basis of the political context in which the genocide occurs: (1) postwar, postimperial; (2) postcolonial; (3) postcoup or postrevolution; and (4) conquest. This typology is also of explanatory importance as it suggests that a precondition for genocide is national upheaval due to lost wars, political consolidation, revolution, rebellion, or conquest. If such upheaval occurs in a society with marked ethnic, values, or religious variation, genocide might result, especially if no other societies intervene to prevent or stop it. The presence of marked differences between cultural and religious groups in nearly all nations where genocide has occurred suggests that genocide is a product of plural societies.

Although much current attention is focused on genocides in the twentieth century, the majority of genocides in human history have been genocides of colonialism perpetrated by colonial powers against the indigenous peoples of the New World, Australia, and southern Africa. The majority of victims have been the cultures and native peoples of the Caribbean, North America, Middle America, and South America who beginning with Columbus's second expedition in 1494 were the target of genocidal and ethnocidal policies and acts that in some places continue today. These peoples were first targeted by the colonial governments—Portuguese, Spanish, French, and English—and then by the national cultures that succeeded the colonists as the rulers of the New World. Although the details vary from place to place, genocidal activities usually involved direct government involvement or support; a belief system that defined the native peoples as subhuman; raids and wars to kill native men, women, and children; the public execution of leaders; forced relocations; placement on reservations; removal of children; massacres; the purposeful spread of European diseases such as smallpox from which the native people had no natural immunity; enslavement; and wars between native groups caused either directly or indirectly by government policy or action.

Although the size of the pre-Columbian population is unknown, a comparison of estimates now considered to be reasonably accurate with more recent estimates and census figures indicates the enormity of the New World genocide. Within 100 years of Columbus's arrival, the Caribbean population, composed mainly of about 10 million Arawaks and Caribs, had disappeared entirely. In Middle America, the population was reduced from about 30 million to fewer than 300,000 in less than 100 years. In North America the indigenous population of about 15 million declined to a low of 237,000 in 1900 and has now increased to about 2 million. In South America, a native population of nearly 40 million declined to 443,000 by 1570 and is now about 15 million. Some of these deaths resulted from the nonpurposeful spread of European diseases such as smallpox, measles, mumps, whooping cough, and cholera, among others, but

Group of Tasmanians in the mid-1800s. Following English settlement in 1803, the 2,000–5,000 Tasmanians then living were hunted and killed. The culture has been extinct since the late 1800s.

it is not unreasonable to assume that at least 50 percent were the direct result of genocide or the indirect result of ethnocide. In short, some 95 percent of the population of the New World was exterminated as a result of the arrival of and settlement by Europeans.

The situation is much the same in regard to the disappearance of New World cultures, although it is impossible to estimate how many actually existed in 1492. It is likely though, that in North America at the time of European contact, at least 1,000 different languages were spoken, a number that has decreased to about 100, although efforts are underway to revive the use of some that had fallen into disuse. In South America and Middle America numerous cultures disappeared and in the Amazon they continue to disappear. In the Caribbean there are no surviving native cultures, although some survivors who fled to Middle America merged with other survivors to form new cultures such as the Miskito. (Extinct New World cultures are listed at the end of this article.)

The situation in Australia was much the same, although the number of Aboriginal cultures and individuals was much lower, so there were fewer to be killed off. The Australian genocide that has drawn the most attention was the extermination of the Tasmanians by the English in the nineteenth century. At the time of English arrival in 1803, Tasmania had been inhabited for some 23,000 years. In 1803 the total number of Tasmanians (actually, the island's inhabitants were a number of related though politically distinct groups) was between 2,000 and 5,000. By 1876 the last full-blooded Tasmanian was dead, as the direct result of forced relocation and wars meant to kill off the Tasmanians.

In the twentieth century, the two genocides that have drawn the most attention are the killing of about 1.5 million Armenians by the Turks in 1915–1917 and the killing of about 6 million Jews, and 50,000 Gypsies and members of other groups by the Germans during World War II. The Nazi genocide of Jews, referred to as the Holocaust, led to the ongoing interest in genocide we see today and has also become a matter of controversy as to whether the Holocaust is a singularly unique event in human history or the most extreme case drawn from a human history filled with genocide. Both the Armenians and Jews were middleman minorities, a type of social group that is often the target of discrimination and genocide. A middleman minority is a cultural group that serves in an economic middleman position in a society where it is a cultural minority. Some well-known such groups are the Overseas Chinese throughout Southeast Asia, Asians in Africa, and Jews in Europe.

The following table lists major genocides (not including politicides) of the 20th century.

Major Genocides of the Twentieth Century

Perpetrator	Victim	Year
Germany	Herero	1904
Turks	Armenians	1915–1917
Germany	Jews, Gypsies	1938–1945
USSR	Chechen/Ingush, Karachay, Balkars, Jews, Meskhetian Turks, Crimean Tatars	1943–1968
Pakistan	Baluch	1958–1974
Iraq	Kurds	1959–
Angola	Kongo	1961–1962
Paraguay	Aché	1962–1972
Tutsi (Burundi)	Hutu	1965–
Nigeria	Igbo	1966
Uganda	Karamojong, Acholi, Lango, Asians	1971–1986
Indonesia	Timorese	1975
Myanmar (Burma)	Muslims	1978–
Iran	Baha'i, Kurds	1981–
Serbs	Bosnian Muslims	1992–

The following is a partial list of New World Cultures that are physically or culturally extinct due to genocide and/or ethnocide.

North America

Alsea
Apalachee
Atakapa
Bayogoula
Beothuk
Biloxi
Calusa
Chakchiuma
Chawaska
Chimariko
Coahuilteco
Conestoga
Coos
Costano
Cusabo
Edisto
Hitchiti
Jumano
Kamia
Karankawa
Kwalhiokwa
Mackenzie Inuit
Manso
Mobile
Molala
Mosopelea
Mugulasha
Nicola
Okelousa
Pamilco
Pamunkey
Piro
Quinipissa
Secotan
Siuslaw
Southhampton Inuit
Susquehanna
Takelma
Tangipahoa
Timucua
Tlatskanai
Tolowa
Tsetsaut
Tutelo
Umpqua
Wappinger
Washa
Wenrohonron
Yamasee
Yana
Yuki

Middle America and the Caribbean

Acaxee
Aguacadibe
Ameyao
Arawak
Bainoa
Bani
Barbacoa
Bayamo
Bayaquitiri
Boyaca
Cahibo
Caizcimu
Camaguey
Carib
Cayaguayo
Chiapanec
Ciboney
Ciguayo
Cochimi
Cubanacan
Cuciba
Guaimaro
Guamahaya
Guanachahibe
Guaniguanico
Hanamana
Havana
Hubabo
Huereo
Igneri
Jaqua
Lucayans
Macorizc
Maguan
Maguana
Marien
Marisi
Mayaguez
Ornoray
Pai-Pai
Paya
Sabaneque
Tahue
Taino
Totorame
Xixime

South America

Arikêm Atsawaka
Ayomén
Bisaniwa
Boanarí
Botocudos
Buijana-Piri
Care
Chaima
Chandinawa
Ciguaje
Eno
Fa-al
Garú
Genambi
Icaguate
Imihita
Iñapari
Jurí
Kabixiéna
Kamaka
Karamanta
Karirí
Kénkateye
Kiyasinga
Koëruna
Kokonuko
Kueretú
Makawahe
Makusa
Manitsawá
Mariaté
Mekka
Mongoyó
Morike
Mura
Nobenidza
Ona
Pamiwa
Pasé
Purí
Riama
Shaninawa
Shereu
Siary
Sura
Tamanako
Tapiira
Tapuya
Taruma
Tekiraka
Tiniwa
Toromona
Tupinamba
Uantuya
Urumi
Wainumá
Warpe
Yabaana
Yahgan
Yakaroa
Yapua
Yura

See also ETHNOCIDE; PACIFICATION; TOTAL WAR.

Davis, Shelton. (1977) *Victims of the Miracle: Development and the Indians of Brazil.*

Dobyns, Henry F. (1966) "Estimating Aboriginal American Population." *Current Anthropology* 7: 395–416.

Dow, James. (1995) *The Encyclopedia of World Cultures. Volume 8. Middle America and the Caribbean.*

Fein, Helen, ed. (1992) *Genocide Watch.*

Gutman, Israel, ed. (1990) *The Encyclopedia of the Holocaust.* 4 vols.

Jaimes, M. Annette, ed. (1992) *The State of Native America: Genocide, Colonization, and Resistance.*

Jonassohn, Kurt, and Frank Chalk. (1987) "A Typology of Genocide and Some Implications for the Human Rights Agenda." In Walliman and Dobkowski, 3–20.

Kuper, Leo. (1985) *The Prevention of Genocide.*

Lemkin, Raphael. (1944) *Axis Rule in Occupied Europe.*

Lizarralde, Manuel. (1992) "Index and Map of the Contemporary South American Indigenous Peoples." Unpublished manuscript, University of California at Berkeley.

O'Leary, Timothy J., and David Levinson, eds. (1990) *The Encyclopedia of World Cultures. Volume 1. North America.*

Reynolds, Henry. (1981) *The Other Side of the Frontier.*

Rummel, R. J. (1991) *China's Bloody Century: Genocide and Mass Murder since 1900.*

Stannard, David E. (1992) *American Holocaust: Columbus and the Conquest of the New World.*

Ternon, Yves. (1981) *The Armenians: History of a Genocide.*

Walliman, Isidor, and Michael N. Dobkowski, eds. (1987) *Genocide and the Modern Age.*

GERONTOCIDE

Gerontocide is the socially acceptable disposal of the aged through killing or abandonment. Surveys suggest that gerontocide occurs in about 20 to 25 percent of societies. This is a lower percentage than the 36 percent of societies with death-hastening behavior, as death-hastening behavior is a broader concept that includes killing and abandoning as well as forsaking and other behaviors such as suicide by the aged. Gerontocide is found in societies in all regions of the world, except for southern Europe, although it occurred there in the past. It was customary in a greater percentage of societies in North and South America prior to Europeanization of the continents and in Africa than elsewhere in the world. This distributional pattern seems to reflect the more-frequent presence of gerontocide in seminomadic hunting, fishing, and herding cultures, which were most common in these three parts of the world. Today, gerontocide is no longer customary in most of these societies as they are now sedentary and integrated, in some cases only marginally, into industrialized economic systems of the nations where they live. For example, the Saami (Lapps) once but no longer practice gerontocide.

Traditional explanations for gerontocide emphasized the severe climate, nomadic lifestyle, irregular food supply, and weak kinship ties that presumably were characteristic of societies with geronticide. The Eskimo and Inuit peoples were often cited as a classic example of a gerontocide society and the image of the aged Eskimo willingly drifting off on an ice floe became a popular myth. Recent research suggests that these factors do not cause gerontocide. Rather, societies with gerontocide seem to be ones that are seminomadic (seasonal movements following food sources) with a "loose" community structure that does not allow for the sharing of resources to support the aged. In societies with a "tight" structure based on close ties and reciprocal obligations between kin, support for the aged is easier. Additionally, gerontocide is customary only when the aged are defined as decrepit, which may result from a deterioration in their health or a change in community circumstances that prevents them from being socially productive members of the community. For example, the Copper Eskimo of Canada routinely provided the aged with food and clothing and transported those who could not do so themselves from camp to camp on sleds. However, in times of starvation, the aged would be abandoned.

See also Death-Hastening Behavior.

Glascock, Anthony P., and Richard A. Wagner. (1986) *HRAF Research Series in Quantitative Cross-Cultural Data. Vol. II: Life Cycle Data.*

Jenness, Diamond. (1922) *Report of the Canadian Arctic Expedition, 1913–1918, Vol. XII, Part A.*

Maxwell, Robert J., and Philip Silverman. (1989) "Gerontocide." In *The Contents of Culture: Constants and Variants: Studies in Honor of John M. Roberts,* edited by Ralph Bolton, 511–523.

Gossip

Gossip is a form of interpersonal communication that involves the transfer of information that may or may not be factual. At its core, gossip requires two or more participants, an account of an event, and evaluative comments about the event or its participants. Defining a particular communication event as gossip—in contrast to other types of communication—requires a consideration of the individual's intentions in transmitting the information, the type of information transmitted, and the information provider's and the listener's right to the information. Among the defining features of gossip are that the information is usually derogatory, the person gossiped about is not present, and the person transmitting the information and the person receiving it share an understanding of what constitutes correct behavior. Gossip is closely related to rumor and scandal, with the major difference being that the life cycle of a gossip event and gossip information is relatively short.

Gossip is the most common form of verbal aggression around the world. It is a form of verbal aggression in that an individual's purpose in gossiping is often to bring harm to the reputation and status of the individual gossiped about. For example, in cultures where wrongdoers are shunned or banished, the initial charge of misconduct is usually made through gossip, which leads to a more public, more open discussion of the wrongdoer's behavior. Gossip can be especially malicious, particularly when it takes the form of claiming that a person is a witch or evil sorcerer—crimes that may result in the alleged witch or sorcerer being killed. Because gossip can cause serious conflict between individuals and groups, in some cultures gossip is prohibited.

Despite its potential to cause conflict, gossip is also an important mechanism of social control in primary social groups. In complex societies, primary groups where gossip is important include families, cliques, work groups, neighborhoods, communities, and professional organizations. In small-scale societies, gossip is often a key mechanism of social control for the culture as a whole, especially in societies that rely exclusively on coordinate, self-help mechanisms of social control. However, gossip occurs and serves as a mechanism of social control in all societies. As John B. Haviland (1977:68) points out, for residents of the municipality of Zinacantan in southeast Mexico, what people "gossip about is a good index of what they worry about." In Zinacantan the ten things people gossip about most are: drunkenness, divorce, illicit sexual relations, jail and punishment, wealth and poverty, kin disputes, courtship, adultery, fighting, and stealing—all things they also worry about. Additionally, their gossip emphasizes events that they also fight about, and especially matters that are the subject of litigation in the local courts. Although gossip has not been studied systematically across cultures, Haviland's conclusion that the implicit subject of gossip is the rules of morality that underlie correct behavior seems to be the case in all cultures and primary social groups. This means that gossip reinforces social cohesion by enabling individuals to express their shared understanding of the core values of their culture.

Much of the anthropological interest in gossip has focused on the functions of gossip. There are two major views as to the major function of gossip in social groups. In one view, gossip is seen as a mechanism of social control and social boundary maintenance, sanctioning the behavior of group members and indicating the boundaries of the group to insiders and outsiders. Within this framework, the ability to participate in gossip is seen as a key marker of an individual membership in the group and thus helps to indicate who is a member and who is not. In fact, people living in cultures other than their own often learn quickly that their inability to participate in gossip or their exclusion from gossip events marks them as an outsider. For example, criticism of how a person wears his hair is an overt attempt to control that individual's behavior and an implicit statement about how members of the group wear their hair as compared to nonmembers. This, of course, points directly to the underlying nature of gossip as a shared understanding of the basic rules of morality that govern behavior in the group.

In the second view of the primary function of gossip, gossip is conceptualized as a tool that groups use to achieve their own interests when those interests conflict with the self-interests of others. In this view, gossip is a form of impression management with the goal of creating a negative image of rival groups and a positive image of one's own group. In conflict situations gossip is also used to define the issues in dispute in a way that casts the other party in a negative light. Gossip is especially prevalent in conflicts involving two political factions in a single culture or community. Each faction uses gossip to describe the rival group in negative terms, to attribute sinister motives to the other group, and to suggest that the other group's position and actions will harm the group as a whole. Thus, in this view, gossip is seen as a form of conflict rather than as a mechanism of group cohesion.

In fact, it seems clear that gossip can and often does play a variety of functions in social groups and cultures, including the discharge of aggressive feelings, the sanctioning of individual behavior, defining the group boundary, creating impressions of one's own and other groups, and as a tool for achieving one's goals in conflict situations.

Besnier, Niko. (1989) "Information Withholding as a Manipulative and Collusive Strategy in Nukulaelae Gossip." *Language and Society* 18: 315–341.

Brison, Karen J. (1992) *Just Talk: Gossip, Meetings, and Power in a Papua New Guinea Village.*

Cox, Bruce A. (1970) "What is Hopi Gossip About? Information Management and Hopi Factions." *Man* 5: 88–98.

Gluckman, Max. (1963) "Gossip and Scandal." *Current Anthropology* 4:307–316.

Haviland, John B. (1977) *Gossip, Reputation, and Knowledge in Zinacantan.*

Paine, Robert. (1967) "What Is Gossip About? An Alternative Hypothesis." *Man* 2: 278–285.

Rosnow, Ralph L., and Gary A. Fine. (1976) *Rumor and Gossip: The Social Psychology of Hearsay.*

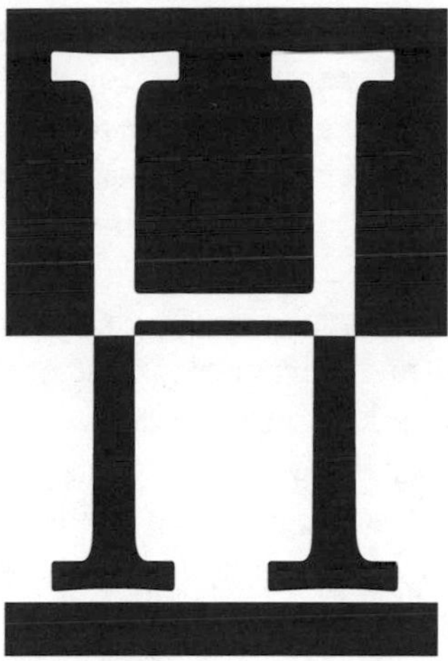

Harangue

A harangue is a form of verbal behavior used to express a grievance. The harangue has been described mainly in cultures in Melanesia, although similar behaviors occur elsewhere, as among the Ona of South America. A harangue generally takes place at night, when the person who believes he has been wronged by another stands outside and shouts his charges so that the accused and all others in the community can hear. For example, a Trobriand Islands man whose nephew had been erroneously imprisoned harangued the chief whom he held responsible:

> Namwana Guya'u, you are a cause of trouble. We, the Tabali of Omarakana, allowed you to stay here, to live among us. You had plenty of food in Omarakana, you ate of our food, you partook of the pigs brought to us as a tribute and of the fish. You sailed in our canoe. You built a hut on our soil. Now you have done us harm. You have told lies. Mitakata is in prison. We do not want you to stay here. This is our village! You are a stranger here. Go away! We chase you away! We chase you out of Omarakana.

This harangue was followed by similar statements shouted by other relatives of the imprisoned man. The chief sat in his hut in silence and shame and left the village for good before dawn. Although in this case the harangue was delivered against a chief, often it is a chief who delivers it, thereby giving it the weight of local authority and making it likely that the accused will correct his behavior or leave the community, either temporarily or permanently.

It is the sense of individual shame in the context of the entire community knowing about the wrongdoing that is the key element in the harangue. Shame, as it is experienced by Melanesian peoples, is difficult to translate cross-culturally as it is a far deeper and more powerful emotional and moral experience than what is experienced as guilt or shame in Western cultures. The harangue invokes shame in the guilty wrongdoer who must then alter his behavior or leave the community. In this way, the harangue is an especially effective mechanism of social control.

See also Banishment; Self-Punishment; Shunning.

Malinowski, Bronislaw. (1926) *Crime and Custom in Savage Society.*

Young, Michael. (1971) *Fighting with Food: Leadership, Values and Social Control in a Massim Society.*

Head-Hunting

Head-hunting is the practice of going to war or raiding other communities or societies for the purpose of cutting off and bringing back heads of the enemy. Although there is no worldwide survey of head-hunting, information in the ethnographic record indicates that it was an activity mainly of some cultures in Indonesia, especially on the islands of Borneo and the Celebes; in the Philippines where it is best-described for some cultures in northern Luzon but also reported for cultures on the southern island of Mindanao; New Guinea; and in tropical South America, where head-hunting by the Jivaro of Ecuador is well described. In other parts of the world, head-hunting was either absent or unusual, although some scholars suggest that the scalping found in North America is related to head-hunting. Head-hunting largely disappeared in the early part of the twentieth century, although it was still practiced by some isolated groups in all four regions into the 1960s or 1970s. Early accounts of head-hunting reported by missionaries, soldiers, and government officials overdramatized the activity and also overestimated its frequency. In fact, the number of heads taken was probably relatively few. One count from four Ifugao villages in the Philippines in the late 1880s shows that only six heads were taken by a population of 600 people in a five-year period.

There are both similarities and differences across the regions in the reasons why head-hunting was done and in the practice itself. The two basic similarities are that the taking of heads was a major reason (or even the sole reason) for making war or raiding and that heads were taken from other groups, rarely from members of one's own group and never from kin. A third similarity was that the taking of heads was a source of prestige and status for the warrior. In this regard, head-hunting is similar to other customs associated with warfare such as counting coup, trophy cannibalism, human sacrifice, scalping, and torture. Prestige was the primary reason for head-hunting by the Jivaro of Ecuador, but only one of a number of reasons for head-hunting by groups in Southeast Asia.

The practice was probably most elaborate in Indonesia. There warriors took heads for three reasons. First, to gain prestige for themselves as brave warriors. The more heads a man took, the more glory he brought to himself. Renowned hunters were decorated with special tattoos on their chests and ornaments such as panther teeth. Second, to take revenge against other groups. Heads were taken purposefully both to seek revenge and for the other reasons and also in the aftermath of combat. Since the loss of a head was a major blow to a group, it would seek revenge at some later date. Third, and perhaps most importantly, to gain control of the magical power that resides in the head. The idea that a human head is sacred or has supernatural power was a common belief in Indonesia and the head was thought of as the repository of magical power. Thus, when misfortune such as a poor crop or epidemics struck, the people looked to increase their store of magic power to strengthen themselves and to ward off evil spirits. The heads of enemies provided this power. Heads that were taken for use at a funeral were placed on the grave so that the soul of the slain warrior could serve the deceased in the afterlife. Heads taken to bring good fortune to the community were cleaned and then displayed in a house where the soul would act as guardian spirit.

In the Philippines, head-hunting groups also saw the heads as a source of glory for the hunter and good fortune for the community, although only some men were head-hunters and the practice seems to have been more limited than in Indonesia. In both regions the loss of a head caused great distress to the community, which sought to recover the body and dispose of it without the usual funeral rites so as to ward off misfortune. Misfortune might result because the loss of the head meant the loss of the power of the head to the community. Thus, the primary motivation for revenge attacks was to recover some of the lost power.

For the Jivaro of Ecuador, the primary purpose of taking heads was to increase the warrior's prestige, friends, and the obligations of others to him through public recognition of the warrior as a successful fighter and generous host. They also believed that possession of the head increased the power of the women in the warrior's household, although there was no general belief in the magical power of the head. A man's prestige was built not so much by the actual taking of the head—which could be a man's, woman's, or child's—but from the three feasts that he hosted over a three-year period after the head-hunting. By proving that he was a generous host to the community he enhanced his prestige, made new friends, and obligated others to reciprocate his generosity.

Aside from the people's own beliefs about why they took heads, there has been little research into possible deeper or broader explanations, such as the role of head-taking in the political, economic, or social systems of these cultures. One possibility is that head-hunting plays a psychological role as a way for men to discharge intense feelings of anger and envy and turn those feelings into more positive feelings of pride and admiration from the community.

See also CANNIBALISM; COUNTING COUP; HUMAN SACRIFICE; SCALPING; TORTURING THE ENEMY.

Barton, Roy F. (1919) *Ifugao Law.* California University Publications in American Archaeology and Ethnology 15: 1–187.

Harner, Michael J. (1972) *The Jivaro: People of the Sacred Waterfalls.*

Kennedy, Raymond. (1942). *The Ageless Indies.*

Rosaldo, Michelle Z. (1977) "Skulls and Causality." *Man* (n.s.) 12: 168–169.

Sanday, Peggy R. (1986) *Divine Hunger: Cannibalism as a Cultural System.*

HOMICIDE

Homicides are "those interpersonal assaults and other acts directed against another person (for example, poisonings) that occur outside the context of warfare, and that prove fatal" (Daly and Wilson 1988: 14). While Western conceptions of homicide usually assume that some direct physical action such as shooting, stabbing, poisoning, or hitting with a vehicle must occur for a homicide to take place, in many cultures homicide may also take place through witchcraft or sorcery. That is, an individual calls upon supernatural forces to kill another individual, usually through making them ill or by causing them to have an accident. In cultures where people use witchcraft or sorcery to harm others, it does not matter whether or not witchcraft or sorcery in fact does cause a person to die or whether it only explains a death that resulted from another cause such as illness or a serious injury. What does matter and what qualifies witchcraft and sorcery as forms of homicide in some cultures is that the people believe that they can kill another individual or that they can be killed by these means. For example, the Kapauku of New Guinea use witchcraft and sorcery to kill enemies, who are usually people from other communities, but sometimes also from one's own village. In one case, a Kapauku groom died shortly after his wedding and the death was attributed to the actions of a jealous sorcerer. The sorcerer was judged guilty by the village leader and executed by the victim's older brother.

How often homicides are committed in a society is a question that is difficult to measure in cultures around the world. In part, this is because of different definitions of what behaviors constitute a homicide from culture to culture and also because of wide variations on how reliably homicides are reported. In Western cultures, for example, homicides caused by witchcraft are not classified in government crime statistics as homicides because most people do not believe that one person can cause another to die by using witchcraft. However, in cultures where witchcraft beliefs are strong, not counting homicides due to witchcraft might result in a large underreporting of the number of homicides. For example, among the Tzeltal, deaths are commonly attributed to the actions of witches and revenge for witchcraft is the most common reason people kill each other. To give a general sense of how frequent homicide is in cultures around the world, in one survey of 186 cultures in which all types of homicide except infanticide were counted, homicide was considered to be infrequent in 55 percent of cultures, more frequent in 35 percent and very frequent in 10 percent. In another survey of 40 cultures in which only premeditated homicides were counted and homicides in self-defense were not counted, 48 percent-cultures were found to have high homicide rates and 52 percent had low rates. Homicide information for some nations is somewhat more reliable than that for cultures, but again variations in definitions and variations in the quality of national crime statistics make comparisons across nations difficult. The two general conclusions that can be stated with some certainty about homicide rates are that homicide occurs in all cultures and in all cultures at least some types of homicide are considered to be crimes.

In most cultures the norms that govern social behavior and the legal system delineate different types of homicide. The three criteria used most often to differentiate among types of homicide are intent, premeditation, and the closeness of the relationship between the murderer and the victim. Intent means that the killer wanted the victim to die. Premeditation means that the killer thought about killing the victim before acting and planned the homicide. Closeness has to do with whether the killer and the victim were blood relatives, relatives by marriage, neighbors, members of the same community, members of the same society, or members of different societies.

Western legal systems differentiate on the basis of intent and premeditation (as in legal concepts such as manslaughter, murder, and homicide) and also differentiate on the basis of relationship, as indicated by the use of specific words for certain types of homicide such as infanticide, matricide, and gerontocide. Western legal systems also differentiate on the basis of the status and role of the victim in the community. For example, the punishment for killing a police officer is often more severe than the punishment for killing a civilian, indicating that killing a police officer is a more serious form of homicide.

In most non-Western cultures, similar sets of rules distinguish among types of homicide although these rules may not always be codified into a set of written laws. These rules are not important just because they differentiate among types of homicide and indicate which are acceptable and which are criminal but also because they determine the severity of punishment meted out to the killer. For example, the Ifugao of the Philippines recognize four types of homicide and have different levels of punishment for each (Barton 1919: 78):

> (a) The taking of life when there is an entire absence of both intent and carelessness. As for example . . . when a party of hunters have a wild boar at bay. The boar . . . charges the most advanced of the hunters, and in retreating backwards, the latter jabs one of his companions with the shod point of his spear handle. There is no penalty for such a taking of life.
>
> (b) The taking of life when there is clearly an absence of intent, but a degree of carelessness. For example, a number of men are throwing spears at a mark. A child runs in

the way, and is killed. The penalty is a fine varying from one-third to two-thirds the amount of the full fine for homicide according to the degree of carelessness.

(c) Intentional taking of the life of another, under the impression that he is an enemy when in reality he is a co-villager or a companion. In case the killer can make the family of the slain understand the circumstances, only a fine is assessed. This fine is called *labod.* If the killer be unrelated to the slain, the full amount of the *labod* is demanded: if related, the amount is usually lessened.

Example: Dumauwat of Baay was irrigating his fields at night. Some of his companions told him that there were some head-hunters from an enemy village near. In the darkness, Dumauwat encountered another man. Likyayu, the betrothed of his daughter. He asked him who was there. On account of the noise of water falling from the rice fields, Likyayu did not hear the inquiry, and said nothing. Dumauwat speared him. Likyayu cried out. Dumauwat recognized his voice, and carried him home. He furnished animals for sacrifice to secure Likyayu's recovery. Likyayu recovered. Had he died, Dumauwat would have been called on for the full amount of the fine; but had Likyayu been firmly engaged to Dumauwat's daughter, that is, had the *bango* ceremony been performed the full amount of the *labod* fine would not have been demanded, since the relationship would have been an extenuating circumstance.

(d) The taking of life by persons in a brawl or by an intoxicated or insane person. In case the slain died before his slayer could agree to provide animals for sacrifice, the latter would probably be killed by the kin of the slain if he were of a foreign district. He might be killed if a nonrelated co-villager. He would be fined the *labod* if a kinsman. He would probably go scot free if a brother or uncle.

The Ifugao also differentiate attempted murder from actual murder, with punishment again inversely related to the closeness of the relationship of the murderer and the intended victim.

In many cultures, whether or not the killer and victim are kin or are members of the same political community is a major consideration in determining whether a homicide is considered to be a crime. For example, the Kapauku consider the premeditated murder of a member of one's own kin group or political confederacy a crime and execute the killer. However, killing a member of another confederacy is not considered a crime and the killer is not punished, although it might lead to a war between the confederacies. Because the killing of a close relative is an especially serious offense in many cultures, those who kill their children or parents or any close kin in kin-based cultures are often thought to be insane, which sometimes though not always excuses their behavior and forestalls punishment. For example, among the Ona a woman who kills her infant is considered insane and the behavior excused. Among the Dogon, "the murderer is an unfortunate person, the object of pity as much as of repulsion, who could only act as he did at a moment when an unknown force dominated him . . . ." (Paulme 1940: 113). However, a Dogon murderer does not escape punishment and is banished from the community often for life and he is considered to be dead, with his wife allowed to remarry and his property divided among his relatives.

Criminologists and others who study homicide often distinguish among different general types of homicide, some of which are listed below:

assassination—the killing of a political leader or other important public figure for a political purpose

capital punishment—the killing of a criminal that is approved of by the political community *familicide*—the killing of an entire nuclear family by a member of the family, usually the husband/father who then kills himself

feuding (blood revenge)—after a homicide, the killing of the murderer or a member of his kin group by the kin of the victim

filicide—the killing of a son or daughter by a parent

fratricide—the killing of a brother by a brother

gerontocide—the killing of the aged

infanticide—the killing of an infant, usually by a parent, a relative, or with the parents' approval

mass murder—the killing of a number of individuals at the same time in the same place usually by one individual

matricide—the killing of a mother by her child

parricide—the killing of a parent by his or her child

serial killing—the killing of a number of individuals over a period of time by one individual

spousal homicide—the killing of a spouse by a spouse

suicide—killing oneself

terrorism—the killing of civilians by a political group for a political purpose

A number of these types involve one blood relative killing another blood relative, a general type of homicide that is often though of as being quite common. In fact, as the survey of homicides throughout history and across cultures by the biologist-psychologist team of Martin Daly and Margo Wilson shows, the killing of blood relatives is actually unusual and is quite rare when we consider the frequency and closeness of interaction among blood relatives relative to that among nonrelatives. For example, the two most common forms of killing of blood relatives—infanticide and gerontocide—are both considered acceptable under certain circumstances in some societies but occur only rarely in those societies and then only when the survival of an infant or aged person threatens the survival of others in the family or community.

Efforts to explain homicide across cultures as well as in specific cultures have been hampered by the definitional and information reliability problems mentioned above. Instead, most explanations seek to account for only specific types of homicide as discussed in the relevant articles throughout this volume. At the same time, two general frameworks have been used to explain homicide in a broad sense. One framework is known as the culture pattern of violence or legitimacy of violence model. This model suggests that within and across cultures, homicide exists as part of a broader cultural pattern of violence and violent conflict resolution. Cross-culturally, homicide is more frequent in cultures that are more often at war, where capital punishment is used more often, where assaults are common, where people often compete against each other in combative sports, and where boys are raised to behave aggressively.

The second framework is the evolutionary psychology model in which social and individual behavior including homicide is explained at least in part by principles derived from evolutionary biology. The central principles are those of natural selection, fitness, and self-interest. Natural selection is the evolutionary process through which certain traits survive over time while others disappear. Those that survive are ones that have adaptive value in that they enable organisms to compete successfully in their environment. Fitness refers to the degree to which a particular trait provides survival value for a particular organism or species. Self-interest, within this framework, means that individuals will behave in ways that increase their fitness, primarily by passing their genes on to future generations through their children or other blood kin such as nieces and nephews. Thus, homicide can be conceptualized as a mechanism produced by the natural selection process that is used (unconsciously) by human beings to maximize their fitness. While this framework has only recently been used to explain homicide, it is likely to prove useful for explaining why specific types of homicide occur as well as answering other questions about homicide around the world, such as why most homicides are committed by men and why blood relatives of the killer are less often the victim than are nonblood relatives.

See also CAPITAL PUNISHMENT; CRIME; DEATH-HASTENING BEHAVIOR; FEUDING; GERONTOCIDE; INFANTICIDE; SORCERY; SUICIDE; WITCHCRAFT.

Archer, Dane, and Rosemary Gartner. (1984) *Violence and Crime in Cross-National Perspective.*

Barton, Roy F. (1919) *Ifugao Law.* California University Publications in American Archaeology and Ethnology 15: 1–187.

Daly, Martin, and Margo Wilson. (1988) *Homicide.*

Ember, Carol R., and Melvin Ember. (1992) "Warfare, Aggression and Resource Problems: Cross-Cultural Codes." *Behavior Science Research* 26: 169–226.

Nash, June. (1967) "Death as a Way of Life: The Increasing Resort to Homicide in a Maya Indian Community." *American Anthropologist* 69: 455–470.

Palmer, Stuart. (1965) "Murder and Suicide in Forty Non-Literate Societies." *The Journal of Criminal Law, Criminology, and Police Science* 56: 320–324.

Paulme, Denise. (1940) *Social Organization of the Dogon.*

Pospisil, Leopold. (1958) *Kapauku Papuans and Their Law.*

HUMAN SACRIFICE

Sacrifice is a form of nonverbal communication between human beings and the supernatural world. It is an exchange of goods meant to influence the supernatural to behave in a way that is beneficial to the humans offering the sacrifice. Sacrifice comes in three major forms: animal; plant foods such as rice, wheat, or corn; and human. A common feature of all three forms is that what is sacrificed is of economic value to the person making the sacrifice. In cultures where animals are sacrificed, the species sacrificed are those that are economically important; in cultures where it is food, it is staple crops; and in cultures where it is humans, it is usually in cultures where humans are an important source of energy. Animal and plant sacrifice (which is sometimes classified as an offering rather than a sacrifice) are far more common than human sacrifice, although all forms have been found throughout human history in all regions of the world.

A survey of 107 cultures shows that human sacrifice occurred commonly in 17 percent of cultures and sporadically in 14 percent in the nineteenth and early twentieth centuries. Thus, it was not customary in 69 percent, making it relatively rare compared to most other forms of behavior that result in death for the victim such as homicide or capital punishment. Human sacrifice was concentrated in cultures in Africa (50 percent of those with human sacrifice) and Oceania (30 percent), for reasons discussed below.

Humans are sacrificed only for the most important requests to the supernatural. Among the Marquesas Islanders in Polynesia these reasons included success in war, to end a drought, to secure a plentiful harvest, to consecrate a new house or canoe, and to mark special events in the life of the chief such as his being ill or departing on a voyage. For the Bambara of West Africa, the reasons were the chief's running short on money, his having problems governing, and

Aztec sacrifice involved tearing out the heart to give blood to the sun.

a family suffering many deaths. Humans who were sacrificed in most cultures were outsiders such as slaves or war captives or those who did not fit in, such as albinos. When members of one's own culture were sacrificed, women and children were more likely to be the victims than were men.

Cultures with human sacrifice are mostly ones with an advanced horticultural economy and political organization—a common type of culture in Oceania and West Africa. In these cultures people subsist primarily from food grown in large gardens and groves, live in large, relatively permanent villages, and are governed by a chief who might be supported by a cadre of public servants. In this type of culture, human labor is the major source of energy to plant and tend the gardens, build houses, construct tools, etc. Two indicators of the importance of human energy were the use of slaves and the presence of specialized craftsmen such as potters and leatherworkers. Thus, when an important request was made to the supernatural, it was often accompanied by a sacrifice of what was most important economically—a human life. It has been suggested that human sacrifice did not occur in other types of societies such as foraging, farming, or industrial ones because for these, human labor is not such an important commodity. In farming cultures it is food crops that are offered, indicating their economic importance.

The culture that has drawn the most attention for its use of human sacrifice is the Aztec State of pre-Columbian Mexico. Compared to any other known culture, the Aztec were at the far extreme in the use of human sacrifice and also in the practice of cannibalism. Sacrifice was a central feature of the Aztec religious system, with the human heart and blood believed to be the ultimate source of power for the sun and Aztec deities. During the two annual ceremonial cycles of 365 and 260 days, it is estimated that about 20,000 humans were sacrificed in hundreds of temples throughout the Aztec empire. There were at least 80 such temples in the capital city of Tenochtitlán. The victims were usually warriors captured and kept alive to be sacrificed or become slaves. While a variety of killing methods was used, the preferred method was cutting the victim open on a stone slab, removing the heart and placing it in a ceremonial vessel, smearing blood on the carved image of the god, and placing the skull on a skull rack alongside thousands of others. Aztec sacrifice was allegedly accompanied by cannibalism, with at least three of the limbs going to the warrior who captured the victim and the torso fed to animals in the royal zoo.

Various explanations have been suggested for Aztec human sacrifice. Older explanations emphasized the central role of sacrifice in Aztec religion and the Aztec sacrifice complex that developed around it. This complex included the religious beliefs and myths, the stone temples, ceremonial platforms and equipment such as the skull racks, the sacrifice rituals that lasted three days, the ceremonial cycle, cannibalism, and warfare that was waged primarily to capture sacrificial victims. Both the archaeological and historical record point to the central role of human sacrifice in Aztec culture.

More recent attempts to explain Aztec sacrifice move beyond the Aztec's own beliefs and the cultural manifestation of those beliefs and cite both environmental and political forces. The environmental explanation suggests that the vitality and survival of the Aztec state may have been threatened by overpopulation because of the limited food resources available in Central Mexico. The Aztec lived mainly on foods derived from corn; there was a severe shortage of wild animals to hunt for meat and no domestic food-producing and supplying animals. Thus, in this explanation, sacrifice is seen as a form of population control (one estimate suggests that 250,000 people or the equivalent of 10 percent of the regional population may have been sacrificed each year) while cannibalism provided protein that could not be obtained from other food sources. The political explanation suggests that sacrifice and cannibalism were but one of a number of political strategies used by the Aztec monarchs to control the noble class and maintain control of the military. In this view, human sacrifices were a form of wealth given to and consolidated among the nobles, who otherwise might rebel against the monarch. Whatever the causes of Aztec sacrifice and cannibalism, both ended with the Spanish conquest in the sixteenth century.

See also CANNIBALISM; RAIDING FOR SLAVES.

Dieterlen, Germaine. (1951) *An Essay on the Religion of the Bambara.*

Handy, E. S. Craighill. (1923) *The Native Culture of the Marquesas.* Bernice P. Bishop Museum, Bulletin 9.

Harner, Michael. (1977) "The Ecological Basis for Aztec Sacrifice." *American Ethnologist* 4: 117–135.

Price, Barbara J. (1978) "Demystification, Enriddlement, and Aztec Cannibalism: A Materialist Rejoinder to Harner." *American Ethnologist* 5: 98–115.

Sheils, Dean. (1980) "A Comparative Study of Human Sacrifice." *Behavior Science Research* 15: 245–262.

Soustelle, Jacques. (1962) *Daily Life of the Aztecs.*

HUMOR

Humor is a cultural universal. A survey of 75 cultures shows that all had some form of humor and only in two were people generally not humorous. Beneath this broad generalization, humor varies very widely in content, form of expression, and topics considered humorous from one culture to another. Similarly, the relationship between humor and aggression and conflict varies widely from one culture to another, with relatively little known about the role humor plays in both the expression and control of aggression and conflict.

Regardless of humor's exact relationship to aggression, it seems quite clear that humor is found in all cultures because it is a form of entertainment and amusement that is enjoyable and pleasurable. Its role in expressing aggression and conflict is likely to be secondary to this broader role in the human experience, although in some cultures the role of humor in controlling aggression is of considerable importance.

Humor comes in a wide variety of forms around the world. The major ones are:

Joking
Satire
Riddles
Puns
Rhymes
Proverbs
Mocking
Insults
Ridicule
Teasing
Imitation
Satire
Slapstick
Caricatures
Clowning
Burlesque
Practical joking
Pranks
Mock aggression (horseplay)
Tickling

To this list we must add joking relationships and ethnic humor, two forms of humor that clearly have a role in the expression and control of aggression. Additionally, song duels and word duels both have major humor components in that the behavior of the participants amuses the audience.

Although little is now known about the relationship between humor and aggression around the world, information from individual cultures suggests that humor can and often is a mechanism through which aggression is displayed and conflict controlled. Whether or not humor serves this function in a specific culture is determined by a mix of factors including the types and levels of aggression in the culture, the types of humor typically used, other outlets for the expression of aggression, and the level of conflict both within the culture and with other cultures. It does seem, however, that the use of aggressive forms of humor is one component of a broader cultural patterning of the expression of aggression. In cultures where aggressive behavior is controlled, humor is less aggressive, with the opposite holding for cultures that permit the open expression of aggression. Additionally, the more aggressive forms of humor such as horseplay, practical jokes, pranks, and insults are found more commonly in small, close-knit communities where there is relative social equality among the people and where most relationships are close or intimate. In this type of community, the direct expression of aggression toward those with whom one has to interact daily may be problematic and aggression expressed in humor acts as a safety valve.

Psychological interpretations of the role of humor proceed from the assumption that humor is a mechanism for meeting the human need to express aggressive drives or feelings. In this view humor serves both drive discharge and social control functions by allowing for the expression of aggression in ways that reduce individual tension and social conflict. Ridicule, ritualized insults, telling of jokes, and practical joking are especially important in this regard. For example, among the Amhara of Ethiopia servants will often play practical jokes on their masters, jokes which the masters appreciate and find amusing, especially when they are clever. This form of joking allows the servants to express anger that might result from their inferior status in a socially acceptable way that allows for the smooth continuation of master-servant relations. Among the San of Botswana, joking is understood and used to alleviate tensions in social situations and is seen as a preferable alternative to losing one's temper. Similarly, the Navajo of the American Southwest turn to joking as a way of appearing harmless and therefore avoiding conflict when in the company of strangers.

Sociocultural interpretations of humor stress the dual role humor can play in maintaining social control within the group and creating group solidarity in reference to other groups. This control/solidarity function can occur in groups of any size and composition. Cross-culturally, this pattern manifests itself in a variety of ways in different cultures. As regards social control, humor functions in some cultures much like gossip in that it expresses approval of group norms, encourages identification with the group, creates a positive self image for the group, and calls attention to deviant behavior. On Nissan Island in Oceania, for example, people engage in a form of gossip in which they criticize and laugh about other people's misbehavior or misfortune behind their backs. Besides providing amusement and a means of expressing anger for the participants, this form of gossip also reinforces group norms and punishes those who violate the rules by shaming them. Chicanos in South Texas use humorous wordplay and irony to emphasize the differences between themselves and their white neighbors. One form of wordplay is the literal translation of people's names from Spanish into English which dramatically demonstrates the differences between the cultures as when Casimiro Flores is rendered in English as "I Almost See Flowers."

Humor also encourages intragroup harmony by allowing for the public discussion or display of topics that are forbidden otherwise. Ritual clowning, burlesque, and caricature are especially important in this regard and all three are usually expressions of what is called ritual humor. Ritual humor is a form of humor in which some of the normal rules of conduct are suspended or even reversed. Usually, ritual humor takes the form of public dramatic performances conducted by ritual humor specialists such as clowns or fools. The reversal of normal behavior (called contrary behavior by anthropologists) is a tension-reducing mechanism as it allows people to make fun of or to be amused by behaviors of other people who normally are immune from such treatment. Contrary behavior includes ridiculing high status people in the community, men dressing and acting like women, acting in contrary ways such as walking backwards, giving wrong answers to obvious questions, and ridiculing outsiders.

Intergroup conflict often involves a broad category of humor that is called ethnic humor. Manifestations of ethnic humor include satire, sarcasm, caricature, ritual clowning, burlesque, and jokes. All of these are relatively safe mechanisms for the expression of conflict between different ethnic groups. By stereotyping and ridiculing the other group, people create solidarity and a positive self-image for their own group while damaging the reputation of the other group. Such humor seems to be culturally universal and occurs in all ethnic groups in contact with one another. The level of hostility beneath the humor, of course, varies widely around the world.

Although the indirect role of humor in expressing aggression and controlling conflict has been stressed, it also possible for aggression to be expressed directly through humor. Insults, ridicule, and mocking are often direct forms of verbal aggression. For example, in disputes between Kpelle (Liberia) men, the disputants will try to weaken the status of their opponent by using insulting jokes to embarrass the other man and damage his reputation. This pattern of insulting is learned by young Kpelle boys who often trade such insults with each other, even when they do not fully understand the meanings of the jokes. Perhaps the most striking aspect of the relationship between humor and aggression is the clear sex difference in the expression of humor. Women rarely engage in public displays of aggressive humor such as word and song duels, practical jokes, pranks, and ritual clowning. Although there are a few cultures where women regularly participate in song and word duels, the regular public use of aggressive humor by women occurs only in a few polygynous societies—

societies that have markedly high levels of female aggression in general. For example, among the Dogon of Mali, co-wives often publicly taunt and insult each other, behavior that causes their children to hide in shame and their husband to flee the scene, but which is of much amusement to others in the community. Dogon wives also often engage in word duels, trading of insults, and sarcasm with their husbands both in private and public, with all participants believing it better to express anger indirectly through humor rather than expressing such feelings directly and possibly precipitating violence.

See also INSULTS; JOKING RELATIONSHIPS; SEX DIFFERENCES IN AGGRESSION; SOCIALIZATION OF AGGRESSION; SONG DUELS; WORD DUELS.

Alford, Finnegan, and Richard D. Alford. (1981) "A Holo-Cultural Study of Humor." *Ethos* 9: 149–164.

Apte, Mahadev L. (1985) *Humor and Laughter: An Anthropological Approach.*

Bricker, Victoria R. (1973) *Ritual Humor in Highland Chiapas.*

Calame-Griaule, Genevieve. (1986) *Words and the Dogon World.*

Lancy, David F. (1975) *Work, Play and Learning in a Kpelle Town.*

Levine, Donald N. (1965) *Wax and Gold: Tradition and Innovation in Ethiopian Culture.*

McAllester, David P. (1954) *Enemy Way Music: A Study of Social and Esthetic Values as seen in Navaho Music.*

Marshall, Lorna J. (1976) *The !Kung of Nyae Nyae.*

Nachman, Steven R. (1986) "Discomforting Laughter: Schadenfreude among Melanesians." *Journal of Anthropological Research* 42: 53–67.

West, Stanley A., and June Macklin, eds. (1979) *The Chicano Experience.*

HUSBAND BEATING

Husband beating is physical violence by a woman directed at her husband. It can range in severity from a push or shove to hitting with the hand to assault with a weapon to murder. A survey of 90 cultures indicates that wives beat their husbands in 27 percent of cultures, although it occurs in a majority of households in only 6.7 percent of societies. This is far less than the 84.5 percent of societies where wife beating occurs and the 74 percent of societies where children are physically punished. Thus, within the residential family, men are the least likely family member to be the object of violence by other members of the family. Husband beating is found only in societies where wife beating also occurs and in most societies occurs less often and is less likely to cause serious physical harm than is wife beating.

Adultery or a suspicion of adultery is the most frequent cause of husband beating. Unlike wife beating, there are very few cultures where it is considered proper for a wife to beat her husband just because she believes that he is failing to meet his obligations to her or the family. And in those few cultures where there are acceptable reasons for beating a husband, there is often a double standard. For example, the Toradja of Indonesia permit spouse beating when one party is "guilty" of not meeting family obligations. However, the obligations of a wife are far greater than those of a husband and a wife can be beaten for being late with the evening meal, while a husband is not "guilty" if he comes late to the meal or chooses to dine elsewhere.

See also AGGRESSION BY WOMEN; WIFE BEATING.

Adriani, N., and A. C. Krutz. (1951) *The Bare'e-Speaking Toradja of Central Celebes (The East Toradja).*

Levinson, David. (1989) *Family Violence in Cross-Cultural Perspective.*

Infanticide

Infanticide is the purposeful termination of an infant's life. In accord with Judeo-Christian beliefs, infanticide has been treated as a particularly abhorrent crime by Western culture for nearly 2,000 years. However, at various times in Western history the penalties imposed have been less severe than those for other types of homicide and the laws banning infanticide have sometimes been enforced inconsistently. In the non-Western world prior to the imposition of Christianity and Western legal systems, the majority of non-Western societies allowed infanticide for various reasons. In many of these societies, infanticide clearly served as a form of birth control in the absence of other methods that could be used to prevent conception or terminate a pregnancy before birth without harm to the mother. The underlying purpose was to space births to allow scarce resources, including the mother's time and energy, to be given to the existing children. A half-dozen cross-cultural surveys estimate the percentage of such societies at between 53 and 78 percent, depending on how precisely infanticide is defined and how the cases are counted. At the same time, of course, there were numerous societies that forbid infanticide. For example, infanticide by the Ona of the Tierra del Fuego at the southern tip of South America was described by ethnographer Martin Gusinde as ". . . out of the question and inconceivable, so to speak." He then recounts the story of a mother who drowned her daughter and then hid from the group to conceal her crime. When her crime was eventually discovered she was ostracized and then allowed to rejoin the group although she was now seen as being mentally ill—the only possible explanation for her actions. Mental illness is also a common explanation for infanticide in the Western world today, although often without validity and often at the cost of masking the real reasons leading a parent to kill his or her child.

Little is known about who kills the infant, largely because ethnographers wrote little about it, perhaps for fear of getting native people in trouble with colonial officials who considered infanticide a crime. What is known is that in the majority of societies the killing was done by the mother, usually through means such as abandonment, smothering, poisoning, or burial. Midwives often do the killing in some societies, while fathers and other relatives do so in a small minority of cultures. In general, however, parents usually kill the infant, a major difference between infanticide by humans as compared to that by nonhuman primates, among whom the killing is more often done by a male unrelated to the infant.

In a sample of 57 societies, the reasons commonly given for infanticide are:

Illegitimate conception (adultery, unwed mother, rape, father from other society or kinship group)	53%
A twin or triplet	40%
Infant unfit (ill, weak, handicapped)	53%
Abnormal birth (breech, premature)	20%

Birth control (too many children, too close birth spacing, poverty)	23%
Infant unwanted (family problems, mother too old)	27%
Infant a girl	17%
Infant a boy	7%
Other	3%

Infanticide has been explained as a form of after-the-fact birth control, used in a variety of situations as listed above, virtually all of which are circumstances that interfere in some way with a parent's willingness or ability to devote sufficient resources to raising the child. This birth control explanation is supported by the timing of the actual act of killing the infant. In 90 percent of societies that permitted infanticide, the killing took place before the performance of a birth ceremony. Since a birth ceremony publicly defines the infant as a social being and as fully "human," killing before the ceremony means that the act is not a crime—the infant is not human—and perhaps also makes it somewhat easier emotionally for a mother to kill or lose her child. Other possible explanations, which draw heavily on observations of nonhuman primates such as gorillas, emphasize the use of the infant's body for food (very rare in humans), the role of nonbiological parents (stepparents) who have less biological investment in the infant or child, competition between men that results in their killing one another's offspring, and mental illness on the part of the perpetrator.

Twin infanticide and female infanticide are special forms of infanticide. Twin or triplet infanticide, where only one infant is allowed to survive, occurs in anywhere from 25 percent to 40 percent of the societies where infanticide occurs. However, the rule is often not rigidly enforced, as among the Guarani of Brazil where in some communities one of the twins is killed, but in other communities both twins are allowed to live. Whether or not a twin is killed depends mostly on the resources available to the mother to rear two children of the same age. Only when she has much other work to perform and cannot count on child care help from relatives is it likely that a twin will be sacrificed.

Female infanticide, while the subject of much discussion, is not as widespread as many believe, reported in only about 17 percent of societies. Why some societies choose to dispose of female infants more readily than male infants is unclear, although the practice is clearly motivated by a perceived need on the part of the parents to produce sons or at least more sons than daughters. A variety of situations can give rise to this preference for sons. One is the need to produce a steady stream of warriors to battle other communities or societies. Another is a need to produce male heirs when there is much wealth in the family and inheritance and continuation of the family name is through the male line. Finally, in many societies in traditional times, it was easier to replace women by taking women or girls as war captives and then integrating them into the society through marriage than it was to replace men with war captives. Perhaps this is one reason why societies that raided or traded for slaves took far more female slaves than male slaves.

Daly, Martin, and Margo Wilson. (1988) *Homicide.*

Granzberg, Gary. (1973) "Twin Infanticide—A Cross-Cultural Test of a Materialistic Explanation." *Ethos* 4: 405–412.

Gusinde, Martin. (1931) *The Fireland Indians. Vol. 1. The Selk'nam: On the Life and Thought of a Hunting People of the Great Island of Tierra del Fuego.*

Hausfater, G., and S. Blaffer Hardy, eds. (1984) *Infanticide: Comparative and Evolutionary Perspectives.*

Langer, William L. (1974) "Infanticide: A Historical Survey." *History of Childhood Quarterly: The Journal of Psychohistory* 1: 353–365.

Levinson, David. (1989) *Family Violence in Cross-Cultural Perspective.*

Minturn, Leigh, and Jerry Stashak. (1982) "Infanticide as a Terminal Abortion Procedure." *Behavior Science Research* 17: 70–90.

Schaden, Egon. (1962) *Fundamental Aspects of Guarani Culture.*

INSULTS

Insults are a form of communication in which through words or actions one person attempts to degrade another. Insults are a very common feature of interpersonal relations in many, if not all, cultures of the world, although not all people in all cultures insult others. Insults are usually a form of verbal aggression in that they are motivated by a desire to embarrass, humiliate, dominate, defeat, or damage the reputation of another person. Insults generally call attention to real or fantasized behaviors or personality traits that are considered unacceptable in the culture. Thus, in all cultures, some insults are considered more extreme than others, depending on the relationship between the individuals, the subject of the insult, and the context in which it is made. Accusations of witchcraft and sorcery are extreme insults in cultures with these customs. Insults are often public behavior, with the audience finding the insults quite humorous.

Insults can be either verbal or nonverbal. Nonverbal insults are often communicated through motions of the fingers, hand, or arm. Other types of nonverbal insults include showing one's buttocks, a woman exposing her vagina to another woman, spitting, pulling down one's eyelid, and adopting particular body language. For example, a Dogon girl will call an adult lazy by jumping in place twice with her arms crossed in front of her body and then once with her arms spread open.

Not all insulting behavior expresses anger or harms the other person, as among certain categories of intimates in some cultures, the exchange of insults signifies closeness and friendship. For example, Punjabi men from northwestern India who encounter each other after a long interval will exchange insults, call each other names, and engage in horseplay as signs of friendship. On a broader scale, insults as a means of expressing closeness are one feature of the joking relationships between various categories of kin and nonkin in many cultures. Insults tend to be most common in small, primary social groups where the participants are relative equals or among intimates in larger groups. Thus, insults are a more common feature of social interaction and aggression in small-scale non-Western cultures than in modern, urbanized cultures. In urbanized cultures, insults are most often traded by members of primary groups, such as coworkers or adolescent boys. In all cultures, insulting is primarily a male activity. The major exception to this generalization are polygynous cultures where co-wives as part of their broader pattern of hostile interaction often insult one another.

Insults are commonly expressed around the world in the assigning of nicknames. Nicknaming is a very common custom—a survey of 60 cultures indicates that at least some people assign nicknames to others in about two-thirds of cultures. Nicknames are often preferred because they more clearly identify individuals than do given names. Nicknames generally describe individuals on the basis of personality traits or behavioral abnormalities, physical appearance including physical abnormalities, place of birth or origin, and occupation. Derogatory nicknames are far more common than positive or neutral ones, being used in 50 percent of cultures. Derogatory nicknames are most often based on physical or behavioral abnormalities; in a sense labeling the person with a permanent insult.

In some cultures where insulting is a major means of expressing anger, insulting is but one aspect of a broader pattern of verbal aggression. For example, the Amhara of Ethiopia have been described as a culture characterized by a high level of verbal aggression. Nonverbal insults hurled by Amhara men at each other include sticking out one's tongue and spitting on the ground in front of another man. A theme of cannibalism (perhaps a symbolic expression of verbal aggression) runs through Amhara art, myth, games, and riddles. Anger is expressed through gossip, insulting, arguing, and litigation. Even nonaggressive conversation is characterized by an assertive speaking style, disagreements, and arguments. Finally, Amhara disputes frequently end up in court, where the opportunity to argue and insult one's rival is more important than resolving the case.

While most insults are communicated as part of day-to-day interaction, some, such as word and song duels, are a highly ritualized and institutionalized form of insulting. Words duels are an organized form of competition in which the competitors attempt to better or humiliate one another in front of an audience. Insults are also a component of ethnic humor. In some societies, members of the dominant culture will openly insult members of the subordinate one, often by assigning them a derogatory term of reference or referring to their behavior and personalities in negative, stereotypical terms. People from two cultures where neither is dominant may also engage in the same insulting behavior, although here the insulting is reciprocal and is perhaps done to demonstrate cultural differences and the ethnic solidarity of members of each group rather than to reinforce social or economic superiority.

See also Joking Relationships; Song Duels; Word Duels.

Alford, Finnegan, and Richard D. Alford. (1981) "A Holo-Cultural Study of Humor." *Ethos* 9: 149–164.

Alford, Richard D. (1988) *Naming and Identity: A Cross-Cultural Study of Personal Naming Practices.*

Apte, Mahadev L. (1985) *Humor and Laughter: An Anthropological Approach.*

Griaule, Marcel. (1938) *Dogon Games.*

Levine, Donald N. (1965) *Wax and Gold: Tradition and Innovation in Ethiopian Culture.*

Internal Conflict

Internal conflict is the label used for a very broad category of behaviors and practices that involves conflict and violence between people in the same culture. It contrasts with external conflict, which refers to conflict between different cultures. In its broadest definition, internal conflict includes all types of conflict both by and directed at either individuals or groups within a culture. Many of these specific forms of conflict are covered by separate articles in this volume. Because the concept is so broad, various classification schemes have been developed for ordering the various types of internal conflict found in cultures around the world. One classification scheme, applied to interpersonal violence, differentiates types of violence on the basis of the perpetrator-victim relationship—(1) both are members of the same household, (2) both are residents of the same community and know each another, (3) both are strangers to one another (they are residents of different communities). This scheme is useful in research designed to explain specific forms of interpersonal conflict as it draws attention to the relationship between the participants and to the crucial question of who is violent toward whom.

A second classification framework distinguishes between conflict that takes place between individuals (sometimes called interpersonal conflict or violence) and that which occurs between groups. Individual violence includes assault, drunken brawling, and wife beating, while internal conflict between groups includes feuding, raiding, and internal war, although the distinctions between these three are not always clear. This framework is also useful in studying the causes of internal conflict as it allows one to distinguish between internal conflicts that are acceptable to the group and those that are unacceptable. It also enables one to analyze the relationships among different forms of violence.

A third classification framework treats internal conflict as a single phenomenon, but measures its frequency and intensity along a number of dimensions and thus allows for the classification of entire cultures or communities as high, moderate, or low in their levels of internal conflict. Political scientist Marc Howard Ross, for example, uses this approach to measure seven components of internal conflict in cultures around the world:

1. Severity of conflict between communities
2. Acceptability of conflict directed at people in other communities
3. Frequency of internal war
4. Severity of conflict within the community
5. Extent of the use of physical force to settle disputes
6. Degree of acceptability of violence directed at other members of the community
7. Degree of compliance with community norms and community decisions

This scheme allows the rating of different cultures on each of these dimensions and a summing of the scores provides a gross overall estimate of the level of internal conflict in a culture. Applied to a sample of 90 cultures, this approach shows some cultures to be highly conflictual, others in the middle range, and still others having little internal conflict and violence. Highly conflictual cultures are ones like the Somali of East Africa who have much feuding, internal war, and raids between communities, political units, and kin-based clans, and high compliance with community norms due to a need to consolidate community resources so as to fight with other communities. Internal conflict and violence is so endemic among the Somali that in 1992 the United Nations sent troops to the country to control clan and subclan warfare and to insure the delivery of food supplies to nearly 2 million starving Somalis. The Comanche of the Plains are an example of culture with a moderate level of internal violence. Among the Comanche, interpersonal violence among community members was common and physical force was used to settle disputes, but there was little group violence directed at other communities or kin groups. At the low end of the violence scale are cultures such as the Semai of Malaysia who have virtually no violence and who settle disputes in ways that allow the parties to air their grievances publicly and to express anger verbally rather than physically.

Much attention has been directed at explaining why some cultures have high levels of internal violence while others have low levels. Additionally, much attention has been given to answering the same question for specific types of internal violence such as feuding; these are discussed separately in the relevant articles throughout this volume.

Both psychological and sociocultural factors are involved in internal violence. Psychological explanations look to childrearing practices for the basic causes of violence. Cultures with high overall rates of internal violence are ones where boys are raised to be aggressive, either directly by encouraging and rewarding aggressive behavior or indirectly through the use of harsh and restrictive childrearing practices. The debate over whether socialization for aggression causes internal violence or whether internal violence causes socialization for aggression is not settled. The violence-causes-socialization view is based on the assumption that people living in violent cultures will need to raise boys to be aggressive so that they can compete effectively. The socialization-causes-violence view is based on the assumption that the presence of violence-prone boys and men leads to violence. In one variant of this view, it is suggested that societies that often engage in external wars raise boys to be aggressive so that they will be able warriors. This aggression, in times of peace, is then expressed internally rather than externally. There is some evidence for this in regard to modern nations, as the crime rate often increases during and following wars. However, it is not clear that the same pattern holds for non-Western, nonstate societies, although in some societies there is a clear link between the levels of internal and external war.

Sociocultural explanations center on the extent and strength of crosscutting ties between groups within the culture. These groups might be lineages, clans, villages, neighborhoods, or other types of clearly delineated local groups. The idea that crosscutting ties established through intermarriage, trade, cooperation in external warfare, and residence lead to peaceful relations between communities while weak ties of these types allow or encourage conflict goes back over 100 years. Much attention has been given to the role of intermarriage in creating conflicting loyalties between people who have relatives in different communities or from different kin groups and in creating alliances between groups. While it does appear that intermarriage encourages efforts at peacemaking (peacemakers are often women living in the community of their husband, but born into a different community), it does not in general create cross-kin group or community alliances or crosscutting ties that result in low levels of internal violence. Rather, cultures with low levels of internal violence are ones with many different types (marriage, trade, ceremonial obligations, alliances in war against other cultures) of crosscutting ties that create continual interaction between members of different communities. Thus, it is the number and intensity of ties that make cultures internally peaceful. An example of an internally peaceful society is the Iroquois Confederation composed of six nations. The primary motivation for forming the confederation was to stop fighting between the nations so that they could pool resources and direct their attention to war with neighboring societies such as the Erie, Neutral, and Huron. Despite being in a constant state of war with other societies, the Iroquois were mainly peaceful internally and maintained regular intermarriage between nations and between clans within the nations, cooperated in warfare, traded, exchanged slaves, and cooperated politically at confederacy-wide conferences to deal with important issues.

Cultures that are internally conflictual and violent have weak crosscutting ties and little regular peaceful contact between members of different communities. In addition, some internally violent cultures also have localized kinship groups such as fraternal interest groups, which are groups of related men who support one another in conflict with other like groups. These localized support groups operate only in cultures without strong, centralized leaders. When strong leadership exists, the leaders are able to control the activities of such groups and to manage the conflict process directly. As described above, the Somali have a high level of internal violence. They also lack strong crosscutting ties, and instead of trade, intermarriage, and support, clans and subclans live in a state of open hostility and rivalry for scarce resources such as food, land, and water.

It may be that the psychological and sociocultural causes of internal conflict operate together, with all societies with childrearing practices that produce aggressive adults predisposed toward violence and the strength of crosscutting ties determining whether the violence is directed at others within the society or at other societies. The interplay of these two factors may be especially important in regard to the causes of internal versus external war as discussed in the article on War.

See also ASSAULT; CAPITAL PUNISHMENT; CONFLICT RESOLUTION; FAMILY VIOLENCE; HOMICIDE; PEACE; PEACEMAKING, RAIDING; SOCIALIZATION OF AGGRESSION; WAR.

Archer, Dane, and Rosemary Gartner. (1984) *Violence and Crime in Cross-National Perspective.*

Kang, Gay. (1976) *Solidarity Theory: A Cross-Cultural Test of the Relationships among Exogamy, Cross-Allegiance, Peace, and Survival Value.*

Otterbein, Keith. (1968) "Internal War: A Cross-Cultural Comparison." *American Anthropologist* 70: 277–289.

Ross, Marc H. (1983) "Political Decision-Making and Conflict: Additional Cross-Cultural Codes and Scales." *Ethnology* 22: 169–192.

Ross, Marc H. (1985) "Internal and External Violence and Conflict: Cross-Cultural Evidence and a New Analysis." *Journal of Conflict Resolution* 29: 547–579.

Ross, Marc H. (1986) "A Cross-Cultural Theory of Political Conflict and Violence." *Political Psychology* 7: 427–469.

Tefft, Stanton, and Douglas Reinhardt. (1974) "Warfare Regulation: A Cross-Cultural Test of Hypotheses among Tribal Peoples." *Behavior Science Research* 9: 151–172.

Joking Relationships

A joking relationship is "patterned playful behavior that occurs between two individuals who recognize special kinship or other types of bonds between them . . . ." (Apte 1985: 30–31). Joking relationships generally involve horseplay, obscene remarks, teasing, sexual suggestions, and insults. Joking relationships are both similar to and the opposite of kin avoidances. They are similar in that both are structured, obligatory patterns of behavior between certain categories of kin and that they do not occur among certain categories of blood relatives such as parents and children and siblings. They are also similar in that both customs may serve to control or prevent conflict between individuals, families, or kin groups. But, they are opposite in that joking relationships require the open display of emotions, those categories of kin who are subject to avoidance cannot enter into a joking relationship, and while those who avoid each other are prohibited from marrying one another, those who are required to joke are often potential sexual and marriage partners. Although the emphasis here is on the joking relationship between relatives because of its possible role in conflict management, joking relationships also occur among nonkin, including people from different villages, coworkers, and friends. Among these groups, however, the relationship lacks the formal, obligatory qualities exhibited by relatives and instead is more a form of play and reflects closeness and intimacy.

The three most common forms of joking relationship involving categories of kin who are potential sexual and marriage partners are between a man and his wife's younger sister(s), a woman and her husband's younger brother(s), and between cross-cousins of the opposite sex. A cross-cousin is the child of an individual's parent's siblings of the opposite sex—one's father's sisters' and mother's brothers' children. The husband–wife's sister joking relationship is found mainly in cultures which also have the levirate—the custom that a widower must marry his wife's (usually younger) sister. In one survey, 22 of 24 cultures with this form of joking also have the levirate; these cultures are mainly Native American ones. The wife–husband's brother joking relationship is found mainly in cultures with the sororate—the custom that a widow must marry her husband's (usually younger) brother. In the same survey, 18 of 19 cultures with this form of joking also have the sororate, and, again nearly all are in North America. Thus, in these two forms it is clear that the persons who joke are potential marriage partners and the nature of their joking that often includes horseplay, sexual innuendo, sexual suggestions, and teasing suggests that the anxiety and potential conflict created by the potential marital relationship is managed by acknowledging the possibility of the relationship publicly and by releasing the tension through the custom of joking. However, it is not correct to conclude that these joking relationships are caused by the levirate and the sororate, as there are numerous cultures with these latter customs who do not have joking relationships. This suggests that in some cultures the levirate and sororate are not necessarily sources of tension or that other mechanisms control the tension caused by these customs.

The third type of joking relationship that seems related to marriage practices is joking between cross-cousins of the opposite sex who are potential or, in many cultures, preferred marriage partners. Cultures with a preference for cross-cousin marriage are ones with unilineal descent—that is, individuals trace their kinship ties only through one parental line—their father's (the most common form) or their mother's. In some of these cultures cross-cousin joking relationships are institutionalized, although, as with other forms of joking, there are many cultures with cross-cousin marriage but without joking. An example of a culture with cross-cousin joking is found on Manus in Polynesia. The relationship is between a man and his father's sister's daughter; the man will publicly fondle her breasts and tease her about her marital status. Such behavior is not allowed in private and if a man goes too far he is subject to supernatural punishment.

The most common forms of joking among individuals who are not potential spouses are between grandparents and grandchildren, between brothers-in-law, and between a woman's brother and her son (uncle and nephew). In all of these situations, the joking partners are individuals whose relationship to each another is mediated by another person. For grandparents and grandchildren it is the child's mother or father, for brothers-in-law it their wife/sister, and for the uncle and nephew it is their sister/mother. Of course, potential marriage is not a source of tension or conflict in these relationships. However, all involve the possibility of conflict between the joking pairs and with the intermediary person over authority, control, power, wealth, etc. in the family or kinship group. Thus, these joking relationships may provide structure in situations where cooperation is important and conflict possible.

The social or psychological forces that cause joking relations are unknown, despite considerable speculation by social scientists. Most efforts to explain joking relationships are functional ones and emphasize the role of joking relationships in maintaining order in kin-based societies and in providing a mechanism for the release of tension. However, these are essentially speculations and it may well be that for each type of joking relationship there is a distinct explanation.

As mentioned above, joking relationships among nonrelatives are common and are usually a sign of friendship and closeness rather than a mechanism for controlling conflict in potentially disruptive relationships. Probably the most elaborate form of joking among nonkin is the joking relationships of members of different clans and different cultures in Africa. Interclan joking relationships probably have a long history in some African cultures and served as a formal mechanism for the creation of bonds between individuals from different kin groups in the same cultures. After the end of colonial rule and with the migration of peoples from different cultures to cities where they had to live and work together, interclan joking was probably extended to members of different cultures, especially when the cultures had been enemies in the past. In East Africa, such joking is known as *utani* and involves not just the usual behaviors associated with joking but also an expectation that joking partners will be generous and helpful to each other. Thus, in the modern context in East Africa, joking is a mechanism for the creation of social cohesion among peoples who formerly had no or perhaps hostile relations with one another.

See also HUMOR; INSULTS; KIN AVOIDANCE; SONG DUELS; WORD DUELS.

Apte, Mahadev L. (1985) *Humor and Laughter: An Anthropological Approach.*

Brant, Charles S. (1972) "A Preliminary Study of Cross-Sexual Joking Relationships in Primitive Society." *Behavior Science Notes* 7: 313–330.

Mead, Margaret. (1934) *Kinship in the Admiralty Islands.* Anthropological Papers of the American Museum of Natural History, vol. 34, pt. 2, 180–358.

Murdock, George P. (1949) *Social Structure.*

Radcliffe-Brown, Arthur R. (1965) *Structure and Function in Primitive Society.*

Kin Avoidance

Kin avoidances are restrictions on physical or social contact between certain categories of relatives. Kin avoidance differs from the day-to-day avoidance of, or withdrawal from, conflict situations that is typical of people in some cultures in that kin avoidance rules are prescribed and enforced by the cultural group. Thus, these rules limit the degree of contact between sets of individuals. Kin avoidance is found in cultures around the world, although it is most common in North American Indian cultures. In all cultures with kin avoidance and in all its forms sexual relations between the individuals are prohibited. Beyond that one prohibition, cultures vary widely in other restricted behaviors, which might include seeing each other naked, being in the same room together, using the other's name, eating together, looking at each other, or speaking to each other.

The most common forms of avoidance are mother-in-law, daughter-in-law, and brother-sister. In mother-in-law avoidance the restrictions apply to a husband and his wife's mother; in daughter-in-law avoidance to a wife and her husband's father, and in brother-sister avoidance to adolescent and adult brothers and sisters. There are also some categories of kin who are almost never the object of avoidance, including grandparents, parents, children, aunts and uncles, and nieces and nephews. Mother-in-law avoidance is the most common form of avoidance, with brother-sister second, and daughter-in-law third. These avoidances are all reciprocal, in that the restrictions that apply to one of the individuals in the pair also apply to the other. At the cultural level, cultures can be categorized as being either "high avoidance" or "low avoidance." For example, the Fijians are "high" as they have strict mother-in-law, father-in-law, and brother-sister avoidances as well as avoidances for other sets of kin, while the Hopi are "low" as they have no avoidances at all.

The actual behaviors restricted vary from culture to culture, with common restrictions being on looking eye-to-eye, talking to each other, eating together, seeing each other, sleeping in the same room, touching each other, touching each other's possessions, being alone together, being in the same house together, and discussing sex in front of the other. The more restrictive a culture is, the more restrictions there are likely to be, with the most restrictive cultures generally prohibiting individuals in an avoidance relationship from eating together and from looking at each other. And, if these are prohibited, it is likely that they will also be prohibited from talking to each other and from talking about sex in front of each other.

The Lau Fijians restrict contact between brothers and sisters beyond the age of seven or eight, who from then on are not allowed to play together or to speak to one another. As is common in other cultures, this restriction is extended to include other categories of kin, for the Lau it is a boy's parallel cousins—these are his cousins through his father's line and are members of his kinship group and thus, like sisters, not available as sexual or marriage partners. Evidently, underlying brother-sister avoidance and its extension to other kin is a powerful fear of incest and the resulting need to prevent incestuous sexual relations between close kin. Brother-sister avoidance and its extension to other categories of kin who are not potential sex or marriage partners is one such mechanism for controlling incest and preventing violations of the incest taboo, which in many cultures is a particularly serious crime. The idea that brother-sister avoidance is customary in cultures where there is some concern about incest between close relatives is supported by the absence among the Lau and other cultures of restrictions on contact between individuals who are potential sex or marriage partners.

In cultures with brother-sister avoidance, the avoidance rules usually go into effect when the siblings approach or reach puberty. Despite the avoidances, siblings often remain emotionally close to one another, provide economic and other assistance to each other, and take much interest in each other's children. Sibling avoidance is also common in cultures where, upon marriage, the husband moves to the house or village of the wife and where the husband and not the wife's brother has authority over the wife. Here, the avoidance might help control competition and conflict between the brother and his sister's husband.

Like the Lau, the Arapaho also require brother-sister avoidance, with the two not allowed to speak to one another, a sister expected to keep her distance from her brother and neither allowed to discuss sexual matters in the presence of the other. And the Arapaho also restrict contact between a son-in-law and his mother-in-law, with the two not allowed to look at or speak to each other or be in the same room together. If they need to communicate it must be indirectly through the wife/daughter. As with brother-sister avoidance, mother-in-law avoidance serves in many cultures to prevent conflict in the family, in this case conflict that might arise when a daughter marries and the husband moves in with her family. Technically, this is called matrilocal postmarital residence and is customary in about 8 percent of cultures around the world. Avoidance allows the husband to adjust to living near or with his mother-in-law and it allows her to adjust to his presence, as well as preventing conflict between the two over control of her daughter and his wife (the same woman). After a suitable period of time, the son and mother-in-law exchange gifts and their relationship shifts from one of avoidance to one of respect.

The Arapaho and other cultures such as the Kiowa Apache also have daughter-in-law avoidance, although among the Arapaho the restrictions are not as great as for a son and mother-in-law. Among the Kiowa Apache, mother-in-law and daughter-in-law avoidance is equally strict and these two in-laws are prohibited from touching, looking at, being alone with, talking to, or using each other's name. In cultures like these with both forms of in-law avoidance, relations between parents and their adult children are often ambiguous; perhaps avoidance restricts contact between parents and their children and children-in-law and thus frees adult children from parental control.

Although, as described above, avoidance customs play a role in defining or limiting social relations among certain categories of kin and thereby prevent conflict between these and other individuals, there are no general explanations that account for the presence of avoidance in cultures around the world. It may be that different explanations account for different forms of avoidance. It is clear that avoidance is not the only mechanism for controlling potential conflict in certain family relationships, as avoidance does not occur in all cultures, suggesting that in some cultures in-law or brother-sister relationships are not especially troublesome or that other mechanisms serve the same purpose as avoidance.

See also JOKING RELATIONSHIPS.

Eggan, Fred, ed. (1955) *Social Anthropology of North American Tribes.*

Murdock, George P. (1949) *Social Structure.*

Schlegel, Alice. (1972) *Male Dominance and Female Autonomy.*

Stephens, William, and Roy G. D'Andrade. (1962) "Kin-Avoidance." In *The Oedipus Complex: Cross-Cultural Evidence,* by William N. Stephens, 124–150.

Thompson, Laura. (1940) *Fijian Frontier.*

Witkowski, Stanley R. (1972) "A Cross-Cultural Test of the Proximity Hypothesis." *Behavior Science Notes* 7: 243–263.

Machoism

Machoism is a general term for a pattern of behavior exhibited by men in some cultures. It is also referred to as defensive masculinity, ultramasculinity, protest masculinity, and compensatory machoism. All of these terms refer to a culturally or subculturally institutionalized pattern of male behavior that often includes heavy alcohol consumption, drunken brawling, cursing, sexual aggressiveness, bragging, and the commission of violent crimes such as rape, assault, and murder.

Some central features of machoism that are found in many cultures are displayed by Chicano men in South Texas (Madsen 1973: 22): "The better man is the one who can drink more, defend himself best, have more sex relations, and have more sons borne by his wife. If unmarried, the better man is the one who has the most girl friends; if married, the one who deceives his wife the most." While sexual prowess is stressed in the Chicano definition of machoism, in other cultures aggressive behavior may also be important and sometimes even more important, although both sexual performance and aggressiveness are usually of some importance.

Machoism is found mainly in cultures where men are dominant, both outside the home and in the family; where male and female roles are clearly differentiated; and where boys spend large amounts of time with their mothers and other women and little time with their fathers. In some cultures, this set of circumstances creates a cross-gender identity problem for boys: because they are raised by women, they identify with women; but at adolescence, they are expected to begin acting like men, a developmental task for which they are neither socially nor emotionally prepared. Machoism develops then as a mechanism by which adolescents and men publicly display their masculinity in exaggerated ways to compensate for their own feelings of femininity. These exaggerated ways include committing violent crimes, sexually exploiting women, controlling and dominating women, engaging in sexual rivalries with other men, and out-of-control drinking. For example, among the Khalapur of India and the Nyasongo of Kenya, two groups with little father-child contact, there is much emphasis on warfare and bravery and a high rate of assault and murder in the community. Similarly, the high rate of violence among teenage gang members in the United States has been attributed by some to compensatory machoism. Machoism has also been linked to a high rate of internal war in a cultural group, although here the raising of boys to be aggressive may be more deliberate in order to produce warriors.

Compensatory machoism is one of a number of social and psychocultural mechanisms used in cultures around the world to help boys shift from a female to a male gender identity. Two other common ones are painful initiation ceremonies at puberty, which publicly define boys as men, and the couvade (sympathetic labor), through which men can identity with women by experiencing and acting out some of the elements of childbirth. However, these other mechanisms are not always totally effective, and machoism can be found in cultures with these customs. This is often the case in cultures where the initiation ceremony also involves a long period of separation and education in "being a man" in the culture, with manliness equated with aggression, violence, and dominance. Of course, in societies where male and female roles are not rigidly defined, and where boys have frequent contact with their fathers during infancy and childhood, there is no pressing need to resolve male gender role identity conflicts.

One form of machoism is a pattern of male behavior and male-female relations typical of what have been called "brideservice societies." These are mainly small, lightly populated societies in which people subsist mainly by hunting, gathering, or limited gardening. In these cultures, such as the Shavante in Brazil, male aggression and sexual behavior are linked, and men are dominant over women. In such societies, as in ones associated with machoism, men and women have mostly separate lives, with male activities considered more important than those of females, and female freedom of movement, association, and speech restricted. Additionally, male behavior is expected to be violent and aggressive and dominance over other men and women is expected.

See also Painful Initiation Rites; Word Duels.

Bacon, Margaret M., Irvin L. Child, and Herbert Barry, III. (1963) "A Cross-Cultural Study of Correlates of Crime." *Journal of Abnormal and Social Psychology* 66: 291–300.

Collier, J., and M. Rosaldo. (1981) "Politics and Gender in Simple Societies." In *Sexual Meanings,* edited by S. Ortner and H. Whitehead.

Madsen, William. (1973) *Mexican Americans of South Texas.*

Munroe, Ruth H., Robert L. Munroe, and Beatrice B. Whiting. (1981) *Handbook of Cross-Cultural Human Development.*

Overing, Joanna. (1989) "Styles of Manhood: An Amazonian Contrast in Tranquility and Violence." In *Societies at Peace: Anthropological Perspectives,* edited by Signe Howell and Roy Willis, 79–99.

Segall, Marshall H., et al. (1990) *Human Behavior in Global Perspective.*

Whiting, Beatrice B. (1965) "Sex Identity Conflict and Physical Violence: A Comparative Study." *American Anthropologist* 67: 123–140.

Mass Killing

See Genocide; Omnicide; Torturing the Enemy; Total War; War.

Mediation

Mediation is a form of conflict resolution in which a third party intervenes to help the two disputants settle the conflict. Mediation is a triadic mechanism in that it involves three parties, as opposed to a dyadic process, which is a self-help mechanism involving only the two disputants. Mediation differs from self-help and advisor-based methods of conflict resolution in that in mediation the parties are under some community pressure to use a mediator, self-help may only be used if mediation fails, and the mediator has some authority to force a settlement to be reached. Mediation also differs from council and court-based conflict resolution because mediators, unlike chiefs and councils, cannot rule a settlement nor can they enforce one. A mediator's authority is mainly implicit and informal and derives from social pressures in the community to end the dispute and restore harmony. While mediation has the immediate function of settling the dispute between the two parties, it also has the more general effect of restoring harmony and ensuring that people can get along peacefully in the community. One manifestation of this general effect is that after the mediation yields a successful resolution, the parties "forget" the dispute and do not discuss it publicly.

This function of mediation in restoring group harmony is especially important in small, tightly-knit communities where internal conflict might make the community or culture vulnerable to attack by outsiders. For the example, the Abkhazians of the Caucasus in the former Soviet Union have long been embroiled in a conflict (which has recently turned violent) with neighboring Georgians over Abkhazian autonomy and survival as a distinct people. The Abkhazian elders who serve as mediators, as well as the disputants, realize that a rapid settlement is in the group's interest. Toward this end, mediators often make comments such as "We've come at the request of society. Have you anything against us?" Or "Are you an *apsua* (Abkhazian)? If so then you must do this." Or "How can you do this to another Abkhazian; there are so few of us as it is?" (Garb 1993). Comments such as these coming from respected elders emphasize the function of mediation as a mechanism for restoring group harmony, which must take precedence over the desires of the disputants.

Mediation is used by individuals and groups in all types of cultures around the world, from small hunter/gatherer societies to modern nation-states. It is used most often to settle disputes between people who already know one another and who reside in the same community. Societies that rely heavily on mediation and less on other conflict resolution methods to solve disputes are ones with wealth differences between people but without true social classes as exist in the modern Western world.

Mediation comes in two major forms: inclusive or exclusive. Inclusive mediation is used mostly in small, close-knit communities where the mediator is known to both parties and where his or her knowledge of the situation and rules of conduct are what drive the resolution process. Exclusive mediation is more characteristic of complex societies and involves a mediator whose neutrality derives from his or her not knowing either party and where his or her expertise and knowledge of rules applicable to the dispute drive the resolution process.

Whether inclusive or exclusive, the mediation process can take one of two forms. In one form, the parties stay apart while the mediator shuttles between them to settle the dispute. In some cases, this may involve the mediator serving as a messenger, delivering counterproposals between the two parties until both agree. In other situations, his role may be more direct. For example, among the Dogon of Mali in West Africa, the blacksmith, a highly respected person in the village, acts as the mediator. When one person wrongs another, the blacksmith is informed. He goes to the offended person's house and, standing outside the door, rattles his maul three times, pronouncing the offender's name. The offended party must then accept the other's apology and the matter is resolved.

In the second form, the mediator meets face-to-face with the two parties and works with them to settle the dispute. The Navajo of the American Southwest, for example, call upon the *nataani,* the local leader, to help settle disputes that cannot be resolved by the disputants. He meets with them, offers solutions, encourages them to settle, and sometimes includes other influential individuals in the discussions to help obtain a settlement. However, he has no authority to order a settlement and the participants are not bound to follow his suggestions, although they often do, for the alternative choice of adjudicating the matter before the Navajo Tribal Court is often less desirable.

Although societies differ in which individuals typically play the role of mediator, in most cultures it is someone who is respected both in the community and by the disputants, who is thought to be wise, and is seen as disinterested or neutral. Also important are the mediator's personality, style as a mediator, reputation, and knowledge of the subject of the dispute. A mediator is usually a respected elder, a kin group leader, a village leader, or a member of the community elite such as a wealthy landowner. Although mediators are often described as disinterested or neutral, this is an idealized image; in reality, they often are not totally disinterested. Rather, because they are usually important individuals in the community, they may have a personal stake in the terms of the settlement, and they always have the more general interest of restoring harmony to the community in addition to resolving the dispute to the satisfaction of both parties. For example, in rural Taiwanese villages, wealthy landowners traditionally mediated local disputes. They were preferred as mediators because of their high position in the social hierarchy, despite the fact that disputes about land or irrigation might involve their own self-interest. In recent years, as education and wage labor opportunities have leveled wealth distinctions in villages, the status of the landowners has declined and they are no longer sought as mediators. And mediation itself has become less important, as villagers begin to place self-interest over the desire to maintain community harmony.

Depending on the subject of the dispute, the nature of the parties to it, and his own style, a mediator can act in a number of different ways to encourage a settlement. He can be a passive listener, giving both parties a chance to voice their positions and express their anger. He can act as a chairman, directing the process toward a resolution. Or he can be an active enunciator and set the rules and procedures for the discussions. Beyond being an enunciator, he can also take the role of the active promoter of a solution by encouraging discussion meant to yield a resolution. Finally, he can act as the leader by making actual recommendations and encouraging their acceptance. However, a mediator cannot impose a settlement on the parties.

See also ADVISORS; APOLOGY; CONFLICT RESOLUTION; COUNCILS; SELF-HELP CONFLICT RESOLUTION.

Calame-Griaule, Genevieve. (1986) *Words and the Dogon World.*

Gallin, Bernard. (1966) *Hsin Hsing, Taiwan: A Chinese Village in Change.*

Garb, Paula. (1993) "Abkhazians: Growing in Age and Wisdom." In *Portraits of Culture: Ethnographic Originals,* edited by Melvin Ember, Carol R. Ember, and David Levinson.

Greenhouse, Carol J. (1985) "Mediation: A Comparative Approach." *Man* (n. s.) 20: 90–114.

Gulliver, P. H. (1979) *Disputes and Negotiations: A Cross-Cultural Perspective.*

Newman, Katherine S. (1983) *Law and Economic Organization: A Comparative Study of Preindustrial Societies.*

Pearson, Keith L. (1985) *Process of Political Development in a Navajo Community.*

MILITARISM

The concept of militarism combines two other concepts having to do with war: military glory and military sophistication. Military glory refers to beliefs or cus-

Societies that are militaristic often display their military power in public rituals as with this military parade in Red Square in 1985.

toms that base prestige or social status on the killing of enemy warriors or the display of bravery in warfare. Military sophistication refers to the manner in which warfare is conducted by a society. A society is considered militaristic when it engages in warfare frequently; when it devotes considerable resources to preparing for war; when its soldiers kill, torture, or mutilate the enemy; and when pursuit of military glory is an objective of combat.

An important component of militarism is the training and maintenance of a professional military. In societies that are militaristic—such as the Plains Indians, East African pastoral societies, or nation-states such as the Aztec or Thai—there is usually some form of professional military organization. A professional military can take the form of a standing army, age-sets, military societies, or mercenaries. Only large, complex societies such as modern societies or ancient civilizations can afford to maintain a professional army and have the type of centralized government necessary to control and coordinate the activities of a standing army. One major cost to a society of maintaining a standing army is the loss of manpower to the society, as full-time soldiers cannot be called upon to provide other types of service to the society. A second major cost is the direct economic cost of supporting the army: housing and provisioning the soldiers, equipping the army, and paying the soldiers. Given the societal investment it takes to maintain a standing army, it is not surprising that societies with standing armies are often at war with other societies. Contrary to much popular thinking, maintaining a large army does not lead to less war; quite the opposite, it seems to encourage societies to engage in aggressive wars.

In societies that wage war often but without the resources to maintain a standing army, other means are used to insure the availability of a professional military force. The three most common mechanisms are military societies, age-sets, and a belief that the role of warrior is part of the male role for all men. A military society is a type of voluntary organization found among the Plains Indians of North America. Although they varied from culture to culture, military societies were generally composed of men or boys who had either been in combat or considered themselves ready for combat. Membership in such societies usually cut across kin groups and families, thus creating a ready fighting force. The Cheyenne, for example, at various times had from five to seven societies, with the five original being the Fox, Dog, Shield, Elk, and Bowstring. In times of peace, a military society might act as a police force within the greater society.

Age-sets are groups of individuals of the same sex and of about the same age who are grouped together as a social unit and are expected to move through life's stages and transitions (puberty, adult status, participation in warfare, marriage) as a group. Although not organized as explicitly for military purposes as military societies, age-sets provide a society with a pool of males who are socially and ceremonially linked to each other and thus will fight together against other groups. This type of age-set is found among cattle-herding cultures in East Africa. In cultures that frequently engage in raiding or war, training boys to be warriors is an important function of the age-set.

The third mechanism that allows societies without a standing army to have a readily available supply of warriors is an ethos that defines military prowess as a component of the male role. In some cultures, all males are expected to be warriors, while in others only some males are expected to be warriors. Cultures that are militaristic and do not have a standing army often require all or some men to be warriors. In some of these cultures, age-sets and military societies organize men into military units; in others, such as the Iroquois, participation in warfare was more a matter of individual choice. Although it is mainly warlike cultures that require men to serve as warriors and train boys to be aggressive, sometimes generally peaceful cultures must do the same in order to defend themselves. For example, all Papago boys were trained to fight and all men were required to be warriors even though the Papago fought only to defend themselves against the Apache, who often raided their villages.

A fourth mechanism for raising a professional army is the hiring of mercenaries from another society. Mercenaries seem to be used mainly when the culture does not have a professional military or when its military is weaker than that of the enemy. For example, a renowned Jivaro warrior may be hired by a neighboring society to raid a third society and take heads and capture women. The Jivaro warrior and his party are provided safe passage through the other society's territory and paid with a shotgun or some other valuable item for a successful raid.

Societies that are militarily successful—those that expand their boundaries by taking territory from other societies—are militaristic and have a strong, centralized government. Militaristic societies frequently attack other cultures, maintain a professional military, and reward military achievements. A strong, centralized government is capable of controlling internal conflict and directing societal resources against other societies.

See also MILITARY GLORY; MILITARY SOPHISTICATION; WAR.

Carter, Harold, Jr. (1977) "Military Organization as a Response to Residence and Size of

Population: A Cross-Cultural Study." *Behavior Science Research* 12: 271–290.

Eckhardt, William. (1973) "Anthropological Correlates of Primitive Militarism." *Peace Research* 5: 5–10.

Goldschmidt, Walter. (1986) "Personal Motivation and Institutionalized Conflict." In *Peace and War: Cross-Cultural Perspectives,* edited by Mary LeCron Foster and Robert A. Rubinstein, 3–14.

Harner, Michael J. (1973) *The Jivaro: People of the Sacred Waterfalls.*

Hoebel, A. Adamson. (1960) *The Cheyennes: Indians of the Great Plains.*

Naroll, Raoul, Vern L. Bullough, and Frada Naroll. (1974) *Military Deterrence in History.*

Otterbein, Keith F. (1985) *The Evolution of War.* 3rd edition.

Russell, Elbert W. (1973) "An Additional Warfare Element in Territorial Expansion." *Behavior Science Notes* 8: 201–207.

Underhill, Ruth M. (1946) *Papago Indian Religion.*

MILITARY GLORY

Military glory refers to beliefs or customs that base personal prestige and social status on the killing of enemy warriors or the display of bravery in warfare. Military glory is characteristic of cultures that are warlike; that is, those cultures that engage in wars often and that wage war aggressively. A survey of 159 cultures indicates that in 83 percent prestige is associated with being a warrior or soldier and that in 62 percent warriors are usually or

Descendants of Ukrainian Cossacks at folk art festival, 1991.

always rewarded. On the other hand, military glory is not important in cultures that are mostly peaceful and cultures that fight primarily to defend themselves. Military glory can be achieved in a variety of ways, including counting coup, scalping, taking enemy heads, trophy cannibalism, and demonstrating bravery, ferocity, or military prowess. Glory is also socially recognized in a number of ways, including feasts for victorious warriors, warriors boasting about their exploits, the awarding of medals or trophies, the wearing of special clothing or ornaments, membership in warrior societies, warriors serving as role models for others, warriors chosen as political leaders, warriors portrayed as culture heroes in folktales and myths, and special honors for those killed in war.

See also CANNIBALISM; COUNTING COUP; DEINDIVIDUATION; HEAD-HUNTING; HUMAN SACRIFICE; SCALPING; TORTURING THE ENEMY; WAR.

Nammour, Valerie W. (1975) *Drums and Guns: A Cross-Cultural Study of the Nature of War.*

Russell, Elbert W. (1972) "Factors in Human Aggression: A Cross-Cultural Factor Analysis of Characteristics Related to Warfare and Crime." *Behavior Science Notes* 7: 275–312.

MILITARY SOPHISTICATION

Military sophistication is a concept developed by anthropologist Keith Otterbein that describes in summary fashion the manner in which warfare is conducted by a society. A survey of 46 societies shows that 17 percent have a high level of military sophistication, 41 percent a moderate level and 41 percent a low level. A high level of military sophistication is typical of cultures with a large population and a centralized political system. Throughout human history these have often been societies ruled by a monarch, such as the Thai, the Japanese prior to World War II, ancient Hawaiians, the Aztec, and the Egyptians, in addition to subgroups within those societies, such as principalities ruled by a duke or prince.

A high level of military sophistication is indicated by the presence of all or many of the following eleven military practices: (1) a professional military composed of military societies or a standing army, (2) a high level of subordination within the army, (3) the initiation of war through an official announcement, (4) cessation of warfare by diplomatic negotiations, (5) use of line formations and ambush tactics, (6) use of shock weapons, (7) use of shields and body armor for protection, (8) field fortifications, (9) use of cavalry in battle, (10) fortified villages, and (11) war motivated by political goals such as subjugating or extracting tribute from the enemy.

The Thai are an example of a society with a high level of military sophistication. Prior to their involvement in international politics and world wars, Thai kingdoms fought with others for land, tribute, and plunder. Princes maintained a standing army (although many men paid their way out of service); its professional officers relied on a mix of tactics including lines, attacks from fortified locations, and a cavalry using elephants; and diplomatic negotiations were used to end or sometimes prevent war. At the other extreme in terms of military sophistication are the Andaman Islanders, a small hunter/gatherer society who maintained no army, rarely attacked other villages, wore no armor, used no fortifications, and terminated raids by killing or capturing all members of the enemy community.

The level of military sophistication of a society is related to how successful the society is at waging war. More sophisticated societies more

A group of refugees in southern Rwanda watches a French armored vehicle. A professional military and specialized equipment are typical of societies with a high level of military sophistication.

often attack their neighbors, are more often victorious, and have higher casualty rates than less sophisticated societies. And, because they are usually the victors, as an outcome of war they often expand their territory by taking land from the losers.

See also MILITARISM; WAR.

Man, Edward H. (1932) *On the Aboriginal Inhabitants of the Andaman Islands.*

Otterbein, Keith. (1985) *The Evolution of War.* 3rd edition.

Thompson, Virginia M. (1941) *Thailand: The New Siam.*

Nonconfrontational Conflict Management

Conflict management refers to behaviors that occur in reaction to an actual or potential conflict situation. Conflict management can involve actions taken to resolve the conflict, actions taken to avoid a conflict, or even actions that inadvertently prolong or intensify the conflict. Nonconfrontational management of interpersonal conflict relies on actions that prevent or restrict direct contact between the conflicting parties. Therefore, nonconfrontational conflict management does not necessarily lead to a rapid resolution of the conflict. Instead, it often helps the disputants manage emotions such as anger, frustration, guilt, shame, betrayal, and hatred that often accompany conflict. The successful management of these emotions is an important part of the conflict resolution process, and in families or small communities the conflict may not be resolvable until strong emotions such as these are vented or controlled.

There are seven major types of nonconfrontational conflict management: anticipatory avoidance, withdrawal, situation code switching, triadic management, displacement, self-punishment, and acceptance.

In anticipatory avoidance, conflict is prevented from ever occurring because an individual avoids social situations that may involve him or her in a conflict. For example, among the Highland Quechua of Ecuador men know that group drinking will often lead to fights, so men who want to avoid fighting stay clear of community festivals where such drinking always occurs.

In withdrawal, a person avoids open conflict by withdrawing from the social situation and indicating his or her displeasure by silence or avoidance of the other person.

Situational code switching is used by conflicting parties who must interact. In certain situations where their conflict will disrupt the group, such as a family meeting, they will interact in a friendly way, but they will ignore each other in other situations.

Triadic management refers to the use of a mediator or go-between to settle the dispute.

In displacement, the offended party acts out his feelings by getting angry with or blaming some innocent third party rather than the appropriate target of the anger. Displacement is commonly used when the appropriate target is too powerful to be approached directly.

Self-punishment refers to a number of behavior patterns, ranging from over-compliance to the wishes of another to destroying one's own property to self-mutilation to suicide.

In acceptance the conflict is resolved because the individual accepts the conflict situation and the unfavorable outcome.

See also Apology; Avoidance and Withdrawal; Mediation; Self-Punishment; Shunning; Suicide.

Lebra, Takie S. (1984) "Nonconfrontational Strategies for Management of Interpersonal

Conflicts." In *Conflict in Japan*, edited by Ellis S. Krauss, Thomas P. Rohlen, and Patricia G. Steinhoff, 41–60.

NONVIOLENT COMMUNITIES

There are probably no cultures in the world where violence between residents of the same community never occurs. A survey of 136 cultures shows that in 54 percent people believe that violent means will solve their problems. This still leaves 46 percent of cultures believing that nonviolence is the solution; within this group are a small number of cultures where violence between people or groups rarely occurs and where violence is strongly discouraged. In a survey of 186 cultures, 8 percent were identified as having little violence among individuals (trespass, theft, assault, and homicide); 2.5 percent as having little violence by groups; and 2 percent little violence of either type. In another survey of 90 cultures, family violence (wife beating, husband beating, sibling fighting, and physical punishment of children) rarely occurred in 18 percent of the cultures. While nonviolent cultures are often defined as such in terms of the frequency and intensity of violent behavior involving members of the culture, cross-culturally it is perhaps more useful to think of nonviolent cultures as cultures where violence does not occur often, where it is not valued and is openly discouraged, where violence-inducing events in other cultures are reacted to nonviolently, and where violence is considered deviant. Cultures that are nonviolent in this sense include the Buid of the Philippines, the Semai of Malaysia, and the Papago of Arizona, among others.

The identification of cultures where people rarely fight with one another has played a role in the ongoing debate over whether humans are innately aggressive or whether aggression is learned. Proponents of the learning view cite these nonviolent cultures as "proof" that aggression is not innate in humans. However, it is also possible the individuals in these cultures do have aggressive feelings and wishes but what they learn is how to control or channel these impulses so that they are not expressed in the form of physical violence. This is true of the Buid, who feel hostility toward outsiders, and the Semai, who have proved to be capable soldiers and able to retaliate against incursions by outsiders, although within the context of Semai culture, the Semai find their violence directed against outsiders as beyond comprehension.

While nonviolent cultures are found in all regions of the world, about 40 percent are foraging cultures. Foraging cultures are ones in which people subsist primarily from foodstuffs they acquire through hunting or gathering. Among foraging cultures with low levels of violence are the Papago of Arizona, the Vedda of Sri Lanka, and the Semai of Malaysia. In addition to their basic food-getting strategies, foraging societies are similar to one another in that the basic social unit is the nuclear family, communities consist of a group of families, social relations are egalitarian, there are no formal leaders, and individual autonomy is valued. In addition, it is not unusual in foraging societies for individuals or families who feel slighted or angry to simply leave the community and join another one. All of these factors encourage the development and perpetuation of nonviolent interpersonal relations, as cooperation at the family and community levels are important for group survival. This does not mean that all foraging cultures are nonviolent nor that they do not fight with other cultures. And, as the above percentages suggest, not all nonviolent cultures are foraging ones; among nonviolent nonforagers are the Central Thai, Rotumans in Fiji, and rural Haitians. In these cultures, as with foragers, a need for community solidarity seems to be an important factor in fostering nonviolence.

Beyond the structural features of a society that may encourage nonviolence, there are six categories of factors that operate in nonviolent cultures to encourage nonviolence: (1) socialization for nonviolence, (2) redefinition and expression of anger, (3) supernatural punishment, (4) avoidance, (5) gossip and public opinion, and (6) nonviolent expression of anger.

Parents in nonviolent cultures raise their children to behave nonviolently. They may do so in a variety of ways. First, parents in nonviolent cultures rarely hit their children. Thus, children grow up modeling their behavior on the nonaggressive behavior of adults. Second, parents actively discourage aggressive behavior by discouraging fights between children, punishing aggressive behavior, or by ignoring angry and violent behavior. Third, parents encourage nonviolent, nonconflictual behavior such as cooperation in play and work groups, sharing, obedience, and respect for seniority and authority. Fourth, parents encourage humility and discourage bragging and calling attention to oneself. Arrogance, bragging, showing off, and like behaviors and attitudes often cause others to get angry in cultures where conformity, cooperation, and equality are valued. Thus, the childrearing process in nonviolent cultures is geared toward producing adults who can control their own aggressive feelings when angry with others and behave in ways that will not cause others to get angry with them.

As part of growing up, individuals in some nonviolent cultures also learn to redefine emotions such as anger or frustration as "fear." In this context, the person they fear is the person they are angry with and what they fear is that person becoming angry with and harming them. In psychodynamic terms, this is termed projection, as it involves an individual attributing his or her own wishes or feelings to another person. In these cultures fear of retaliation by others is a primary factor in people not expressing anger.

In some cultures fear is not just of other people but is also projected onto supernatural forces that will be made angry by aggressive acts and then punish the aggressor. As with fear of other individuals, fear of the supernatural controls violence because the angry person fears supernatural punishment that will make him become ill, have an accident, or even die. Fear of supernatural punishment takes other forms as well. For example, bad luck may be attributed to angry thoughts or, more concretely, people may fear that those they are angry with will use witchcraft or sorcery to seek revenge. This suggests that the control of aggression through fear of others or the supernatural might have the high cost of making people generally suspicious and mistrustful of others.

The use of belief in the supernatural to control or express anger and aggression constitutes what has been called a "culturally constituted mechanism of defense." These mechanisms are culturally appropriate means of expressing aggression that allow the individual to express his or her feelings in a way that does not disrupt the community. For example, the Zapotec in Mexico, noted for their nonviolent ethos, sometimes express anger through illness. One who feels mildly angry is *muina,* and can relieve the mild discomfort by expressing anger. Someone who is more upset is *coraje,* and the anger may spill over into a loud argument or a fight. And, the long-term suppression of anger causes *bilis,* a serious disease of the liver or gallbladder, which must be relieved through violent behavior that is excused because the person is so ill.

Since in nonviolent cultures children are socialized to act nonviolently and in many cultures people do not express angry feelings for fear of punishment, it follows that individuals will try to avoid situations where anger might be expressed. Thus, in nonviolent cultures, individuals prefer flight to fight and will ignore or avoid others with whom they are angry, sometimes for short periods of time, but in cases of serious offenses, for long periods. And in some cultures, such as the Papago, fear of one's own anger and the anger of others is so great that an individual who feels wronged will never confront the person believed or even known to have committed the wrong. At most, the wronged person might indicate his or her displeasure by avoiding the other person or treating him or her coldly.

Related to flight is the use in some cultures of nonviolent means to express aggressive feelings. These include mediators to settle disputes peacefully, hurling of verbal insults, word duels, formal apology, and public hearings to air grievances and vent feelings. Among the Semai, for example, a grievance is aired in a public forum before the village headman. The forum might last for days, with the time consumed by lengthy speeches by all who wish to speak. Eventually, it becomes clear which side is in the right, and the headman settles the dispute. The process, in addition to settling the dispute in accord with the facts, also allows the disputants to express their feelings and work out feelings of anger and frustration that might otherwise lead to aggression.

The final mechanism that encourages nonviolence is the heavy use of gossip and public opinion in nonviolent cultures. A frequent reaction to feeling wronged by another is to tell others in the community about it. Since the community is small, everyone will quickly hear about what happened. If public opinion supports the accuser, the wrongdoer will then have little recourse but to make amends and act differently in the future. Since in small communities an individual's well-being is tied to the community, failure to conform can lead to ostracism or shunning.

See also APOLOGY; CONFLICT RESOLUTION; FEUDING; GOSSIP; INTERNAL CONFLICT; MEDIATION; PEACE; PEACEMAKING; SOCIALIZATION OF AGGRESSION; WORD DUELS

Dentan, Robert K. (1968) *The Semai.*

Dentan, Robert K. (1978) "Notes on Childhood in a Non-Violent Context: The Semai Case." In *Learning Non-Aggression,* edited by Ashley Montagu, 94–143.

Ember, Carol R., and Melvin Ember. (1992) "Warfare, Aggression, and Resource Problems: Cross-Cultural Codes." *Behavior Science Research* 26: 169–226.

Gibson, Thomas. (1989) "Symbolic Representations of Tranquility and Aggression among the Buid." In *Societies at Peace: Anthropological Perspectives,* edited by Signe Howell and Roy Willis, 60–78.

Howard, Alan. (1990) "Dispute Management in Rotuma." *Journal of Anthropological Research* 46: 263–292.

Levinson, David. (1989) *Family Violence in Cross-Cultural Perspective.*

Mitchell, William E. (1992) "Why Wape Men Don't Beat Their Wives: Constraints Toward Domestic Tranquility." In *Sanctions and Sanctuary: Cultural Perspectives on the Beating of Wives,* edited by Dorothy A. Counts, Judith K. Brown, and Jacquelyn C. Campbell, 89–98.

Montagu, Ashley, ed. (1978) *Learning Non-Aggression.*

Namour, Valerie W. (1975) *Drums and Guns: A Cross-Cultural Study of the Nature of War.*

O'Nell, Carl W. (1986) "Primary and Secondary Effects of Violence Control among the Nonviolent Zapotec." *Anthropoligical Quarterly* 59: 184-190.

Phillips, Herbert P. (1966) *Thai Peasant Personality: The Patterning of Interpersonal Behavior in the Village of Bang Chan.*

Robarchek, Clayton A. (1978) *Semai Nonviolence: A Systems Approach to Understanding.*

Spiro, Melford. (1965) "Religious Systems as Culturally Constituted Defense Mechanism." In *Context and Meaning in Cultural Anthropology,* edited by Melford Spiro.

Underhill, Ruth M. (1936) *Social Organization of the Papago Indians.* Columbia University Contributions to Anthropology 30: 1–280.

Oaths

Oaths are a solemn calling upon the supernatural to witness the truth of what a person says. The underlying principle is that an individual's truthfulness will be judged by supernatural beings who will cause harm to those who are dishonest. In cultures where people believe strongly in the power of the supernatural to influence the lives of the living, oaths can be an important way of encouraging compliance and settling disputes. Oaths are used for a variety of purposes and in a variety of contexts. In the United States they are used to encourage witnesses to tell the truth in judicial proceedings, to encourage compliance and allegiance among members of restricted membership organizations such as fraternal organizations and the military, and to hold public officials to high standards of conduct. Elsewhere, oaths are often used to settle disputes and to maintain social order, a common use for oaths in non-Western cultures.

A cross-cultural survey of oaths in 150 cultures shows that oaths are used in 37 percent of cultures. In 19 percent, oaths alone are used, while in 18 percent both ordeals and oaths are used to settle disputes. Unlike ordeals, which are not distributed around the world, oaths are used by cultures in all regions. However, as with ordeals, oaths are found more often in cultures in sub-Saharan Africa and Asia. It is likely that both oaths and ordeals, which are similar ways of settling disputes, developed in the Old World and then spread elsewhere. Oaths are most commonly used to settle disputes in which members of the community can not easily decide which party is telling the truth. For example, among the Wolof and Tiv of West Africa, a person's willingness to take an oath is taken as a sign that he is telling the truth while resistance is a sign that he is not telling the truth. The dispute is then likely to be resolved in favor of the oath-taker. Oaths are an effective conflict resolution mechanism only when people are generally truthful and when they believe that the supernatural will harm them if they lie under oath. It is, of course, the belief that they will be punished for lying that causes them to be truthful. Thus, it not surprising that societies that rely on oaths are ones in which children are reared to be responsible, an emphasis that likely produces adults who are truthful. Additionally, people in societies with oaths generally believe strongly in a high God and they share the belief that those who lie while under oath will be punished. For example, the Crow Indians believed that those who lied would be cursed and that they or their children would be punished. As with ordeals, it seems that oaths occur mainly in societies where the political leadership is weak and the group is fragmented into a number of different subgroups, usually kinship groups such as lineages or clans. In these cultures, oaths allow the weak leadership to maintain control by appealing to a higher authority in judicial decision making.

See also Ordeals; Supernatural Aggression.

Roberts, John M. (1967) "Oaths, Autonomic Ordeals, and Power." In *Cross-Cultural Approaches,* edited by Clelland S. Ford, 169–195.

OMNICIDE

Omnicide means the destruction of all of humankind either through mass killing or mass destruction of such magnitude that it threatens all of human life. Such destruction might result from (1) destruction and killing through the use of nuclear weapons, (2) a nuclear winter that would threaten food production and produce genetic effects in survivors that might reduce their chances of reproducing, or (3) biological warfare that spreads deadly diseases. Interest in and concern about omnicide arose mostly in response to nuclearism—the development, building, stockpiling, threatened use, and actual use of nuclear weapons by one nation to annihilate its enemies. Another development creating a threat of omnicide is a failure since World War II for nations at war to distinguish between military personnel and civilians as appropriate targets. This suggests a lessening of concern for human life in general and a willingness by governments to use extraordinary military efforts to achieve their ends. Recently, concern about omnicide has lessened with the end of the Soviet Union–United States cold war rivalry, the emergence of the United States as an unrivaled world military power, and the development of military technology that allows the often precise targeting of military and other targets and the sparing of civilians. The major threat now is the spread of nuclear weapon capability to many nations and their possible use in internal and regional wars that might escalate into a global nuclear war.

See also ETHNOCIDE; GENOCIDE; PACIFICATION; TOTAL WAR; WAR.

Kuper, Leo. (1992) "Genocide." In *Encyclopedia of Sociology,* edited by Edgar Borgatta, vol. 2: 757–761.

Lifton, Robert J., and Erik Markusen. (1990) *The Genocidal Mentality: Nazi Holocaust and Nuclear Threat.*

ORDEALS

Ordeals are used to determine guilt or innocence by submitting the accused to painful or dangerous tests. The underlying principle is that the tests are controlled by supernatural beings who will intervene to protect the innocent from harm and allow the guilty to suffer. Thus, failure to pass the test proves guilt. There are a variety of types of ordeals, including those where the outcome is based on chance or the knowledge or skill of the participants and those used as part of initiation rites or to prepare men for combat. Ordeals are also used to settle disputes and maintain social order, a category of ordeals called autonomic ordeals. In autonomic ordeals the outcome is determined by the involuntary reactions of the participants to painful or dangerous stimuli. The reactions are usually physiological responses to painful or dangerous situations as the ordeals often involve burning, scalding, bleeding, or drowning.

Autonomic ordeals were common in Medieval Europe and often involved fire and heat, water, and direct appeals to God. For example, a individual was judged guilty if his hand was burned after insertion in boiling water or by carrying a red-hot piece of iron. In water ordeals, the guilty were thought to float and the innocent to sink. These tests were not especially reliable. Direct appeals to God were more contests than ordeals—the innocent party was the one who could stand longest in front of a cross with his hands upraised. Ordeals faded from use in Europe when they were replaced by more rational legal procedures such as trials and the use of evidence.

A cross-cultural survey of ordeals in 150 cultures in more recent times indicates that autonomic ordeals are used in 26 percent of cultures. Ordeals are not distributed uniformly around the world. Rather, two-thirds of societies with ordeals are in sub-Saharan Africa and no native North or South American culture is known to have ever used ordeals. Ordeals are usually the method of final resort, called for by those in power only when other methods of resolving a dispute or discovering the facts have proved fruitless. The Rundi of Zaire are a society that traditionally made heavy use of ordeals in judicial proceedings. The preferred ordeal was one in which the accused was forced to inhale a poisonous powder mixed with water and tobacco. The mix causes some to have siezures and hallucinations, proving their guilt. Those who confess immediately are administered an antidote that reverses the effects of the poison. Other ordeals include ingesting materials such as cow dung or certain plants that will cause sickness; immersing a hand in boiling water; sitting a person in a basket into which others thrust spears; and more benign methods that do not subject the accused to harm. The severity of the ordeal often reflected the severity of the wrong being investigated. Thus, not all were as harsh as those just described. For example, the Dogon of Mali determined if a boy stole sorrel by tickling along the spine of his back with a stick of straw. If he could not control his laughter, he was considered guilty. These ordeals are now a custom of the past among the Rundi and Dogon and in Africa in general; they were banned by the European colonial powers, who instituted their own legal systems, which have now been replaced by the legal systems of the African nations.

Little is known about why some cultures use ordeals and others do not, although it is clear that they fall into disuse when a formal legal system becomes the primary means of settling disputes in a society. In Africa and Medieval Europe, it seems that ordeals occured mainly in societies where the political leadership was weak, the group was fragmented into a number of different subgroups such as kinship groups, and there was a strong belief in the supernatural. In this context, ordeals allowed the weak leadership to maintain control by appealing to a a higher authority in judicial decision making.

See also Oaths; Painful Initiation Rites; Peacemaking.

Griaule, Marcel. (1938) *Dogon Games.*

Pagès, G. (1933) *A Hamitic Kingdom in the Center of Africa: In Ruanda on the Shores of Lake Kiva (Belgian Congo).*

Roberts, John M. (1967) "Oaths, Autonomic Ordeals, and Power." In *Cross-Cultural Approaches,* edited by Clelland S. Ford, 169–195.

Teksbury, William J. (1967) "The Ordeal as a Vehicle for Divine Intervention in Medieval Europe." In *Law and Warfare: Studies in the Anthropology of Conflict,* edited by Paul Bohannan, 267–270.

Pacification

Pacification refers both to the process and the end result of that process in which a culture is forced or chooses to "abandon warfare and cede control over the use of military force to a group perceived as more powerful. . . ." (Rodman 1983: 1). Along with conquest, colonization, genocide, and ethnocide, pacification is a major strategy used by colonial powers and modern nations to subjugate indigenous peoples and acquire ownership or control of the natural resources in their traditional homelands. While the four other strategies involve cultural change or disruption in a general sense, pacification usually refers to government action designed specifically by the national government or a colonial power to end warfare waged by indigenous peoples. For example, pacification efforts in the twentieth century were undertaken on a broad scale by the British in Melanesia, the Australians in New Guinea, and the Brazilian government in the Amazon region. However, pacification efforts are always only one component of a broader agenda ultimately designed to transfer control of local resources from the native cultures to the dominant (usually national) society and also part of a broader pattern of culture change that affects all aspects of native life. Pacification has been justified by colonists as a humane and morally correct strategy, and in some situations, as in early efforts in Brazil and by some missionaries in Melanesia, this was a major motivation. However, economic and political domination was always the primary goal, if not for those carrying out the pacification, then for the government officials and developers interested in political and economic control of the region and the native peoples living there.

The term *pacification* is used somewhat inconsistently by social scientists and government officials, and is appropriate only in reference to those situations where the explicit government policy is to "pacify" indigenous cultures rather than to conquer or destroy them. Thus, the term is used primarily in reference to one aspect of native-colonial or government relations in Melanesia and South America, and not used in reference to native-colonial or government relations in North America or Africa. In North America the native peoples were conquered and displaced onto reservations while in Africa they were encouraged initially to raid for slaves, were then colonized or exploited as a labor force, and eventually achieved political independence.

Another confusion about the term is that warfare practices that are the target of pacification efforts may vary from one situation to another. Pacification efforts assume, of course, that the culture to be pacified is already warlike, an assumption that may not necessarily be true. Thus, one form of warfare to be controlled through pacification is that of indigenous peoples reacting in a warlike fashion to the encroaching dominant culture. For this reason, pacification always precedes intensive efforts to develop the resources in the territories of the pacified peoples. A second type of warfare to be controlled by pacification is warfare between indigenous people. When the culture (or cultures) to be pacified is known or strongly suspected of being warlike (which is often the situation), the wars that are meant to be prevented are those between the culture and other native peoples, which do not directly threaten the colonists but are an impediment to their controlling the region and governing the native peoples.

The major arenas for pacification have been South America—especially Brazil—and New Guinea and the associated islands of Melanesia in the South Pacific. Comparison of pacification efforts in these two regions illustrates the major objectives, causes, techniques, and outcomes of pacification around the world.

Pacification in Brazil

Although localized efforts by traders, missionaries, land agents, and government officers had occurred previously, full-scale pacification began in Brazil in the early 1900s under the direction of the government's Indian Protection Service (SPI) for the express purpose of protecting the Indian cultures from traders, land developers, and others. The SPI strategy was to make contact with hostile tribes and to convince them to end hostilities directed at outsiders and to convince them to trust the government to protect them and their interests. Beginning in the early 1900s, teams of unarmed SPI agents would approach an Indian village, leave gifts such as beads, mirrors, and steel machetes at the entrance and then wait weeks or months for the Indians to accept the gifts. After again waiting some period of time, the agents would enter the village with an interpreter and convince the Indians to cease hostilities and to trust the government agents to protect their interests. The agents were pacifists and patient and operated under the dictum: "Die if it be necessary, but never kill." (Davis 1977: 4). This approach to pacification is referred to as "classic pacification."

Such classic pacification was successful and over 60 tribes were pacified, 67 Indian posts established in the region, and no Indians and only a few agents killed. However, the long-term effects of this pacification effort were devastating to the Indians. Between 1900 and 1957 more than 80 tribes were destroyed by disease, and others fled to the interior or were placed on small, resource-poor reservations (called "Parks"). The traditional territories of the pacified groups are now coffee and rubber plantations, and the sites of towns, farms, factories, and mineral extraction operations. In addition, many of the surviving groups exist on the margins of Brazilian society and have lost their native languages, beliefs, and customs.

Beginning about 1950 pacification efforts became overtly linked to Brazilian development and economic policy with protection of Indians no longer a major consideration. Economic development of the Amazon Basin was the driving force, with the emphasis on building roads, mining, farming, establishment of towns and industry and settlement by non-Indians. The government's Indian policy stressed pacification followed by relocation on small reservations isolated from areas of development. However, when existing reservations were in the way of development, they were further reduced in size or divided by roads. As with the more humanely motivated pacification of the early 1900s, the Indian tribes were devastated. For example, the highway program that began in 1970 has resulted in the disappearance, relocation, fleeing, or deculturation of all 29 tribes living in the vicinity of the proposed roads. The policy today is a combination of placement on reservations and integration into mainstream society through a combination of pacification, genocide, and ethnocide.

Pacification in Melanesia

Melanesia is that portion of the south Pacific Ocean that includes the large island of New Guinea and adjacent, smaller islands and archipelagos such as the Solomon Islands. Pacification of insular Melanesia and the large island of

New Guinea took somewhat different courses due to the different nature of contact with European colonists. On the islands, pacification by the British began after 1850. For the previous 50 years there was little interest in pacifying the local cultures, as the islands were mainly a source of laborers who were supplied by coastal peoples to European recruiters to work for three years on the sugar plantations in Fiji and Queensland. Pacification began after 1850 only when the British sought to colonize the islands, establish local plantations, and make the colonies self-sufficient. To do so they moved to end warfare among indigenous cultures and to prevent violent resistance to British settlement. With the aid of missionaries who had previously been seeking pacification on their own, all native cultures were pacified through the use or show of force or pacified peacefully and all came under British control. Unlike in Brazil, pacification was encouraged and supported but not directly managed by the colonial government. Instead, it was managed by the local colonial officials who used small European police forces sometimes supplemented by native police, missionaries, influential local leaders, the imposition of taxes, and other means to end indigenous warfare and to limit resistance to European control.

On New Guinea warfare was a ubiquitous feature of life among many of the distinct and numerous groups who lived in the highlands, although peaceful contact involving trade and marriage was also common. As with the islands, early European contact was confined to the coast and pacification of the interior highlands did not begin until after 1900 and was not achieved in most places until between 1930 and the 1960s. In the highlands pacification meant the cessation of fighting between native cultures and the prevention of raids against the colonists and was motivated by Australian interest in developing the interior. As on the islands, pacification was managed by local officials (although the process was strongly supported by the Australian government) who used military patrols and military posts in pacified regions to maintain peace.

The pacification process was accelerated and spread further to the interior during World War II when it was motivated by the perceived need to secure the region and keep the local population under control. In all locales, successful pacification was followed by the establishment of plantations, military posts, towns, roads, airstrips, the introduction of a nationally administered legal system, and an economy based on wage labor. While most groups have remained pacified, beginning in about 1970 and continuing since New Guinea independence in 1975, some groups have resumed fighting with each other and have resisted government efforts to repacify them. It is unclear why fighting has resumed, but important causes include (1) a weakening of peaceful trade and marriage relations between groups, which may have controlled warfare in the past, (2) new political alliances among the groups, (3) the survival of traditional warfare patterns and associated beliefs such as political leadership based on the achievement of military glory, (4) a doubting of the ability of the national government to manage local conflicts, and (5) the failure of the government to replace warfare with other nonviolent conflict resolution mechanisms.

Compared to pacification in Brazil, pacification in Melanesia did not destroy many of the native cultures and has also not been permanent in all regions. Of course, one of the major differences between the two regions has been the political independence achieved by native peoples in Melanesia versus the political domination or destruction of Indians in Brazil.

The Melanesian experience also points to another important component of pacification—the need to replace indigenous warfare as a means of settling conflicts with nonviolent conflict resolution mechanisms. In New Guinea and elsewhere, new, nonviolent mechanisms include the use of village and regional courts, fighting with property as among the Goodenough Islanders in Melanesia or the Tlingit in North America, and the institutionalization of a legal system based on individual property rights.

See also Ethnocide; Fighting with Property; Genocide; Peace; Peacemaking; War.

Brown, Paula. (1986) "Simbu Aggression and the Drive to Win." *Anthropological Quarterly* 59: 165–170.

Davis, Shelton H. (1977) *Victims of the Miracle: Development and the Indians of Brazil.*

Podolefsky, Aaron. (1984) "Contemporary Warfare in the New Guinea Highlands." *Ethnology* 23: 73–87.

Rodman, Margaret, and Matthew Cooper, eds. (1983) *The Pacification of Melanesia.*

Painful Initiation Rites

Initiation rites are ceremonies that mark the transition from childhood or adolescence to adulthood. Such ceremonies occur in about 55 percent of the cultures in a survey of 90 world cultures. Some cultures have rites only for girls, some only for boys, and some for both. Rites for girls occur in a larger number of cultures, while those for boys are often more elaborate and dramatic. The rites are usually public and in addition to the final ceremony, feast, or dance, often involve training, education, and other activities to teach the initiates appropriate adult behavior. In 65 percent of those cultures with initiation rites, the rites also include activities that cause physical harm or pain to the initiates. In 37 percent of these cultures the pain is incurred as part of a genital operation such as circumcision or clitoridectomy, in 53 percent the pain results from various forms of rough treatment, and in 13 percent of cultures both rough treatment and genital operations cause pain. Genital operations have drawn special attention from researchers and are discussed in the article on Genital Mutilation.

Pain infliction other than genital operations results from food restrictions or fasting (25 percent of cultures with rites), tattooing or scarification (16 percent), piercing a body part such as the nose, ear, or lip (16 percent), immersion in cold water (10 percent), beating or whipping (10 percent), ordeals such as isolation in the wilderness (10 percent), traumatic sex (5 percent), smearing with dirt (5 percent), dancing until fatigued (4 percent), and burning, running until exhausted, and tooth extraction (2 percent each). While painful procedures such as these are found in some cultures in all parts of the world, they were most common among American Indian cultures in North and South America where genital operations were nonexistent. Elsewhere, operations were more common and remain common in Africa and Oceania. Pain infliction on girls during initiation rites occurs mostly in cultures that also rely on physical punishment to discipline children and in which men frequently beat their wives. For example, in the course of raising their children, the Goajiro of Colombia slap them, beat them with whips and sticks, and even make them vomit by spinning them around in mesh bags suspended from the ceiling of the communal houses. At their first menstruation, girls are given a drink to make them vomit and then suspended in the bag for three to five days. During this period girls are given neither food nor drink and are expected to remain motionless. The rite is completed with a month-long period of seclusion during which the girl is taught how to be an adult Goajiro woman, with a public feast then held to celebrate her achievement of that new status. As an adult woman she

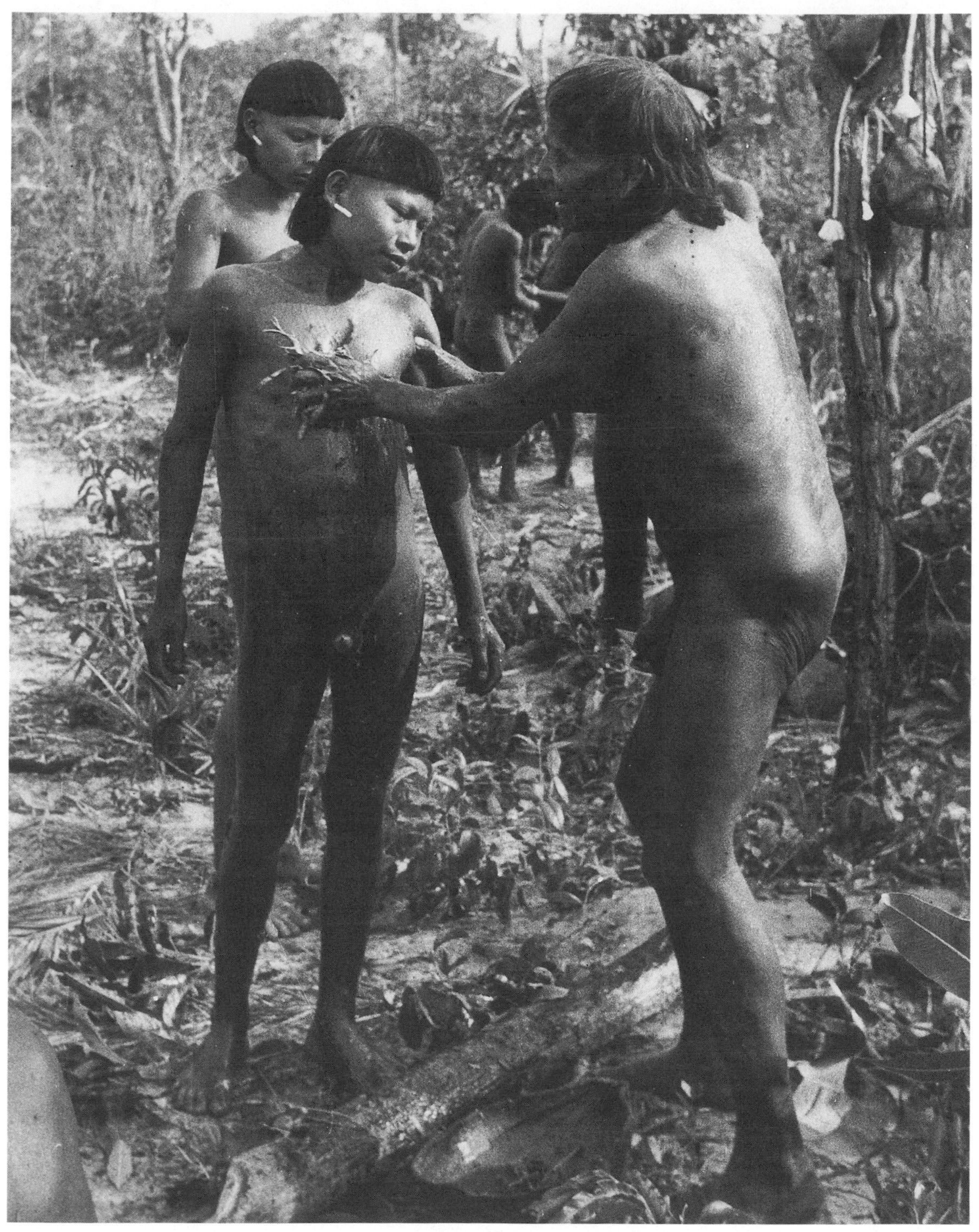

Xavante boys during their initiation rite marking adult status.

can expect her husband to regularly beat her for whatever reason he finds appropriate. Evidently, painful initiation for girls in cultures like the Goajiro is a means of preparing them for an adult life filled with physical violence, both by them toward their children and by their husbands toward them. Painful initiation is part of a more general cultural pattern that favors the use of physical violence in many types of relationships.

Painful initiation of boys including circumcision has generally been explained as a sociocultural mechanism used to inculcate masculine personality traits in boys who because of close contact with their mothers and little contact with their fathers have grown up with a feminine identity. These rites might also be used to teach boys to be compliant in societies where boyhood aggression is unchecked during childhood. These explanations assume that the dramatic and traumatic rite will reverse behavior that is not considered appropriate for men. An alternative explanation suggests that such rites serve to create solidarity among men and therefore are found in societies where men must work closely together.

See also Genital Mutilation; Machoism.

Barry, Herbert III, and Alice Schlegel, eds. (1980) *Cross-Cultural Samples and Codes.*

Granzberg, Gary. (1973) "The Psychological Integration of Culture: A Cross-Cultural Study of Hopi Type Initiation Rites." *Journal of Social Psychology* 90: 3–7.

Gutierrez de Pineda, V. (1950) *Social Organization in La Guajira.*

Levinson, David. (1989) *Family Violence in Cross-Cultural Perspective.*

Levinson, David, and Martin J. Malone. (1980) *Toward Explaining Human Culture.*

Peace

Peace is a type of relationship between political communities that is characterized by the absence of violent conflict. A peaceful society is one that is not at war with other societies. It may be peaceful because it does not have contact with other societies (and thus there is no opportunity for war to occur) or because its relations with all other societies are peaceful. This definition of peace distinguishes between peace between political communities and "peace" within communities. The latter is more appropriately defined as nonviolence and is treated separately in the article Nonviolent Communities. Thus, societies can be characterized as internally peaceful (there is no warfare between political communities within the society) or externally peaceful (there is no warfare between political communities from different societies), or both internally and externally peaceful. Some societies are only internally peaceful, others only externally peaceful, and the majority of peaceful societies are both internally and externally peaceful.

Most attempts to measure the frequency of peacefulness within or across societies do not define peace as an absolute. Instead, peace is treated as a variable condition and is usually gauged in terms of the time duration of peace periods. For example, in one survey societies are considered to be peaceful if they are engaged in war less often than once every ten years, while in another survey societies are considered peaceful it they go to war less than once every two years. Because peace is often measured in these different ways, the results of cross-cultural surveys of peace are not entirely consistent. However, taken together, these surveys do provide a broad estimate of the number of peaceful societies around the world. It seems that from 33 to 56 percent of societies are internally peaceful, 22 to 43 percent are externally peaceful, and 30 percent are both internally and externally peaceful. These percentages are based on peace being defined in terms of the duration of periods of peace. If we take a more absolute view of peace and define it as the complete absence of war, the number of peaceful societies is far fewer. For example, in a survey of 50 non-Western cultures only one, the Copper Eskimo of Canada, were found to be completely peaceful. To this one we may add a few others also described as peaceful—the San of Botswana and Namibia, Buid of the Philippines, Xinguano in Brazil, Tikopia in Oceania, and the Dorobo in Kenya. These few societies are, of course, only a tiny percentage of the 2,000 or so societies known to exist over the past 200 years.

Peace is also rare among nations. A survey of peace throughout human history identifies only 52 nation-states as having continuous peace periods of at least 100 years. The longest is the Icelandic peace period which by 1990 had lasted for 734 years. However, in this survey, peace was defined as internal peace, and wars waged outside the nation's home territory were not considered to indicate that the society was nonpeaceful. When these external war nations are removed from the list of 52, the number of nation-states with peace periods of more 100 years decreases to fewer than 20. Similarly, in the world today, there are at least 50 nations experiencing continual, violent internal conflicts usually involving ethnic separatism movements.

Despite the confusion over defining and counting peaceful societies, it is possible to offer some general conclusions about the frequency of peace. First, only a small minority of societies known throughout human history has been completely peaceful. Second, most societies are more peaceful than they are warlike, that is, they experience longer periods of peace than they do periods of war. Third, a sizeable minority of societies are mostly peaceful, that is they experience much longer periods of peace than they do periods of war.

Why are some cultures more peaceful than others? As with the question of how many cultures are peaceful, there is as yet no clear answer to this question. What we do know is that military deterrence—preparedness for war—contrary to popular belief, does not make for peace. It now seems clear that both non-Western cultures and modern nations that prepare for war are not more peaceful than cultures that do not prepare for war. We also know that contact and alliances between cultures do not necessarily cause those cultures to be peaceful, although extensive contact through trade, marriage, and reciprocal ceremonial obligations between political communities within a society does make for longer periods of peace between those communities.

That many of the most peaceful cultures are hunter-gatherers suggests that some feature or features of the hunter-gatherer way of life might make them more peaceful. The hunter-gatherer experience points to two factors associated with peace: isolation from other groups and the occupation of a region that contains no resources of interest to others. Isolation means little or no contact with other societies or with only a few other societies, reducing the opportunity for war to develop. Few desirable resources such as arable land, cattle, or water means that other societies have little reason to attack the hunter-gatherer society, again insuring peace. While most completely peaceful societies are hunter-gatherers, only a minority of hunter-gatherers are peaceful. These are mainly ones that live in isolated, resource poor regions.

See also ALLIANCES; FISSIONING; INTERNAL CONFLICT; NONVIOLENT COMMUNITIES; PEACEMAKING; WAR.

Ember, Carol R. (1978) "Myths about Hunter-Gatherers." *Ethnology* 17: 439–448.

Ember, Carol R., and Melvin Ember. (1992) "Warfare, Aggression, and Resource Problems: Cross-Cultural Codes." *Behavior Science Research* 26: 169–226.

Ember, Carol R., Melvin Ember, and Bruce M. Russett. (1992) "Peace between Participatory Polities: A Cross-Cultural Test of the 'Democracies Rarely Fight Each Other' Hypothesis." *World Politics* 44: 573–599.

Fabbro, D. (1978) "Peaceful Societies: An Introduction." *Journal of Peace Research* 12: 67–84.

Haas, Jonathan, ed. (1990) *The Anthropology of War.*

Kang, Gay E. (1976) *Solidarity Theory: A Cross-Cultural Test of the Relationships among Exogamy, Cross-Allegiance, Peace, and Survival Value.*

Loftin, Colin K. (1971) *Warfare and Societal Complexity: A Cross-Cultural Study of Organized Fighting in Preindustrial Societies.*

Melko, Matthew. (1973) *52 Peaceful Societies.*

Nammour, Valerie W. (1975) *Drums and Guns: A Cross-Cultural Study of the Nature of War.*

Naroll, Raoul, Vern L. Bullough, and Frada Naroll. (1974) *Military Deterrence in History.*

Otterbein, Keith F. (1989) *The Evolution of War.* 3d edition.

Ross, Marc H. (1983) "Political Decision-Making and Conflict: Additional Cross-Cultural Codes." *Ethnology* 22: 169–192.

Tefft, Stanton K., and Douglas Reinhardt. (1974) "Warfare Regulation: A Cross-Cultural Test of Hypotheses among Tribal Peoples." *Behavior Science Research* 9: 151–172.

Westing, A. (1982) "Warfare as a Human Endeavor: The High Fatality Wars of the Twentieth Century." *Journal of Peace Research* 3: 261–264.

Wiberg, H. (1981) "What Have We Learned about Peace." *Journal of Peace Research* 15: 110–149.

PEACEMAKING

Peacemaking refers to both the process and the mechanisms used to end war or to regulate disputes so as to prevent them from escalating into war. Peacemaking is a common way to end wars and is used to end or prevent both internal war and external war. A survey of 186 societies shows that 46 percent typically end wars through negotiation rather than conquest, annihilation, or displacement of the enemy and a survey of another 50 cultures indicates that 60 percent use diplomacy to end wars. Peace ceremonies are a significant component of the warfare regulation process, with 74 percent of cultures using ceremonies to either achieve peace or to mark peacemaking.

Peacemaking is used more often and is more effective in settling internal wars than external wars. A survey of 49 cultures shows that of those that engage mainly in internal war, 94 percent had institutionalized mechanisms for making peace while only 36 percent of those that waged mainly external wars had such mechanisms. Peacemaking is used more often to end internal wars because the objectives of internal war are more amenable to peaceful resolution than are the objectives of external war. Internal war and other forms of violence between communities in the same society are undertaken for limited objectives such as revenge or honor or to amass military glory, slaves, or ritual plunder such as heads. External war is fought for broader goals such as conquering the enemy, driving them off, or taking many slaves or other plunder, objectives that are inconsistent with making peace. Because it pits community against community, internal war is also more threatening to the survival of the society if it is uncontrolled, making peacemaking especially important.

Peacemaking is also more effective at regulating internal war than external war. Peace-regulating mechanisms are successful (success being defined as wars no more than once every two years) in 73 percent of internal war cultures, but in only 50 percent of external war cultures. Peacemaking is more effective in regulating internal war because the groups at war (lineages, clans, communities, tribes) may already have peaceful ties with one another through marriage, kinship, trade, or reciprocal ceremonial obligations. It is also more effective because the warring groups are culturally similar (they speak the same language and share similar value systems) and perceive themselves as all being members of the same ethnic group as compared to outsiders, whom they classify as members of different ethnic groups. A part of this similarity is also a similarity in how people in communities manage disputes. It seems that in cultures with little internal war, people in communities usually govern themselves through a form of participatory democracy where people "agree to disagree" rather than fight over disagreements. The importance of peacemaking in controlling internal war is indicated by the lexicon of the Maori of New Zealand, a large culture composed of a number of subgroups. The Maori have a god of peace called Rongo and four terms for four different types of peace: *hohou rongo* (a binding peace), *rongo taketake* (permanent peace), *rongo awhore* (peace made through discussions), and *rongo whati-whati* (a peace quickly broken).

The major peacemaking mechanisms found around the world are negotiation, mediation, arbitration, and duels and ordeals. Negotiation is the most common type and generally involves representatives of the two sides discussing and agreeing on conditions to end the conflict, one part of which is an agreement to end the warfare. Negotiators may be the political or military leaders from the two sides, their representatives, respected members of the societies or communities, or, in cases of internal war, individuals who have a prior relationship and therefore will be trusted by the enemy. For example, the Maori of New Zealand used families who were related by marriage as emissaries between warring communities.

Mediation, just as it is used to settle disputes between individuals, relies on an individual whose authority to settle the dispute rests on his status and reputation in the society. Since mediation requires a mediator who is known and trusted by both parties, it is used mainly to settle internal wars. The Nuer of the Sudan rely on the Leopard-Skin Chief to settle disputes between Nuer tribes. He meets with the leaders of the two tribes and negotiates a settlement that is memorialized through the sacrifice of a hornless bull and proclamations by the chief.

Arbitration relies on an arbitrator who is not a member of either group and whose authority rests on his knowledge of the situation and relevant political and legal doctrines. Arbitration is not much used in traditional societies, due to the absence of overarching political bodies with such authority.

Duels and ordeals allow the settlement of the dispute and the end of hostilities through a fight between or the infliction of injury to representatives of the groups. The Murngin of Australia traditionally ended feuds between clans by the clan of the individual who started the feud allowing the other clan to spear the leg of the offending individual and then the two clans making camp together and singing and dancing.

Although women are rarely participants in war, they often play a major role in peacemaking. In some cultures such as the Orokavia they play an emissary role; often the emissaries are women who have married-in from the enemy group and thus have ties to and are trusted by both groups. And, since their husbands and sons may be fighting for one side and their fathers and brothers for the other, they also have a personal interest in ending the bloodshed. Iroquois and Andaman Island women played a more direct role. Iroquois wars with neighboring groups such as the Erie, Huron, and Neutral were often ended by women who spoke so eloquently about the human and economic costs of the fighting that the fighting ended. Andaman women were responsible for making the arrangements for the peace ceremony and bringing the warriors together to make peace through a ritual and dance. Maori women played a variety of roles in settling intratribal wars. As noted above, two families with ties through marriage (of a woman of one group to a man of the other) often served as emissaries. Or, a daughter of one chief might be given to the other chief in marriage to ratify the peace or to end a battle. Additionally, young Maori women and girls played a central role in the peace ceremony where they danced and stood in front of the men to symbolize peace.

As noted above, peace ceremonies are a common component of peacemaking. Ceremonies are important because they provide a public forum for ratifying the peace, they bring the warring groups together in a neutral setting, they can be used to balance publicly the losses suffered by the losers, and they can allow for the release of aggression. Because they are so common and can serve a number of functions, peace ceremonies take a wide variety of forms around the world. For the Andaman Islanders, the peace ceremony allows the losing warriors to vent aggressive feelings about the victors. The victorious warriors assemble in a line and the losing warriors "dance" in front of them, shouting at, threatening, and shaking them back and front, while the victors accept the shaking passively. Their anger released, the two groups camp, hunt, and dance together, exchange gifts, and conclude the ceremony with an exchange of bows.

The Tlingit of the Northwest Coast of North America employed elaborate ceremonies to make peace. While not all wars were resolved by the ceremony, it was commonly used for internal disputes of various types. For the Tlingit, making peace was a legal settlement to resolve the basic causes of conflict, to resolve the reason for the immediate conflict, to provide restitution and compensation to the losing side, and to restore peace in the society. The ceremony was arranged by emissaries who were relatives by marriage and thus had ties to the warring groups. Restitution and compensation took the form of a payment of money, goods, ceremonial objects, and the taking of lives. An important component of the ceremony was the exchange of hostages called "peace-makers" or "peace-dancers." These were men or women of the upper class who were exchanged at the start of the ceremony and kept confined by the enemy group for eight days. During this time they were subject to various behavioral and food restrictions, dressed in special costumes, and had their faces painted. The ninth and tenth days of the ceremony were for a feast and dance and the freeing of the hostages. Through the use of ritual, role-playing, and payment of compensation, the Tlingit peace ceremony served many of the basic functions of peace ceremonies and ultimately was successful because it redefined the losers as winners and left the two parties as relative equals.

See also FEUDING; NONVIOLENT CULTURES; PEACE; RAIDING; WAR.

Best, Eldon. (1924) *The Maori.* 2 vols.

Buck, Peter H. (1952) *The Coming of the Maori.* 2d edition.

Chaseling, Wilbur S. (1957) *Yulengor: Nomads of Arnhem Land.*

Ember, Carol, Melvin Ember, and Bruce M. Russett. (1992) "Peace between Participatory Polities: A Cross-Cultural Test of the 'Democracies Rarely Fight Each Other' Hypothesis." *World Politics* 44: 573–599.

Heckwelder, John G. E. (1819) *An Account of the History, Manners, and Customs of the Indian Nations, Who Once Inhabited Pennsylvania and the Neighboring States.*

Howell, P. P. (1954) *A Manual of Nuer Law: Being an Account of Customary Law, Its Evolution and Development in the Courts Established by the Sudan Government.*

Laguna, Frederica de. (1972) *Under Mount Saint Elias: The History and Culture of the Yakutat Tlingit.*

Nammour, Valerie W. (1975) *Drums and Guns: A Cross-Cultural Study of the Nature of War.*

Otterbein, Keith. (1989) *The Evolution of War.* 3d edition.

Radcliffe-Brown, Alfred R. (1922) *The Andaman Islanders: A Study in Social Anthropology.*

Tefft, Stanton K., and Douglas Reinhardt. (1974) "Warfare Regulation: A Cross-Cultural Test of Hypotheses among Tribal Peoples." *Behavior Science Research* 9: 151–172.

Williams, Francis E. (1930) *Orokaiva Society.*

Physical Duels

Physical duels are a form of self-help conflict resolution in which the dispute is settled through physical combat between the disputing parties. The combat can be direct such as in boxing or wrestling matches or involve the use of weapons such as swords, knives, spears, bow and arrow, clubs, or guns. The winner of the duel is the individual with greater physical strength, speed, or skill with the particular weapon. Duels are different than fights in that duels are governed by a set of rules and the behavior is often ritualized. The rules determine what types of disputes are appropriate for settlement by dueling, how the duel is to be conducted, and how a winner is determined. Duels almost always take place in public with supporters of the participants cheering them on.

Although duels of various types—jousts or duels with swords or handguns—have informed the Western imagination at least since the Middle Ages, physical duels are actually uncommon as a way of settling disputes in cultures around the world. In a survey of interpersonal violence in 90 cultures, only 10 percent used duels to settle some types of disputes. This compares to 42 percent of cultures where men fight to settle disputes and 29 percent where women fight. Additionally, physical duels are not used to settle all types of disputes and the rules generally make it clear when a duel is appropriate. For example, the Ifugao of the Philippines settle disputes over the boundaries of rice fields by wrestling, while other disputes are settled by other means. Wrestling is effective in settling boundary disputes as the men engage in a series of bouts along the disputed property line, with the spots where the loser falls creating the new boundary.

Dueling is mainly a male activity. Only among the Aranda of Australia is there frequent dueling between women. This sex difference may result from dueling as opposed to fighting often being undertaken to protect one's or one's family honor, a responsibility that falls to men in nearly all cultures where honor is considered worth fighting for.

In cultures where physical duels are common, they often take a highly conventionalized form. For example, among the Ona of the Tierra del Fuego men would engage in wrestling matches to avenge insults or to defend their honor. These matches began as a loud argument, followed by a challenge to wrestle and then the match itself, with a cheering crowd of kin of the two men spurring them on. A series of matches might take place until one man was soundly beaten or until both were too exhausted to continue. The beaten man might seek revenge through another match at a later date or challenge the victor to a duel with arrows. The arrow duel required the men to take turns shooting arrows at one another while the target person dodged the arrows, moving closer and closer to the archer as the match progressed. Injuries rarely resulted and the crowd picked the winner. The loser, as in wrestling, could request a rematch at a later date.

Another example are the well-described duels of Yanomamö men of Brazil and

Venezuela. Yanomamö men engage in chest pounding, side slapping, and club fights. Chest-pounding duels usually take place in response to minor offenses such as spreading gossip and involve two men alternately punching each other in the chest. Such duels often settle the matter, but if they do not a side-slapping contest may ensue, with the opponents alternately slapping each other on the side. Side slapping more often leads to injury than does chest pounding. For serious offenses such as adultery, men will engage in club fights, hitting each other on the head with 8- to 10-foot-long wooden clubs that open bloody gashes. Such fights often lead to brawls involving supporters of the two combatants. The scars that result from club fights are a marker of prestige for Yanomamö men. Unlike the Ona where a duel often leads to more duels, Yanomamö duels are a relatively harmless way of expressing aggression within and between villages and rarely lead to long-term antagonisms.

See also SELF-HELP CONFLICT RESOLUTION.

Barton, Roy F. (1919) *Ifugao Law.*

Chagnon, Napoleon A. (1968) *Yanomamö: The Fierce People.*

Gusinde, Martin. (1931) *The Fireland Indians. Vol. 1: The Selk'nam, On the Life and Thought of a Hunting People of the Great Island of Tierra del Fuego.*

Levinson, David. (1989) *Family Violence in Cross-Cultural Perspective.*

PHYSICAL PUNISHMENT OF CHILDREN

Physical punishment of children is the use of physical force by parents or other caretakers to discipline, motivate, or punish an infant or child. While there is variation in every society from parent to parent in the use of physical punishment, societies around the world can be ranked on a four-point scale of the relative importance of physical punishment in childrearing. A survey of 90 cultures indicates that physical punishment is not used or is used much less often than other techniques in 26.5 percent of cultures, regularly used but less often than other techniques in about 40 percent, as frequently as other techniques in 21.1 percent, and more often than other techniques in 13.3 percent.

Physical punishment as a method of childrearing falls within the general category of childrearing practices called punishment. Other forms of punishment are teasing, ridiculing, shaming, scolding, and threatening. Cross-cultural surveys indicate that punishment of one of these types is used by caretakers in about 75 percent of societies. A second category of childrearing practices is exhorting, which involves adults setting an example for children, public pressure, verbal commands, lecturing, and moralizing. Setting an example and lecturing are the two most common forms of exhorting. A third category of childrearing methods is rewarding, which includes praising, giving gifts for achievements, hosting celebrations that honor the child as a person, and the conferring of special privileges. From a study of childrearing in 186 cultures, anthropologist Herbert Barry III and his colleagues derived the following list that ranks childrearing techniques in order of frequency, with physical punishment ranked next to last in frequency of use compared to eight other techniques.

1. Setting an example
2. Verbal warning
3. Public pressure
4. Lecturing
5. Teasing
6. Scolding
7. Gift giving

8. Physical punishment
9. Celebrations

In most cultures boys and girls are treated about equally in the use of physical punishment. There is a larger difference in its use with younger and older children, with older boys and girls more likely to be physically punished than younger ones. This is probably because in many cultures parents do not punish their children until they believe that the children are old enough to understand the consequence of their misbehavior.

As suggested by the above statistics, cultures vary widely in the extent to which children are physically punished. Near one extreme are cultures like the Central Thai where parents rarely hit their children and in fact never even threaten their children with "You had better do that or else. . . ." Typical of many cultures are the Highland Quechua of Ecuador where parents resort to slapping only for serious offenses or repeated misbehavior. In most situations, in most cultures physical punishment takes the form of a slap that expresses the parent's sudden rage or loss of control. And at the other extreme are the relatively few cultures where children are regularly reared through physical punishment. One such culture is that of rural Jamaica, where childrearing progresses from slaps to beatings with a switch to floggings with a belt. As the research on socialization of aggression shows, this approach to childrearing is likely to be perpetuated from one generation to the next as routine physical punishment often produces adults who have difficulty controlling their own aggressive behavior. In addition to variation across cultures, there is also variation between regions. Child punishment is used more often in cultures in Africa and the Middle East, somewhat less often in Asia and Europe and Oceania and least often in North and South American Indian groups.

Considerable attention has been given by cross-cultural researchers to explaining cross-cultural variation in the use of physical punishment. From this research a number of clear patterns have emerged. First, physical punishment of children is more typical of societies that are physically punitive in other ways. Thus, in cultures where parents hit their children, older siblings hit younger ones, husbands beat wives, and criminals are subject to corporal punishment more commonly than in cultures where children are rarely hit. This suggests that physical punishment of children is part of a broader cultural pattern that legitimizes the use of physical means by those in power to control the behavior of those who are socially or physically weaker.

Second, physical punishment tends to be used most often by single parents and least often by caretakers in extended family households, where parents are helped by grandparents or one of the parent's adult siblings. Cross-culturally, physical punishment is especially common in polygynous families where the co-wives live in separate houses with their children while the husband they share has his own dwelling. In this context, the day-to-day life of each co-wife is much like that of a single parent as she has no spouse on whom she can reliably count for emotional and physical support. Nuclear family households tend to be in between single-parent and extended family households in their use of physical punishment. Extended family households are notably low in the use of physical punishment because the presence of multiple or alternate caretakers reduces the stress on the parents and provides parents with an adult target for their aggressive feelings (wife beating is more common in extended family households). Regardless of household type, it is also clear that children are less likely to be punished and more likely to be indulged when multiple caretakers are available, and especially when grandparents help raise their grandchildren.

The third factor influencing the use of physical punishment is the level of economic and political complexity of the culture. Adults in complex cultures—those with agricultural economic systems, large communities, and centralized government—often must obey and conform to the wishes of others and therefore they stress conformity and obedience in their children as the personality traits they seek to inculcate through the use of physical punishment for misbehavior.

These three explanations for cultural acceptance and parental use of physical punishment are not necessarily mutually exclusive, and it is likely that a combination of these factors operates to create a social situation that encourages the use of physical punishment rather than other techniques.

See also SOCIALIZATION OF AGGRESSION.

Barry, Herbert III, et al. (1980) "Agents and Techniques for Child Training: Cross-Cultural Codes 6." In *Cross-Cultural Samples and Codes,* edited by Herbert Barry III and Alice Schlegel, 237–276.

Beals, Ralph L. (1966) *Community in Transition: Nayón—Ecuador.*

Cohen, Yehudi A. (1966) *A Study of Interpersonal Relations in a Jamaican Community.*

Levinson, David. (1989) *Family Violence in Cross-Cultural Perspective.*

Munroe, Ruth H., and Robert L. Munroe. (1980) "Household Structure and Socialization Practices." *Journal of Social Psychology* 111: 293–294.

Petersen L. R., G. R. Lee, and G. J. Ellis. (1982) "Social Structure, Socialization Values, and Disciplinary Techniques: A Cross-Cultural Analysis." *Journal of Marriage and the Family* 44: 131–142.

Phillips, Herbert P. (1966) *Thai Peasant Personality: The Patterning of Interpersonal Behavior in the Village of Bang Chan.*

Rohner, Ronald P. (1986) *The Warmth Dimension.*

Raiding

Raiding is a term often used in imprecise or confusing ways in reference to aggressive and hostile relations between different societies or communities within a single society. In its most general sense, raiding refers either to a specific military tactic or to a form of warfare practiced by some societies. Other terms that are sometimes used as synonyms for raiding are feuding, kidnapping, banditry, piracy, thievery, and warfare. Both as a military tactic and as a form of warfare, raiding involves aggression between two distinct political communities. Sometimes political communities are societies, and sometimes they are smaller units such as politically independent tribes or villages within a larger culture. That the aggression involves political communities differentiates raiding from thievery and feuding, which involve individuals or kin groups within a political community.

As a military tactic, raiding is a relatively unstructured attack on an enemy settlement or an incursion into enemy territory for the purpose of destroying property, killing the enemy, or capturing people, animals, or material goods. Raiding usually involves an informally formed war party, a raid can be initiated by anyone with warrior status, and there is relatively little loss of life on both sides. Although it is less structured than other tactics, the raiding party is led by a skilled warrior, the raid is planned, and scouts are often used to locate the enemy settlement or the desired objects. Raiding depends heavily on the element of surprise, and attacks are often launched at dawn.

As a form of warfare characteristic of some societies (although they might also engage in other forms of warfare), raiding focuses on the acquisition of people, animals, or material goods and does not have as its purpose the political domination of another society nor the taking of their territory. Social banditry relies on raiding as a tactic, although social banditry is not raiding per se, as a major motivation of social banditry is political protest and revolt.

Raiding as a form of internal or external war is usually conducted to take goods of social, economic, or religious value; often these goods are in short supply in the raiding society, and raiding is the easiest, least costly, and sometimes the only means of acquiring them. Cross-culturally, the most common social goods taken in raids are women, who are abducted to be used as wives. The most important and most common economic goods taken are humans for use as slaves, livestock, and money or other mediums of exchange. The most common religious goods taken in raids are human heads and humans to be used in sacrifice. Raiding is also a major source of social prestige for men, who earn their reputations and leadership positions by proving themselves as skilled and fearless warriors during raiding expeditions.

See also Banditry; Bride Theft and Raiding; Counting Coup; Feuding; Head-Hunting; Human Sacrifice; Internal Conflict; Military Glory; Raiding for Livestock; Raiding for Slaves; Scalping; War.

RAIDING FOR LIVESTOCK

Raiding to take livestock from neighboring societies has always been a common activity of pastoral cultures around the world. In general, it was nomadic pastoral peoples who relied heavily on one animal (such as cattle, horses, or camels) for economic security who raided other pastoral people. Three regions where raiding for livestock was common that have drawn attention are the Arabian Peninsula, East Africa, and the North American Plains. In Arabia, nomadic Bedouin tribes engaged in continuous raiding against other tribes for camels. In East Africa, the numerous pastoral groups engaged in raiding of varying degrees of intensity to take cattle from one another. And among Native American tribes of the North American Plains, raiding for horses, scalps, and military glory was a major activity prior to the beginning of the Reservation period in the late nineteenth century. Although the capture of economically valuable livestock was a key reason for raiding in all three regions, the actual practice and social organization of raiding varied widely.

The label, Bedouin, refers to nomadic herders of the Syrian, Arabian, and Sahara deserts who traditionally followed a syncretic religion based on Islam and traditional, pre-Islamic beliefs. The Bedouin are composed of politically autonomous tribes governed by chiefs. Bedouin tribes engaged in two types of raiding. Unilateral raiding involved raids against caravans or settled communities for the purpose of capturing whatever valuables were there for the taking. The second form of raiding, reciprocal raiding, involved the taking of camels from other tribes and was an ongoing means of exchanging camels among the tribes. The camel was the Bedouin's major economic resource, providing milk, wool, leather, and transport and serving as a commodity that could be sold or traded to non-Bedouins.

Bedouin tribal raids were carried out almost exclusively to capture camels, did not involve attempts to take land (the desert land not being economically valuable to herders), and the killing of people was avoided. Bedouin camel raiding has been interpreted as an economic adaptation to desert conditions that prevented the tribes from keeping large herds of camels. And, since trade or sale of camels between tribes was forbidden (although they could be given within the tribes as a gift, as blood money payment, or as tribute to the chief), raiding provided the only means of exchanging camels and maintaining or increasing the size of a tribe's herd. Raiding was an ongoing activity among tribes in a region and thereby insured a steady supply of camels for all tribes. Raiding between any two tribes followed a predictable cycle of peace between tribes, followed by thieving, a declaration of hostilities, small- and large-scale raids, an annual ceremonial raid, and then a declaration of peace. The overlap of this cycle across a number of tribes insured a smooth flow of camels. Such raiding has now largely disappeared in Arabia as the Bedouin are no longer mainly nomadic, gas-powered vehicles have replaced the camel, and the national governments in the region exert control over such activities.

The Turkana are one of a number of pastoral groups in East Africa. Prior to pacification by the British in the 1920s, the Turkana were involved in a continuous pattern of raiding with such neighboring peoples as the Karimojong, Jie, Dodo, Samburu, Toposa, Nyangatom, and Merille. The Turkana raided to capture cattle, to gain personal honor and prestige for warriors, and to drive other groups from valuable grazing land or water sources, although the permanent control of this land was not a major goal of raiding. Turkana raids could be either small or large and might be conducted as part of a military expedition into another group's territory. Whether large or small, the fighting was often fierce and enemy men, women, and children were killed. Raiding was a major activity of young men who needed to acquire wealth, in the form of cattle, and reputations as skilled warriors so that they could marry and establish their own homestead. While raiding is now mostly an activity of the past, its ideology remains a part of contemporary Turkana culture.

Raiding by the nomadic Blackfoot Indians of the northern Plains lacked the formal exchange elements of Bedouin raiding but was nonetheless a major economic and social activity. The Blackfoot raided neighboring peoples such as the Cree, Crow, Shoshone, Flathead, and Kutenai. As with the Bedouin, neither conquest of neighboring peoples nor the taking of their land was the goal; rather the Blackfoot raided for horses, for military glory, and for scalps. Horses were vital to the Blackfoot for transport, hunting bison, and as an indicator of a warrior's wealth and bravery. Blackfoot raids were conducted by small, volunteer parties under the leadership of skilled warriors and often resulted in considerable loss of life on both sides.

While pointing to some variation in raiding for livestock around the world, these three examples also show how raiding provides valuable resources both for the raiding society and for the individual raiders. For the society, the resources gained are vital economic ones: camels, horses, and cattle that cannot be raised or kept in large herds by nomadic peoples. For the raiders, the resources gained are individual wealth and prestige, which are required by young men in order to be accepted as full adult members of the community and by older men to gain a leadership role in the community.

Dyson-Hudson, Rada, and Terrence McCabe. (1985) *South Turkana Nomadism: Coping with an Unpredictably Varying Environment.*

Ewers, John C. (1967) "Blackfoot Raiding for Horses and Scalps." In *Law and Warfare: Studies in the Anthropology of Conflict,* edited by Paul Bohannan, 327–344.

Gulliver, Philip H. (1951) *A Preliminary Survey of the Turkana.* Cape Town: University of Cape Town.

Sweet, Louise E. (1965) "Camel Raiding of North Arabian Bedouin: A Mechanism of Ecological Adaptation." *American Anthropologist* 67: 1132–1150.

RAIDING FOR SLAVES

Raiding for slaves, sometimes called kidnapping, is one of the means through which people have been enslaved in societies around the world. The primary way a person has become a slave throughout human history has been by birth. The primary mechanism societies used to acquire slaves was the enslavement of captives taken in raids or warfare. Enslavement can be either direct through enslaving captives or indirect through the purchase or trading of slaves taken as captives by other societies. The taking of slaves has been a fairly common practice throughout human history and across cultures because slavery was also fairly common. Two surveys of non-Western cultures indicate that about 36 percent of cultures had slavery. The majority of these cultures practiced domestic slavery. Slaves were most often women who were used for domestic work; they were often taken as wives and over a generation or two their children often became full members of the culture. A minority (7 percent in a survey of 186 societies) also had chattel slavery, where slavery was a vital component of the social and economic fabric of the society. When we add to this list the long list of preindustrial and industrialized nations that also had slavery—the Romans, Greeks, Egyptians, Ottomans, English, French, Portuguese, Malays, Chinese, to name a few—it is obvious that slavery and raiding for slaves have been common activities around the world.

Raiding for slaves can be conceptualized as differing from capturing slaves in warfare in that raiding was not usually a society-wide activity, it might involve taking slaves from another group within the same society (such as a village, kinship group, or tribe), and the purpose of the raid was mainly to take captives for enslavement. For example, among the Goajiro of Colombia raiding for slaves was a form of revenge in feuds between clans who raided each other for women and girls. The women were used in domestic work and might be married to a nonslave or a slave, while the girls were often sold to outsiders for use as prostitutes. Similarly, the Ifugao of Luzon Island in the Philippines raided internally for slaves, who were then sold to other societies to the south. The Ifugao rarely kept slaves for their own use.

In small-scale non-Western cultures, raiding was second in importance only to warfare as a means of acquiring slaves. Taking slaves through warfare or raiding was especially important in small-scale societies because many children of slave women and free men became nonslaves, which necessitated a continual flow of new slaves taken from other societies and thereby created an ongoing demand for more slaves.

In both capture through warfare and raiding, persons taken as slaves were usually taken from groups the raiding society defined as different than itself. In warfare this was usually another society that occupied a distinct territory, spoke a different language, followed a different set of religious beliefs, and had a different name. In raiding it may also have been a different society or it may have been either a different kinship group (such as a clan) or political unit (such as a tribe or village) within the same society. Virtually all cultures prohibited the enslavement of members of the local community, although some persons might be reduced to slave status to pay off debts or as punishment for a serious crime such as witchcraft.

A striking feature of raiding for slaves is the imbalanced sex ratio of individuals taken, with women taken and enslaved far more frequently than men in the majority of societies with slaves. This is because women (and children) were more easily taken and confined than men, because they could be used as sex or marriage partners and bear children, and because the type of domestic and horticultural work performed by slaves in small-scale societies was usually women's work—weaving, gathering firewood, cleaning, tending fields and garden plots, and caring for children. For example, the Ganda of what is now Uganda raided the neighboring Basoga and Banyoro for women whom Ganda men could then choose to take as wives. These women were considered as equals of Ganda wives, although they had no local kin to support them and their children were not permitted to inherit family property. Similarly, the Somali preferred to take women and girls who performed domestic work and were allowed to marry only low class Somali men. When men were also taken in large numbers, it was because men were needed to perform male work or because the male slaves could be profitably sold. The Kpelle of Liberia and the Tlingit of the northwest coast of North America both took men along with women, with the men forced to do menial work or sold to other societies. Perhaps the one period in human history when the sex ratio of slaves taken was most balanced was during the New World slave trade when slaves were taken by raiding and exported from West Africa. The men were sold to European slave traders for transport to the New World, while the women were more often kept by the raiding societies for their own use.

Because slaves were usually viewed as an economic commodity, raiding practices of a particular society might change in response to external forces that redefined the economic value of slaves. For example, raiding for women had a long history among the Blackfoot of the North American Plains. Before extensive white contact, the Blackfoot captured women for use as wives to bear children. Because Blackfoot battle losses were probably few during this time, raiding for wives was probably limited. Following contact with Europeans the Blackfoot became enmeshed in the regional trade network, and women were now taken as slaves to be sold or traded to European traders. After 1830, when the Blackfoot had adopted the horse and gun and had become nomadic hunters dependent on the bison herds, women were no longer taken to be traded or sold but rather for domestic service in tanning hides and in other work required for participation in the fur trade.

Much of the interest in raiding for slaves has focused on the New World slave trade, where Africans taken mainly from societies in West Africa were brought to European colonies and nations in North America, South America, and the Caribbean to work as slaves on farms and plantations and in households. Some scholars suggest that most were already slaves in African societies and were simply sold by their owners to European slave traders. Others suggest that wars between West African cultures produced the bulk of slaves brought to the New World. A more recent view, based on historical and anthropological research, suggests that raiding produced about 70 percent of the slaves brought to the New World in the seventeenth through the nineteenth centuries. This suggests that West African slave raiders were acting as middleman suppliers for the European traders and, as indicated above, expanded their raiding activities to take men as well as women, because the men could be sold to European slave traders.

See also TREATMENT OF WAR CAPTIVES; WAR.

Barton, Roy F. (1946) *The Religion of the Ifugaos.*

Gutierrez de Pineda, Virginia. (1950) *Social Organization in La Guajira.*

Lewis, Ioan M. (1955) *Peoples of the Horn of Africa.*

Lewis, Oscar. (1942) *The Effects of White Contact upon Blackfoot Culture.*

Mair, Lucy P. (1934) *An African People in the Twentieth Century.*

Patterson, Orlando. (1982) *Slavery and Social Death.*

Pryor, Frederic L. (1977) *The Origins of the Economy.*

Tollefson, Kenneth D. (1976) *The Cultural Foundation of Political Revitalization among the Tlingit.*

Westerman, Diedrich H. (1921) *The Kpelle: A Negro Tribe in Liberia.*

RAPE

Rape is genital contact between a man and a woman when the women has no choice. Absence of choice is indicated by the woman being forced, coerced, or threatened; her being subject to gang rape; a threat of punishment if she does not participate; or intercourse that is physically painful or harmful. Rape is aggression by men directed against women, although there are rare cases of what might be called female rape of males. And there is also homosexual rape where a man is forced to have sexual relations with another man.

The definition above includes both normative rape (rape that is condoned by the society) and nonnormative rape (rape that is not condoned and is considered wrong or a crime). When both normative and nonnormative rape are considered, rape is a cultural universal, occurring in all human societies, although very rarely in some. When only nonnormative rape is considered or only rape that occurs with some frequency, the percentage of societies with rape is about 50 percent.

Societies vary widely in the types of rape they define as criminal and also in the types of punishments used. For example, in traditional Ifugao society in the northern Philippines, forced sexual relations with a girl by an appropriate boy suitor is not generally considered wrong; a rape committed in an open field is more serious than one in private; and rape of a married woman by a married man carries a larger fine than of a married woman by an unmarried man, while the rape of an unmarried woman by an unmarried man is least serious of all. In other cultures, such as the Somali of Africa or the Pawnee Indians of the United States, the most serious type is rape of a girl or an unmarried women. In many cultures where rape or some forms of rape are considered a serious crime it is not just the woman who is seen as being wronged but also her family or her husband. Thus, among the Ifugao, the fine paid by a married man who rapes a married woman is divided among the victim and her family, the victim's husband and his family, and the rapist's wife. There is some evidence that the more harshly rape is punished (some societies kill or ostracize rapists) the less rape there is in that society. However, since rape is present everywhere, a low rate of rape is an indicator that rape is being "regulated" rather than being "prevented."

In her survey of rape in 35 societies, anthropologist Patricia Rozée-Koker identified six common types of normative (condoned) rape. Normative rape occurred in 34 of the 35 societies she surveyed, nonnormative in 63 percent, and both in 60 percent.

Marital Rape (40 percent of societies) is rape that takes place in consummating the marriage or during the marriage.

Exchange Rape (71 percent) is rape that results from sexual access to women who are treated as a trading commodity by men or kin groups. This includes woman-exchange marriage, wife-sharing, wife-loaning, women as gambling prizes, or trading access to women for goods or services.

Punitive Rape (14 percent) is rape used to punish a woman. This includes punishment for resisting male authority, violating societal rules, rejecting a man's sexual advances, or a woman being punished for her husband's crimes. Punitive rape is especially common as a punishment for adultery. Among some Plains Indian groups such as the Blackfoot an adulterous wife might be punished by being gang raped, beaten, and her nose cut off to make her undesirable in the future.

Theft Rape (63 percent) is the abduction of women for sexual use as concubines or prostitutes or as marriage partners. Perhaps the most common form is bride theft, in which a woman is forcibly abducted and raped by a man who wants her as his wife. Because she is no longer a virgin (bride theft occurs mainly in cultures where female virginity is highly valued by men), she will have little chance of finding another man to marry her, so she is compelled to marry her abductor.

Ceremonial Rape (49 percent) includes defloration rituals such as virginity tests, women used to initiate boys to sex, and forced sexual relations as part of ceremonies.

Status Rape (29 percent) is coerced sexual relations between a woman and a man who is her social superior, such as a master, chief, priest, or political leader.

In addition, there are other forms of rape such as rape of enemy women during warfare or practices such as sleepcrawling in some societies in Polynesia in which a man crawls into the hut of a woman at night and has or attempts to have sex with the sleeping woman.

From anthropologist Peggy Sanday's survey of 95 societies, it seems clear that both normative and nonnormative rape occur as part of a more general pattern of male dominance of women and interpersonal aggression. Societies with much rape are ones in which male political authority exceeds that of women, women have fewer rights, men raid other groups for wives, go to war frequently, and fight among themselves. Rape is also more frequent in cultures where male behavior is typified by compulsive masculinity, and where related groups of men band together to fight other groups from other communities. Rape does not, however, occur any more often in societies that restrict sexual freedom or in which men fear sex with women.

See also BRIDE THEFT AND RAIDING; MACHOISM.

Barton, Roy. (1919) *Ifugao Law.* California University Publications in American Archaeology and Ethnology 15: 1–187.

Broude, Gwen, and Sara J. Greene. (1976) "Cross-Cultural Codes on Twenty Sexual Practices." *Ethnology* 15: 409–429.

Otterbein, Keith F. (1979) "A Cross-Cultural Study of Rape." *Aggressive Behavior* 5: 425–435.

Palmer, Craig. (1989) "Is Rape a Cultural Universal? A Re-Examination of the Ethnographic Data." *Ethnology* 28: 1–16.

Rozée-Koker, Patricia. (1987) "Cross-Cultural Codes on Seven Types of Rape." *Behavior Science Research* 21: 101–117.

Sanday, Peggy R. (1981) "The Socio-Cultural Context of Rape: A Cross-Cultural Study." *Journal of Social Issues* 37: 5–27.

RITUALS OF CONFLICT

Rituals of conflict are annual ceremonies or celebrations during which certain categories of people are expected to speak or act antagonistically toward certain other categories of people. Although these rites have been most extensively studied in Africa, they occur all around the world with some frequency. In a survey of 60 societies, 53 percent had annual rituals of conflict, although only 8 percent had them in their full-blown form with actual fighting between adults. These rituals usually take the form of athletic contests, mock battles, relatively harmless attacks against others, pranks, ridicule, and mockery. The people involved are often from different social or economic classes in the society and individuals from the lower of the classes would not normally act antagonistically toward individuals from the superior classes nor would they direct their anger at a person from that class. Thus, the rituals allow for the public display of behavior that is normally controlled and for a reversal of social status. For example, the rites might involve women attacking men, children playing practical jokes on adults, ordinary citizens insulting the chief, in-laws deriding each other, etc. In short, those involved are people who might feel anger at others during the year but are unable to express their feelings due to their subordinate social status.

Annual rituals of conflict are of three types: (1) those involving verbal hostility such as teasing or insulting by adults or aggressive behavior by children; (2) those involving aggressive behavior by adults, short of actual fighting; and (3) those with actual fighting. For example, the Amhara of Ethiopia celebrate the New Year in September when the grain grass begins to mature. As part of the ceremony men engage in mock battles and boys burn scars on their forearms to demonstrate their bravery. Similarly, Tucano men of the Brazilian and Colombian Amazon celebrate their return from the forest with food by whipping each other to see who is the bravest. These rites are so violent that the women and children flee, returning only after the men's cries have subsided.

One of the more dramatic rituals of conflict was the annual Lukang rock fight, which pitted the surname groups against each other in the village of Lukang in Taiwan prior to World War II. On 5 April each year the men in the dozen or so groups would line up around a field and hurl rocks at each other. As they moved toward one another, rock-throwing gave way to punching, kicking, and beatings with sticks. Spectators cheered the fighters on and helped patch up the wounded and send them back into the battle. No one was killed or seriously injured, and no group either won or lost. The purpose was to fight. As one man explained: "People in those days were quite superstitious, and believed that if blood were not shed during the spring, then there would be bad luck during the rest of the year."

Annual rites of conflict are an emotional safety valve and occur most often in societies where opportunities for the expression of individual freedom are limited. These are societies where communal decision making governs a wide range of daily activities and where the social order is rigidly maintained by those in power. Annual rites also occur commonly at harvest time and are especially common and violent in societies where the harvest ends a period of food shortage and hunger. This suggests that annual rituals of conflict provide a release for pent-up feeling of anger resulting both from a lack of individual freedom and from the stress accompanying food shortages and hunger.

See also AGGRESSION IN FOLKTALES; HUMOR.

DeGlopper, Donald R. (1974) *City on the Sands: Social Structure in a Nineteenth-Century Chinese City.*

Dirks, Robert. (1988) "Annual Rituals of Conflict." *American Anthropologist* 90: 856–870.

Gluckman, Max. (1954) *Rituals of Rebellion in South-East Africa.*

RITUALS OF RECONCILIATION

Rituals of reconciliation are a structured mechanism for informally resolving conflicts between individuals. They are structured in comparison to informal dispute management mechanisms such as apology but less structured than some other mechanisms such as oaths, ordeals, or litigation, which often operate within a rigid set of rules and procedures and require the involvement of others beyond the disputants.

While rituals of reconciliation occur in a number of societies around the world (there are no surveys that estimate what percentage) they vary widely both in the categories of people involved and the specific forms the rituals take. However, the constant from society to society is that the individuals who settle disputes through rituals of reconciliation are individuals who live in the same community and normally engage in face-to-face interaction with each other. These individuals are often friends, members of the same social or interest group, or coworkers, and they often belong to the same primary group such as a family, kin group, work team, or set of individuals whose cooperative behavior is important to the community. When these individuals are involved in a dispute that becomes so serious or goes on too long, the cohesion or smooth functioning of the group might be threatened and a ritual of reconciliation is used to resolve the dispute. For example, rituals of reconciliation and formal apology is used by women in Saudi Arabia to settle disputes. Saudi Arabian women play a variety of important community roles (one being the arrangement of marriages) that create deep and long-lasting ties and alliances among families in the community. If disputes between women go unresolved, the basic unity may then be threatened.

Rituals of conflict are often used when one of the disputants chooses to avoid the other, thereby removing any opportunity for the two individuals to settle the problem themselves and also disrupting the normal functioning of the group. Thus, one function of rituals of reconciliation is to control conflict within the social group. A second is to keep the dispute at the local level, protecting the grievants from other more costly approaches such as litigation and from the involvement of outsiders in the group's business.

An example of a highly elaborated ritual of reconciliation is the *i soro* ceremony of the native Fijians. Fiji is a highly stratified society with each person having a distinct rank relative to every other person and also a distinct social role within the community. Violations of social norms governing performance of one's role (carpenter, chief, etc.) or governing relations between people of different (higher and lower) status often leads to disputes that may disrupt village life. *I soro* is used to settle such conflicts as well as other types of disputes. The ritual is performed in its full form for serious offenses and in an abbreviated form for less serious offenses.

In its full form, the offender must first retain the services of an intermediary who is respected by the offended party. As the intermediary must first convince the offended person to participate, the person selected as an intermediary is often an older relative of the offended person, whose presence is likely to encourage the offended party to participate in the ceremony. No one is forced to participate, but social pressure insures that an offended person will almost always accept the intermediary's invitation. At the ceremony, the intermediary speaks for the offender, stating the reason for the visit, emphasizing the need for group harmony, criticizing the behavior being apologized for, asking for forgiveness, and then presenting a small gift (usually a polished whale's tooth) to the offended individual. During the presentation, the offender must "surrender" by wearing formal clothing, sitting in the low-status end of the house, bowing his head, and keeping silent. Following the intermediary's speech, the offended person accepts the gift and also speaks, thus resolving the conflict and signifying reconciliation. The two parties share a drink of *kava* (an alcoholic beverage made from the fermented root of a variety of the pepper plant) and normal relations between the two parties then resume.

See also APOLOGY; MEDIATION; RITUALS OF CONFLICT.

Koch, Klaus-Friedrich, Soraya Altorki, Andrew Arno, and Letitia Hickson. (1977) "Ritual Reconciliation and the Obviation of Grievances: A Comparative Study in the Ethnography of Law." *Ethnology* 16: 269–283.

Scalping

Scalping is the removal of a piece of the skin and hair from an enemy's head. Much attention has been given to scalping as an aspect of American Indian warfare. Prior to European arrival, the scalp of an enemy was taken as a trophy. After warfare practices changed due to the influence of Europeans, the scalp was more often taken as proof that an enemy was killed, in order to get a reward or payment.

At the time of European contact scalping was practiced by the Iroquois and other groups in what is now New York State, northern Pennsylvania, and southern Ontario. It spread to other groups, particularly in the Plains, only after contact with Europeans. The usual method was for a warrior to cut off a patch a skin and hair behind the crown of the skull; the scalp might be taken from a dead warrior or from the living and the procedure was not necessarily fatal. As a trophy, the scalp was preserved, stretched on a circular hoop, painted, the hair decorated, and then carried by women in the victory dance. It then might be retained by a warrior or a woman, or discarded.

Scalping has often been cited as evidence of the vicious nature of warfare as allegedly practiced by American Indians. And, there is little doubt that early settlers were terrified by the thought of marauding Indians on so-called scalping raids. In the 1960s this view of American Indian warfare was challenged by some revisionist scholars who claimed that scalping was not an indigenous practice but was actually taught to the Indians by Europeans. More recently, a review of the evidence proves that scalping was an indigenous practice. The evidence comes from a variety of sources. First, scalping was a one element of a broader complex of customs including the preservation of the scalp, its ritual use, and dancing. If it had been simply borrowed from Europeans, it is unlikely that it would be associated with these other customs, which were not practiced by Europeans. Second, early reports from explorers and missionaries who were the first to come into contact with the native people frequently mention scalping, indicating that it predates European arrival, although these reports probably overdramatized scalping. Third, in the languages of Indian groups that practiced scalping, there are words that describe various aspects of the process, while such precise words were missing from English and French at the time. And, fourth, there is archaeological evidence in the form of scalping marks on skulls (both of individuals who died and those who did not die from the scalping) that demonstrates that scalping was present before the arrival of Europeans.

The presence of scalping before European arrival does not mean that Europeans had no influence on scalping. On the contrary, their influence was major and the European contribution to scalping was twofold. First, as part of their efforts to involve Indians in their wars with European competitors, they encouraged scalping by paying Indians for the scalps taken from individuals of other European nations. This practice began with the Dutch in Manhattan and was used by both the French and English as well. Second, the Europeans adopted scalping themselves and encouraged their soldiers to return with the scalps of Indians. The motive, of course, was to encourage soldiers to kill as many Indians as possible. Thus, while Europeans did not teach American Indians to scalp they were responsible for the spread of the practice to groups outside the East, for making it a goal of warfare, and for using the practice to create an image of American Indians as heartless and ruthless warriors.

See also GENOCIDE; HEAD-HUNTING; MILITARY GLORY; TORTURING THE ENEMY; WESTERN INFLUENCE ON INDIGENOUS WARFARE.

Axtell, James, and William C. Sturtevant. (1986) "The Unkindest Cut, or Who Invented Scalping?" In *The American Indian Past and Present,* edited by Roger L. Nichols, 47–60.

Weatherford, Jack. (1991) *Native Roots: How the Indians Enriched America.*

SELF-HELP CONFLICT RESOLUTION

In self-help or self-redress conflict resolution the two disputants rely on their own actions and the support of those willing to help them to resolve the conflict rather than on formal mechanisms imposed by agents of society. Self-help methods are the only ones that occur in all cultures and they are the predominant form in small, less complex cultures that lack a centralized government. Self-help is rarely used for serious conflicts in social situations where behavior is governed by a firm set of laws. Rather, self-help is used mainly in communities where the unwritten rules and expectations about appropriate behavior are understood by all community members. These rules determine what behaviors are subject to self-help resolution and what are the appropriate self-help measures. For example, a man in the island culture of Tikopia who returns home late at night, suggesting his participation in an adulterous liaison, knows he will receive and will have to accept silently a beating from his wife.

There are five basic types of self-help:

1. Avoidance and withdrawal where one or both persons settle the dispute by avoiding each other for some period of time and then resume relations with no discussion of the wrong that caused the avoidance.
2. Physical reprisal in which the aggrieved party seeks revenge by attacking the other party or his property. So long as the attack is appropriate for the wrong, the offender will not retaliate.
3. Public shaming in which the offender must submit to public ridicule through insults, song duels, or physical duels. Here public pressure plays a role in the settlement, although only the offender and the offended actually participate directly.
4. Negotiation and compensation where the two parties settle their grievance through discussion.
5. Supernatural sanctions in the form of causing the other party to die, fall ill, have an accident, or experience some other misfortune. This is always based on the belief that at least some illnesses are caused by supernatural forces and that such illness might serve as punishment for a wrongdoer. This form of self-help works both as a deterrent to unacceptable behavior because of the fear of falling ill and as a punishment for actual wrongdoing. The offended party may use supernatural force directly by poisoning the offender or more commonly indirectly

through witchcraft or sorcery to cause harm. Or, he or she may work through a ritual specialist such as a shaman or diviner who identifies the cause of the illness by identifying the rule the sick person broke or by identifying the person the sick person offended. In both cases, the conflict is then brought into the open for resolution.

See also Apology, Assault; Avoidance and Withdrawal; Blood Money; Duels; Feuding; Insults; Rituals of Conflict; Rituals of Reconciliation; Self-Punishment; Song Duels; Sorcery; Supernatural Aggression; Witchcraft.

Koch, Klaus-Friedrich, John A. Sodergren, and Susan Campbell. (1976) "Political and Psychological Correlates of Conflict Management: A Cross-Cultural Study." *Law and Society Review* 10: 443–466.

Newman, Katherine S. (1983) *Law and Economic Organization: A Comparative Study of Preindustrial Societies.*

Self-Punishment

Self-punishment is a category of indirect aggression in which an individual who is angry with someone else inflicts injury to him or herself. The two most common forms of self-punishment are suicide, which is often explained as aggression turned inward, and causing physical injury to oneself in reaction to the death of a loved one. In suicide and self-harm in reaction to a death, the aggression is indirect because the appropriate target of the aggression is unavailable. In suicide it is usually because the target person is so physically or socially powerful that the offended person fears confronting him or her directly. For example, Lusi-Kaliai women sometimes try to kill themselves after a beating by their husband as a way of calling the husband's behavior to public attention and also to punish him by depriving him of a wife and publicly shaming him. In reaction to death, aggression must be indirect because the appropriate target is the deceased individual who has angered the survivor by leaving him or her.

In some Melanesian cultures we find another form of self-punishment, although here the intent is to make the offender aware of the wrong he has done, punish him by making him feel ashamed, and get his sympathy. Among the Goodenough Islanders this practice is called *veumaiyiyi* and among the Orokaiva it is called *sisira.* On Orokaiva, a man who has a melon stolen from his field might destroy the entire field, or a man who has something stolen from his house might chop down the house; or for any number of offenses against him he might run away, refuse to eat, or hang himself. All of these actions are to draw attention to the wrong he has suffered, make the offender (who is probably known) feel ashamed of what he has done, and bring sympathy to the offended person. As a mechanism of social control, self-punishment is effective because it replaces and therefore prevents the acting-out of aggression. It is also effective because of the shame it brings the offender, a most serious matter in some Melanesian cultures where it is a deep and more powerful emotional experience than what is meant by the Western conceptualizations of guilt and shame. Because of their fear of being shamed—both for the social stigmatization and the emotional pain shaming causes—individuals will hesitate to harm others.

See also Aggression in Reaction to Death; Fighting with Property; Suicide.

Williams, Francis E. (1930) *Orokaiva Society.*

Young, Michael. (1971) *Fighting with Food: Leadership, Values and Social Control in a Massim Society.*

Sex Differences in Aggression

While there are major differences across cultures in the frequency and intensity of aggressive behavior, cross-cultural studies show that there are only small differences in aggression by boys and men compared to girls and women in most cultures. In 71 percent of societies studied boys aged two to six are somewhat more aggressive than girls of the same age, and in no culture are girls reported to be more aggressive than boys. The same pattern holds for older children, with boys more often encouraged to act aggressively than girls, although in most societies, both boys and girls are reared to be generally nonaggressive. For adults, the sex difference in aggression is even less, with one survey suggesting that both are equally aggressive in most cultures, while in a few cultures men are more aggressive and in a few women are more aggressive.

While aggression in general by men and women might be about the same in many societies, this generalization does not apply to violent aggression that causes harm to others. Cross-culturally, it is clear that men are far more violent than women. All types of the most violently aggressive acts—warfare, homicide, spouse killing, rape, feuding, drunken brawling, violent crimes—are almost exclusively male activities. Compared to men, women only very rarely kill their spouses, kill others, fight in combat, and participate in blood revenge feuds. Instead, most female aggression is directed at other women (this is especially true in polygynous societies) or involves aggression that is culturally defined as appropriate such as infanticide, aggressive reactions to the death of a loved one, or the performance of female genital mutilations. Violence directed at a spouse is a good example of this worldwide pattern of frequent male violence and infrequent female violence. A survey of 90 cultures indicates that wife beating occurs at least in a few marriages in 84 percent of societies, but husband beating occurs in only 27 percent of societies. And, husband beating occurs only in societies where wife beating also occurs and is usually far less violent and causes less harm. The types of aggression that men engage in, as compared to those women engage in, suggest that men are far more likely to act aggressively to advance their own interests than are women and they are far more likely to kill to advance their interests than are women.

While men are more likely than women to use direct, physical aggression, both against women and other men, women across cultures are more likely to use indirect, nonviolent forms of aggression. For example, among the Zapotec of Mexico, men fight with and occasionally kill each other, fight outsiders to protect the community, and in the past have participated in battles between local political factions. Zapotec women, on the other hand, use physical aggression less often and less intensely, with fights rarely amounting to more than pushing, pulling, and slapping. Zapotec women are more prone than men to use indirect forms of aggression such as gossip and insults and are more often accused of causing harm through witchcraft. A similar pattern holds among the Bellonese of the Solomon Islands where husbands freely beat their wives but women express aggression indirectly by insulting, complaining, mocking, and so forth.

A variety of explanations have been offered for sex differences in aggression. Traditional explanations emphasized differential socialization emphases for boys and girls, whereby in some cultures boys are encouraged or taught to act aggressively while girls are more often taught to be passive and compliant. These explanations assume that aggression is a learned behavior, that all individuals—male and female—are born with same potential to behave aggressively or nonaggressively, and that it is cultural factors that determine the form, frequency, and intensity of aggressive behavior. In this view, some social scientists suggest that across cultures females are less directly aggressive than males because in most cultures men dominate women and use physical violence as one mechanism to maintain their power. Recent research, operating from a biological perspective rather than a sociocultural or behavioral one, indicates that physiological, anatomical, and genetic differences between males and females are perhaps a more basic explanation for sex differences in aggression. This does not mean that learning plays no role, but, rather, that the effect of learning is to modify existing genetic predispositions.

See also AGGRESSION BY WOMEN; PEACEMAKING; SOCIALIZATION OF AGGRESSION.

Barry, Herbert III, et al. (1980) "Traits Inculcated in Childhood: Cross-Cultural Codes 5." In *Cross-Cultural Samples and Codes,* edited by Herbert Barry III and Alice Schlegel, 205–236.

Daly, Martin, and Margo Wilson. (1988) *Homicide.*

Fry, Douglas P. (1992) "Female Aggression among the Zapotec of Oaxaca, Mexico." In *Of Mice and Women: Aspects of Female Aggression,* edited by Kaj Björkqvist and Pirkko Niemelä, 187–199.

Glazer, Ilsa M. (1992) "Interfemale Aggression and Resource Scarcity in a Cross-Cultural Perspective." In *Of Mice and Women: Aspects of Female Aggression,* edited by Kaj Björkqvist and Pirkko Niemelä, 163–171.

Kuschel, Rolf. (1992) "'Women Are Women and Men Are Men': How Bellonese Women Get Even." In *Of Mice and Women: Aspects of Female Aggression,* edited by Kaj Björkqvist and Pirkko Niemelä, 173–185.

Levinson, David. (1990) *Family Violence in Cross-Cultural Perspective.*

Rohner, Ronald P. (1976) "Sex Differences in Aggression: Phylogenetic and Enculturation Perspectives." *Ethos* 4: 57–72.

SHUNNING

Shunning is the complete social isolation of a member of a social group. It is used to punish individuals who violate the most important rules of the group. Shunning is used mainly in small, isolated cultures that seek to maintain their traditional life in the context of a larger, dominant culture. In the United States, the Amish and Gypsies are two such groups and both use shunning or the threat of shunning to maintain group identity and social order.

The Amish are a Germanic people who trace their origins to the Swiss Anabaptist movement of 1525–1535. They immigrated to North America in two major waves, 1727–1790 and 1815–1865, and are settled in 20 U.S. states and Canada, with the majority now living in Pennsylvania, Indiana, and Ohio. Amish traditions such as rural farm living, self-sufficiency, simple dress, speaking the German language, in-group marriage, social distance from the surrounding mainstream community, and rigid adherence to community rules called *Ordnung* unify the community and differentiate the Amish from their non-Amish neighbors. Shunning *(Meidung)* is the most severe punishment that can be meted out to those who violate community rules. It is used only for the most serious violations such as adultery, drunkenness, purchasing a gas-powered vehicle, marrying a non-Amish person, or providing more schooling than is needed for one's children. It may also be used when other less severe measures such gossip, admonishments by a deacon, or self-confession fail to change a wrongdoer's behavior. Shunning is a grave action by the community and is instituted only by the unanimous vote of the local church community. The shunned person becomes a social isolate. Others will no longer speak, eat, or sleep with the shunned member. And in some communities, his or her entire family may be shunned as well. Because the Amish maintain no close ties to the outside world, shunning an individual deprives him or her of their entire social and emotional support network, making shunning a very effective punishment and an equally effective deterrent. Not surprisingly, shunned members usually quickly seek to end the ban through public confession and repentance, a painful and humiliating experience for all in a community where violation of rules is a serious matter for all. Because of the severe emotional consequences for the individual, crimes that are subject to punishment by shunning are rarely committed, attesting to the effectiveness of shunning as a mechanism of social control.

Gypsy is a generic term that covers a wide range of peoples found throughout the world who may or may not at some time in human history have all been members of a single cultural group. One such group in North America is the Rom or Romani Gypsies who take their name from their language. Like the Amish, the Rom live outside mainstream society by choice, although, unlike the Amish, they are mistrusted by non-Gypsies. Central to Rom identity is the concept of *marime,* which carries the dual and related meanings of being dirty or polluted and being rejected by the group. To be declared *marime* is the harshest punishment a Rom can experience. It means that anything he wears, touches, or uses is also *marime,* and he is avoided by all others as they fear contamination. A person is declared *marime* informally through the actions of others in the family network or formally at a *kris* (trial). An indicator that one is *marime* is finding that you are being treated like a *gaje* (non-Gypsy). As with shunning by the Amish, *marime* is used rarely and only for very serious offenses such as marrying a *gaje,* raping a Rom woman, or beating up another's wife. The ban is rarely forever, and will be lifted through a second trial or if the person demonstrates exemplary behavior during the *marime* period. *Marime* is effective because it prevents the rejected person from eating with others, which is the main arena of social interaction; is applied to the family of the person; forces the person to interact with non-Gypsies; and causes a loss of respect and status that lasts after reinstatement.

See also BANISHMENT; HARANGUE.

Hostetler, John A. (1980) *Amish Society.* Third edition.

Miller, Carol. (1975) "American Rom and the Ideology of Defilement." In *Gypsies, Tinkers and Other Travelers,* edited by Franham Rehfisch, 41–54.

Nagata, Judith A. (1969) *Continuity and Change among the Old Order Amish of Illinois.*

Schweider, Elmer, and Dorothy Schweider. (1975) *A Peculiar People: Iowa's Old Order Amish.*

Sutherland, Anne. (1975) *Gypsies: The Hidden Americans.*

SIBLING FIGHTING

Physical violence between siblings in childhood is reported as occurring in only 44 percent of societies in a worldwide sample of 90 societies. This is probably an underreporting of the number of societies where fighting does occur between siblings in childhood, although it does seem that the fighting between siblings that is so common in American culture is not typical of all cultures. Sibling violence may be relatively infrequent in some cultures for two reasons. First, children are often segregated by age and sex, diminishing the opportunity for conflict between older and younger siblings and between brothers and sisters. Second, when siblings are not kept apart, older siblings in some cultures play a major role in caring for their younger siblings. And, since parents in many cultures do not routinely physically punish their children, sibling caretakers likely imitate their parents and also use nonviolent means of caring for their siblings.

A factor that may also control sibling fighting is that from an evolutionary point of view siblings have a stake in each other's survival. If we assume that human behavior is motivated in part by one's own interest in passing along one's genes to future generations, nieces and nephews (one's sibling's children) are one way of accomplishing this goal, although not the best way, which is, of course, through one's own children. Thus, individuals have some self-interest in caring for siblings. Similarly, parents have an equal stake in all their children as each child carries the parents' genes so parents have an interest in controlling violence between siblings. At the same time, however, siblings are rivals for their parents' affection, support, and resources and will find means to get the most for themselves, although in many cultures these means are nonviolent.

Violence involving adult siblings is not a common occurrence around the world. It is mainly in societies with matrilineal descent and matrilocal residence that women are at risk of being beaten by their brothers. In these societies individuals trace their lineage only through their mother's line. At marriage men move to the village or house of the wife's parents, with a woman's brother often a powerful person in the family. In this family situation it is not so much a question of whether a woman will be subject to beatings but rather who will do the beating. When her brother is dominant, he, but not her husband, has the right to beat her. When the husband is dominant, both he and the brother may beat a woman although wife beating is more common. When neither is dominant (21 percent of societies in a sample of 66 matrilineal societies), beatings are not allowed.

Fratricide, while a common theme in myths and folktales around the world (for example, the Biblical tale of Cain and Abel), is also relatively infrequent. It seems to occur most often in two types of cultures, both where brothers are rivals. First, it occurs in agricultural societies where brothers are rivals for the family property owned by the father. In these societies there is also conflict between sons and fathers over the property. Second, fratricide takes place in feudal kingdoms where brothers are rivals for the throne. In other societies, where a man's economic well-being is less tied to the family property or status, fratricide is rare.

Siblingship has also been linked to less conflict in two types of families. It is possible that there is less conflict in polygynous families where the co-wives are sisters than in polygynous families where the women are not sisters. Presumably this is because the sisters grew up in the same home together and thus learned how to get along with each other and are not as rivalrous as unrelated women. Similarly, in the few societies with polyandrous marriage (one woman with two or more husbands at the same time), there is less conflict when the husbands are brothers (fraternal polyandry), as they are more likely to cooperate in economic matters.

Daly, Martin, and Margo Wilson. (1988) *Homicide*.

Levine, Nancy. (1992) "Nyinba." In *Encyclopedia of World Cultures. Volume 3. South Asia*, edited by Paul Hocking, 210–213.

Levinson, David. (1989) *Family Violence in Cross-Cultural Perspective.*

Schlegel, Alice. (1972) *Male Dominance and Female Autonomy.*

SOCIAL CONTROL

In its most general sense, social control refers to the ongoing process through which social order and group cohesion is maintained in a culture. Specifically, it refers to the actual beliefs, practices, and processes, both at the individual and group level, that maintain social order. These are generally referred to as mechanisms of social control. Social control mechanisms have two primary functions. First, they allow for the coordination of human behavior in ways that benefit the group. Second, they restrain individual actions that might be harmful to the group.

In every culture the primary mechanism of social control is the socialization process through which children or new members of the group learn and internalize the basic values, rules, and behaviors one must follow to be a functioning member of the culture. As part of the socialization process, children develop individual or internal mechanisms of social control. Chief among these mechanisms are a fear of retaliation by others, a sense of sin over wrongdoing, and a sense of guilt about one's misbehavior. In many cultures, a fear of supernatural sanction also plays a role in the development of these internal control mechanisms. While there is much cross-cultural variation in the relative importance of these controls, they—along with a person's ability to follow culturally prescribed norms—are major factors in governing individual behavior.

At the group level, people in communities and cultures rely on some combination of six primary social control mechanisms: individual self-control, public opinion, reciprocity, supernatural sanction, retaliation, and formal agencies of authority. Cultures can be differentiated on the basis of whether they rely mainly on coordinate control mechanisms or superordinate control mechanisms. Coordinate control is control by peers in the community and involves various self-help conflict resolution mechanisms such as apology and feuding, threat of supernatural sanction through witchcraft or sorcery, or the use of third parties such as mediators. Superordinate control means that social order is maintained through the actions of culturally recognized authorities such as a council, chief, or courts. Superordinate control consists of superordinate justice and superordinate punishment. Justice means that a third-party legal authority is used to arbitrate a dispute or a violation of a law or norm. Punishment means that the legal authority has the power to render and enforce a judicial decision.

The specific mechanisms of social control used vary widely from one culture to another and are discussed in separate articles throughout this volume. In a more general sense though, there is a patterning of social control mechanisms whereby less economically and politically complex cultures rely more often on coordinate mechanisms while more complex cultures rely more on superordinate mechanisms, especially for serious crimes that threaten the well-being of the group. For example, in many traditional farming communities a murder was settled by the kin of the victim retaliating by killing the murderer, or perhaps settling for the payment of compensation, called "blood money." In modern industrial societies, such revenge is rare; instead the police arrest the alleged killer who is then tried before a court and if found guilty is incarcerated or sometimes executed.

See also BLOOD MONEY; SELF-HELP CONFLICT RESOLUTION.

———

Campbell, Donald T. (1983) "Legal and Primary-Group Social Controls." In *Law, Biology and Culture: The Evolution of Law,* edited by Margaret Gruter and Paul Bohannan, 159–171.

Masamura, Wilfred T. (1977) "Law and Violence: A Cross-Cultural Study." *Journal of Anthropological Research* 33: 388–399.

Newman, Katherine S. (1983) *Law and Economic Organization.*

Whiting, Beatrice B. (1950) *Paiute Sorcery.*

Whiting, John W. M. (1967) "Sorcery, Sin and the Superego: A Cross-Cultural Study of Some Mechanisms of Social Control." In *Cross-Cultural Approaches,* edited by Clelland S. Ford, 147–168.

Socialization of Aggression

Socialization of aggression refers to childrearing practices relating to aggressive behavior toward people, animals, or objects. Aggressive behavior can be overtly condoned or encouraged by parents or other caretakers or it can be disapproved of and discouraged. Children being told to stand up for themselves, to retaliate against aggression, exhorted to win in athletic contests, or told heroic myths are all being socialized to behave competitively and aggressively. Similarly, parents who allow their children to fight with their peers until one wins are also encouraging aggression. In cultures where parents encourage their children to be aggressive, they also encourage their children to be fearless and competitive. Since these three emphases in childrearing often go together, they are sometimes lumped together as a single childrearing goal known as toughness. Fearlessness is the suppression of observable reactions to pain, discomfort, and frightening situations. Competitiveness is an emphasis on winning in games, contests, or other endeavors and often involves parents comparing their child's performance to that of other children. At the same time, in cultures where parents want their children to be aggressive, they are much less concerned about their children being industrious, responsible, obedient, and showing self-control. In some cultures where aggressiveness is highly valued, parents do not just ignore these personality traits, but instead discourage their children from behaving in these ways.

A worldwide survey of from 118 to 148 cultures shows that when the cultures are ranked on a ten-point scale, the majority of cultures are either average or below average in the degree to which parents typically socialize young and older children to act aggressively. Thus, in most cultures, parents and other caretakers expect children to control hostility and aggression. For younger children, only in 10 percent of cultures do parents raise both boys and girls to be aggressive. For older children, the percentage for boys increases to 22 percent and for girls to 13 percent. Why a minority of the world's cultures socialize for aggression is not at all clear. It seems likely that biology plays a role with perhaps genetics and physiological factors such as diet especially important, although these possible causes have yet to be studied systematically cross-culturally.

The social environment in which children are raised is also important. In a sample of 25 cultures from all regions of the world where children are socialized for aggression, 56 percent of the cultures have some or many polygynous families (a man with two or more wives at the same time, all living in the same household or nearby households) and another 28 percent have extended families with polygynous marriage. Thus, the polygynous marriage and family environment seems to push parents to encourage their children to be aggressive, a pattern that carries over into adulthood as polygynous families experience more wife beating and fighting between women than do other types of families. In fact, most of the fighting between women around the world occurs in cultures with polygynous marriage. The underlying cause of this seems to be the intense competition between co-wives and among their children who are half-siblings to one another (they share the same father) for access to the husband's wealth, time, and support. For example, Igbo boys in Nigeria are socialized for aggression by their parents and peers. They are expected to compete with other boys of their age in their play groups and are expected to win, with rewards going to the winner. They are expected to fight with boys of the same age from other villages with victories in these fights bringing respect and friends. Aggression is so important that in the days before full-time schooling, boys went through an initiation rite designed to give them "aggressive medicine." Another factor related to socialization for aggression is warfare. In cultures that are frequently at war, boys especially are often raised to be aggressive and fearless, traits that will make them successful warriors.

There are also, of course, many societies where parents mainly raise their children to be nonaggressive and instead to be cooperative, compliant, and to share. These cultures are often ones that subsist by growing crops that must be shared among members of the community, making compliance and cooperation more important personality traits than aggressiveness, which would be disruptive to the social order.

Maasai warriors in Kenya being shaved during their initiation rite, marking their status as warriors.

For example, the Central Thai, the largest ethnic group in Thailand, stress nonaggression in children and adults. Central Thai parents do not use force or threats to coerce their children and adults rarely attempt to force anyone else to do something against their will. As children get older they are punished for fighting with siblings, with other children, and for offenses such as stealing. At the same time, however, frequent violent tantrums by young children including hitting and kicking their mother are tolerated or only mildly scolded, although never reacted to with violence or rewarded. Such behavior by older children, however, is not tolerated. All of this tends to inhibit the expression of aggression and produces adults who do not act aggressively and who avoid rather than respond to aggression by others.

Aside from a conscious effort by parents or other caretakers to raise children to be aggressive, children can learn to act aggressively in three other ways, although in these situations aggressiveness is not necessarily the parent's objective. First they can imitate the aggressive behavior of their parents or other adults. This is called modeling and is a major way in which children learn to behave. When parents routinely hit their children, the children more often than not grow up into adults who are hostile and aggressive. This often happens even when the parents hit their children to control aggression. Second, infants and children experience considerable frustration in attempting to have their needs meet and react to that frustration by acting aggressively—screaming, crying, biting, hitting, etc. Although frustration does not always lead to aggression, it can and often does, particularly when the needs go unmet or when the aggressive behavior is routinely rewarded by the child getting what he or she wants. Third, in some cultures, infants and children are rejected by their parents and react by becoming hostile, aggressive, or passive aggressive. Rejection can be both emotional and physical or both, with physical rejection and, especially, abuse, often causing aggressive behavior in children that often carries over into adulthood.

See also Combative Sports; Genital Mutilation; Machoism; Painful Initiation Rites; Sex Differences in Aggression.

Barry, Herbert III, and Alice Schlegel. (1980) *Cross-Cultural Samples and Codes.*

Ember, Carol, and Melvin Ember. (1992) "Resource Unpredictability, Mistrust, and War." *Journal of Conflict Resolution* 36: 242–262.

Piker, Steven I. (1983) *An Examination of Character and Socialization in a Thai Peasant Community.*

Rohner, Ronald P. (1975) *They Love Me, They Love Me Not.*

Uchendu, Victor C. (1965) *The Igbo of Southeast Nigeria.*

Song Duels

Song duels are a form of duel in which a dispute is brought to public attention and resolved through the communication of grievances and the disparagement of the alleged wrongdoer's behavior in the form of songs written and publicly performed for that purpose. Song duels are one of a number of conflict resolution mechanisms used by the Eskimo and Inuit of North America. Song duels are evidently not part of the conflict resolution repertoire of any other cultures around the world, although a similar though less formal and dramatic custom is used by the Mapuche of Chile. As described in the song of one Eskimo participant, the weapon in a song duel is "the little sharp words, like the wooden splinters which I hack off with my ax." (Rasmussen 1929: 235).

Although there is variation from one Inuit group to another, song duels are used to settle disputes over a wide range of matters, with only murder not usually dealt with in this way. In some Inuit cultures in north-central Canada, song contests are a normal component of friendship and a form of entertainment, with song duels a specialized form of the contests.

Songs are used by the participants to state or deny the grievance, set forth the facts, offer other information—whether true or not—that they think relevant to the alleged grievance, and criticize the behavior and personality of the opponent. The songs are often written for the duel or an already known song may sometimes be used. Both the song and its performance must follow a highly conventionalized style. Generally, the men write and perform their own songs, although a grievant might sometimes hire an especially creative writer or skilled performer to sing on his behalf. Among the Netsilik Inuit, the men write the songs that are then performed by their wives, with the husband providing dance and drumming accompaniment.

Disparaging the behavior and personality of one's opponent is a major part of the duel and any aspect of the other's life—past or present—is a fair target for attack. Various techniques, including direct charges of wrongdoing, innuendo, mockery, burlesque, mimicry, dancing, taunting, self-deprecation, irony, and insult might be used by opponents to attack each other. Each is required to listen to the other's song, responding only at the appropriate break points. Neither is allowed to display anger, either while performing or listening. The duels are always public events performed before the opponents' families and other members of the local community. The outcome is determined by the audience's response to the songs or by the inability of one participant to continue. Factors influencing the audience's decision are the creativity of the song, the singer's skill, and sometimes the facts as set forth in the songs. Once a winner is determined, the dispute is considered settled (the winner is not entitled to any compensation) and the participants are expected to remain friendly. Sometimes, one party is not pleased by the outcome, and then the matter is likely to be settled by a fight. Most song duels are single events that resolve the dispute quickly. Others, however, might go on for years or, more often, for a single year or season. Typical elements of the songs used in duels are shown in the following translation of part of a duel between two men, with K feeling wronged because E had married the woman K had divorced and K now wanted back:

K:

Now shall I split off words—little, sharp words
Like the wooden splinters which I hack off with my ax.
A song from ancient times—a breadth of the ancestors
A song impudent of longing—for my wife.
An impudent, black-skinned oaf has stolen her,
Has tried to belittle her.
A miserable wretch who, loves human flesh—
A cannibal from famine days.

E:

Insolence that takes the breath away
Such laughable arrogance and effrontery.
What a satirical song! Supposed to place blame on me.
You would drive fear into my heart!
I who care not about death.
Hi! You sing about my woman who was your wench.
You weren't so loving then—she was much alone.
You forgot to prize her in song, in stout, contest songs.
Now she is mine.
And never shall she visit singing, false lovers.
Betrayer of women in strange households.

K:

Let me too follow the Umiak as kayak man!
To follow the boat with singers
As if I could be afraid!
As if I were possessed of weak-kneed ways!
When I pursue the kayak paddler.
It is not to be wondered at
That he is pleased,
He who has nearly killed his cousin
He who has nearly harpooned his cousin
No wonder that he was so self-satisfied
That he felt such joy.

E:

But I merely laugh at it
But I but make merry over it
That you K are a murderer
That you are jealous from the ground up.
Given to envy
Because you do not have more than three wives,
And you think them too few
So are you jealous.
You should marry them to some other men.
Then you could have what their husbands bring in.
K, because you do not concern yourself with these things
Because your women eat you out of house and home
So you have taken to murdering your fellow men.

Song duels are a highly effective mechanism for managing conflict in small communities such as traditional Inuit villages where cooperation between men and families is vital for the survival of the group. Song duels resolve disputes and prevent further escalation in a number of ways. First, they provide a public forum for the airing and settlement of disputes. Second, they channel what may be very strong feelings about the wrongdoing into other activities such as song writing, rehearsal, and song performance. Third, they provide a socially nonthreatening nondisruptive way of expressing anger and aggression. And fourth, they provide a way of resolving the dispute.

Mapuche women sing at public gatherings to express displeasure with their husbands. Bystanders will then admonish the husband to mend his ways and he will sing in response. Mapuche society is male and husband-dominated and women are not allowed to criticize their husbands directly. Instead, they use songs to express their displeasure and achieve public support for their complaints. For example, a Mapuche wife will sing (Titiev 1974: 212–213):

> I dreamed of a fox.
> It was bad for me,
> But there is no help for me now,
> Since this is the way it turned out to be.

The song implies that her husband is a thief and bystanders will then admonish the husband and ask him to behave in the future. The husband responds with:

> Things are not as bad as you have said,
> My little cousin (wife).
> If I have done anything wrong,
> It's all over now.
> Only on you do my eyes gaze.
> Let everything bad be ended.

Although song duels do not occur in many cultures, song does a play a role in dispute settlement in some other cultures. The Hopi of Arizona, for example, use grievance chants to express their belief that they have been wronged by another. The Tiv of Nigeria use conventionalized drumming and singing to exchange charges of wrongdoing between people in different villages. This exchange of songs, which might expand to include all members of both communities, does not resolve the conflict directly. Rather, the growing scale of the activity eventually forces the two disputants to meet and settle the matter. In the past, it was settled through fighting; more recently, the dispute is more likely to be mediated.

Balikci, Asen. (1970) *The Netsilik Eskimo.*

Black, Robert A. (1967) "Hopi Grievance Chants: A Mechanism of Social Control." In *Studies in Southwestern Ethnolinguistics,* edited by Dell Hymes and William E. Bittle, 54–67.

Bohannan, Paul. (1957) *Justice and Judgment among the Tiv.*

Hoebel, E. Adamson. (1973) *The Law of Primitive Man.*

Rasmussen, Knud. (1929) *Intellectual Culture of the Iglulik Eskimos.* Fifth Tule Expedition, Report 7, no. 1.

Titiev, Mischa. (1974) "Social Singing among the Mapuche." In *Native South Americans: Ethnology of the Least Known Continent,* edited by Patricia J. Lyon, 208–220.

Sorcery

Although some experts treat sorcery and witchcraft as equivalents, they are different phenomena, and in cultures where both occur the people distinguish between them. A witch (a witch is a female; a male witch is called a warlock) is someone who causes harm to another person by simply wishing the harm to take place. A witch has direct access to the supernatural world and can call on the powers of supernatural forces to cause harm to another. Sorcery, on the other hand, requires the use of a sorcerer who through his of her knowledge of formulae and rituals can direct supernatural power. Sorcerers, unlike witches, cannot innately cause supernatural forces to affect the lives of the living.

Beyond how direct their access is to supernatural power, sorcery and witchcraft differ in other important ways. First, they are found mostly in different cultures. In a survey of 137 cultures, in 47 percent people believed that sorcery was an important cause of illness, in 14 percent people believed that witchcraft was an important cause, in 4 percent people believed that both were important, and in 35 percent people did not believe that either was important. Second, sorcery and witchcraft are found in cultures in different parts of the world. Beliefs in witchcraft as a source of illness predominate in cultures near the Mediterranean Sea, while sorcery beliefs predominate in the New World, in Native American cultures in North and South America. Nearly 50 percent of cultures that attribute illness to sorcery are in the New World. Third, sorcery and witchcraft are found in different types of cultures. Beliefs about sorcery as a cause of illness are found mostly in relatively simple cultures—those with no indigenous writing system, small communities, and an economy based on foraging or horticulture (large-scale gardening). Witchcraft attribution, on the other hand, is found more often in more complex cultures with larger settlements and agriculture. Fourth, unlike witchcraft, sorcery can be used by anyone. A person can become a sorcerer by learning the spells, formulae, incantations, and so on or can hire a known sorcerer. This suggests that sorcery is more likely to flourish in cultures where people have relatively equal access to the supernatural world. This is more typical of relatively simple cultures where there is less social inequality in all spheres of life. Fifth, witchcraft causes only harm while sorcery can be used not only to cause harm, but to cure or to benefit others in various ways. Thus, a witch might cause someone to fall ill or die because witches are intrinsically evil but to cause harm a sorcerer must do so intentionally. While attention is often called to harm caused by sorcery, it seems that sorcerers in most cultures more of-

The victims of sorcery and witchcraft often require the services of a ritual specialist to reverse the harm.

ten use their skills to do good than harm. Most of the sorcerer's work centers on treating illness, not on causing illness. This is especially true in cultures where sorcery is believed to be a major cause of illness, as sorcery is also the major way to cure illness. Sorcerers who cure are usually called medicine men or shamans.

Sorcery is found primarily in cultures that rely on coordinate control to maintain social order and which do not have agencies of superordinate control. Coordinate control means that conflict is resolved through the direct action of the persons involved such as through retaliation, apology, avoidance, etc. Superordinate control means that social order is maintained through the actions of culturally recognized authorities such as a council, chief, or courts. Sorcery acts as a coordinate control in that it causes individuals to pause before causing harm to others for fear that the other person will retaliate by using sorcery to cause them to become ill, have an accident, or even die.

An example of the fear that the threat of sorcery causes is provided by the Toba of Argentina, where sorcery is practiced both in the rural and urban communities. The Toba believe that a sorcerer can cause death through the use of contagious magic, which involves the ritual treatment of physical items associated with the victim—for example, sweat on pieces of clothing, urine, hair, or a cigarette butt. The object is mixed with other objects of magical importance and then burned or buried, causing the victim to become ill and eventually (usually within a month) die. Death is usually inevitable, although the victim can undo the magic by finding a shaman who can "see" the person causing the victim to fall ill. Additionally, a person dying from sorcery can get revenge by identifying the person causing his death just before he dies and then he dies knowing that his death will be avenged. Given the wholesale pattern of aggression and counteraggression sorcery can cause, it is not surprising that the Toba and other cultures prefer to emphasize the beneficial effects of sorcery and use it only selectively to cause harm. In most cultures, the threat of sorcery is enough to maintain social order.

See also EVIL EYE; SUPERNATURAL AGGRESSION; WITCHCRAFT.

Miller, Elmer. (1980) *Harmony and Dissonance in Argentine Toba Society.*

Murdock, George Peter. (1980) *Theories of Illness: A World Survey.*

Whiting, Beatrice B. (1950) *Paiute Sorcery.*

Whiting, John W. M. (1967) "Sorcery, Sin and the Superego: A Cross-Cultural Study of Some Mechanisms of Social Control." In *Cross-Cultural Approaches,* edited by Clelland S. Ford, 147–168.

SUICIDE

Suicide can be either individualistic or institutionalized. Individualistic suicide is motivated by personal factors such as revenge, quarrels, depression, grief, or shame. Institutionalized suicide is approved of or perhaps required by the social group. Well-known examples include hara-kiri, *tsumebara* (enforced hara-kiri), kamikaze, and *raidon* in Japan and suttee (widow sacrifice or suicide) in India. While Westerners view kamikaze and *raidon* as suicide, the pilots (airplane and submarine, respectively) did not believe they were committing suicide; rather they saw themselves as killing enemy soldiers and believed that their own souls were immortal.

Hara-kiri, when not voluntary, is a form of a particular type of suicide known as judicial suicide. Judicial suicide is a type of capital punishment in that a person who is found guilty of a capital crime is forced to kill himself as punishment. Judicial suicide is quite rare with instances reported in only about 8 percent of cultures. It is found only in complex societies with a strong centralized government headed by a powerful monarch or chief who can force a criminal to kill himself. Feudal Japan fits this model as do the Ashanti in Africa and the Trobriand Islanders and Tikopia in Oceania, all of which had judicial suicide. In feudal Japan, the method was through ritual disembowelment with a ceremonial sword, while Trobrianders jumped from a coconut palm tree and Tikopeans paddled out to sea to drown themselves.

Because people often attempt to conceal suicides for personal or religious reasons and because they are hesitant to talk about such matters with outsiders, information on the frequency of suicide is notably unreliable. It is impossible to measure how many societies have suicide and how many do not. And, it is equally difficult to measure the frequency of suicide in a given culture. For example, in a survey of 186 cultures, information about suicide frequency could be obtained for only 47 percent of the cultures, with 4 percent having much suicide, 13 percent a moderate level, and 30 percent very little. The difficulty involved in reliably counting suicides is indicated by comparing these percentages to those obtained in another survey of 35 societies in which suicide was considered frequent in 35 percent, moderate in 37 percent, and rare in 28 percent of the cultures.

Cultures vary in the degree to which they consider suicide to be a wrong—a crime or a sin—or to be acceptable. Unlike U.S. culture, where suicide is generally disapproved of, many cultures classify different types of suicide as either wrong or acceptable. Among the Ashanti of Africa, suicide is treated as a capital crime except in special circumstances, when it is considered honorable. Honorable suicides include killing oneself in war to prevent capture, to accompany a master or mistress to the hereafter, or to remove personal dishonor. Otherwise, the Ashanti believe that a person who commits suicide does so to avoid trial and punishment for committing a crime. But the individual does not escape a trial and punishment, as the corpse is tried, found guilty, and beheaded. The beheading prevents the spirit of the deceased from harming the living, such harm being the basic reason that suicide is considered a capital offense.

Both sociocultural and psychological explanations have been used to explain individualistic suicide cross-culturally. Many sociological explanations are based on French sociologist Emile Durkheim's research in the 1800s, which suggested that suicide was more likely to occur in social groups that were loosely organized and whose members felt alienated. While this formulation might hold for the modern world or nineteenth-century Europe, in non-Western societies it seems that those who kill themselves are people who feel isolated within a closely knit society.

Psychological explanations stress individual motives, especially feelings of anger and the need to get revenge, even if that revenge is achieved through turning one's anger on oneself. Cultural anthropologist Raoul Naroll sought to combine the sociological and psychological explanations into a single explanation, which he called the thwarting disorientation theory of suicide—"thwarting disorientation situations in which a victim blames a person for the victim's loss of social ties, tend to cause suicide." In a sample of 58 cultures, this seems to be the cause, with suicide found more often in cultures where couples do not have free choice in selecting a spouse, divorce for men is easy, wives are often beaten, witches are feared, men get drunk and fight, homicide is common, and the group is often at war with other groups. All of these are situations that might break one's social ties to others or to the community. In addition to thwarting disorientation situations, revenge also plays a role. For example, in rural Taiwan, when a woman marries she leaves her childhood home and moves into her husband's childhood home. There she is forced to compete with her mother-in-law and submit to her wishes. The highest suicide rates for Taiwanese women occurs when the women are in their early twenties, the time period when they marry. A young woman may drink poison, throw herself beneath a train, or leap from a bridge. She is motivated partly by a need to escape a difficult social situation and also by revenge, for it is believed that the ghosts of those who commit suicide will not give up until they bring tragedy to those responsible.

Shame also plays a role in suicide for revenge. Among the Lusi-Kaliai people of Papua New Guinea, women who are beaten by their husbands for what they believe are unfair reasons feel terrible shame and powerlessness and seek revenge by killing themselves. The same situation may apply in contemporary North America where the most frequent event preceding suicide by women is beatings by their husbands.

While suicide may often result from broken social ties, suicide, or at least failed attempts, can also help restore or create ties. Among the !Kung of Botswana, for example, an unhappy young wife might express her feelings by threatening to kill herself. This brings her unhappiness to the attention of other women who rally to offer support.

See also SELF-PUNISHMENT; SUTTEE.

Counts, Dorothy Ayers, Judith K. Brown, and Jacquelyn C. Campbell, eds. (1992) *Sanctions and Sanctuary: Cultural Perspectives on the Beating of Wives.*

Ember, Carol R., and Melvin Ember. (1992) "Warfare, Aggression, and Resource Problems: Cross-Cultural Codes." *Behavior Science Research* 26: 169–226.

Masamura, Wilfred T. (1977) "Social Integration and Suicide: A Test of Durkheim's Theory." *Behavior Science Research* 12: 251–269.

Naroll, Raoul. (1969) "Cultural Determinants and the Concept of the Sick Society." In *Changing Perspectives in Mental Illness,* edited by Stanley C. Plog and Robert B. Edgerton, 128–155.

Otterbein, Keith F. (1986) *The Ultimate Coercive Sanction: A Cross-Cultural Study of Capital Punishment.*

Rattray, R. S. (1929) *Ashanti Law and Constitution.*

Shostak, Marjorie. (1981) *Nisa: The Life and Words of a !Kung Woman.*

Smith, David H., and Linda Hackathorn. (1982) "Some Social and Psychological Factors Related to Suicide in Primitive Societies: A Cross-Cultural Comparative Study." *Suicide and Life-Threatening Behavior* 12: 195–211.

Wolf, Margery. (1972) *Women and the Family in Rural Taiwan.*

Supernatural Aggression

Supernatural aggression is the belief that supernatural beings cause harm to the living. This harm is most often illness or death but may also take other forms such as the ruining of crops, the prevention of rainfall, or destruction of property. A belief in supernatural aggression is similar to a belief in the harmful effects of sorcery, witchcraft, and the evil eye. The major difference is that in supernatural aggression the supernatural spirit acts directly on the living, while in the other three forms supernatural action is indirect through other human beings such as a witch, sorcerer, or a person envious of your success.

Some individuals in all cultures believe that supernatural beings can and will affect the lives of the living. In general, the supreme deity and major deities in all religious belief systems are believed by their adherents to be benevolent, although they are sometimes also believed to cause harm, especially to evildoers. Other types of supernatural beings such as ancestor spirits, ghosts, nature spirits, deceased kin, and lesser gods are more likely to be seen as either benevolent or harmful. For example, in rural Korea there are two categories of spirits. Ancestor spirits are thought to be helpful and promote the welfare of the individual and the kinship group. A second category of vaguely defined spirits, however, is believed to be mostly harmful and is feared as the cause of misfortune, illness, and death.

Across the cultures of the world, beliefs about the influence of spirits can take one of six basic forms:

1. Neutral—no influence on the living
2. Undifferentiated—general belief in their having some influence
3. Malicious-capricious—spirits act arbitrarily and may cause harm
4. Punishing—spirits punish wrongs and are never helpful
5. Rewarding-punishing—spirits are mostly helpful but will punish serious wrongs
6. Benevolent-rewarding—spirits give help and reward good deeds

Rewarding-punishing is the most common type, being typical of 40 percent of cultures; 28 percent have neutral or undifferentiated spirit beliefs, 21 percent malicious-capricious, and 11 percent benevolent-rewarding. In no culture are all spirits believed to be only punishing, although in some, such as the Chukchee of Siberia, spirits are mostly believed to cause harm. Cultures like these are typically found in extremely harsh climates and their belief in punishing spirits is evidently a projection of the uncertain and punishing environment in which they live.

In most cultures, people believe that the harm most often caused by spirits is illness and death. And in nearly all cultures (137 out of 139 cultures in one survey) at least some types of illness are attributed to the actions of supernatural spirits. This belief is found in all regions of the world and is especially strong in cultures in East Asia and the Mediterranean region. Another survey indicates that in 53 percent of traditional non-Western cultures, all or most illness is attributed to supernatural forces, including witchcraft and sorcery. However, strong supernatural aggression beliefs, witchcraft attribution, and sorcery mainly occur in different cultures—if people in a culture believe strongly in one of these, they will probably not believe strongly in the other two. This suggests that the three beliefs are alternative forms of the same basic belief in the potentially harmful effect of the supernatural world. Of course, while a specific culture may be characterized as having a strong belief in the harmful potential of spirits, this does not mean that all people in the culture share the belief nor that they believe that they will be harmed. For example, the Central Thai believe strongly in the potential harm that might be caused by ghosts. But, the majority of people in rural villages say that they personally have not been harmed by ghosts.

A belief in supernatural aggression is accompanied by culturally prescribed means to ward off the harm that will result from that aggression and to control and reverse its effects. Again, there is much variation from culture to culture, with the major means being paying proper respect and homage to the appropriate spirits, praying for intervention by benevolent spirits, using methods for treating illness that remove the cause of the illness, and avoiding places where spirits might exist. Most importantly, people avoid supernatural aggression by following the norms and laws of their culture, as it is wrongdoers who are punished most frequently and most severely. In this way a belief in supernatural aggression acts as a powerful mechanism of social control.

A horseshoe hung over the door is one type of protective object found around the world used to ward off evil.

A belief in supernatural aggression comes from one's childhood experiences. In cultures where infants and children are little indulged, encouraged to take care of themselves, and even neglected, the supernatural world is more likely to be perceived as hostile and aggressive than in cultures where children are looked after and nurtured. These patterns support the more general psychoanalytic interpretation that religious beliefs are to some extent a projection of childhood fantasies about the nature of the world as being either hostile or friendly and that these beliefs are passed on from one generation to the next.

See also EVIL EYE; SORCERY; WITCHCRAFT.

Justinger, Judith M. (1978) *Reaction to Change: A Holocultural Test of Some Theories of Religious Movements.*

Levinson, David, and Martin J. Malone. (1980) *Toward Explaining Human Culture.*

Murdock, George Peter. (1980) *Theories of Illness: A World Theory.*

Schaefer, James M. (1973) *A Hologeistic Study of Family Structure and Sentiment, Supernatural Beliefs, and Drunkenness.*

Tatje, Terence A., and Francis L. K. Hsu. (1969) "Variations in Ancestor Worship and Their Relation to Kinship." *Southwestern Journal of Anthropology* 25: 153–172.

SUTTEE

Suttee (*Sati* in Sanskrit) is the now-extinct custom found in Hindu India that required or forced a widow to burn herself to death on the funeral pyre of her deceased husband at the funeral or shortly thereafter. A related custom was *jauhar,* in which the wife of a warrior killed herself in anticipation of his death in combat. Suttee was prohibited by the Mughal rulers of north India and banned by the British in 1829, although occurrences were reported into the twentieth century and are still occasionally reported in the daily press. Other than when it began to decline and that it was practiced by cultures in both north and south India among such diverse groups as the Tamil in what is the modern state of Tamil Nadu and the Brahmins in Bengali (now mostly the nation of Bangladesh), little is know with certainty about the practice. Some experts believe that it originated in south India and then spread north, others suggest a northern origin, and still others argue that it may have originated independently in the north and south. Wherever it began, it began prior to the Christian era and was present in northwest India by the first century A.D. Some archaeological evidence suggests an earlier presence in south India, although this is not certain. Suttee stones memorializing deceased women are found all over India and have been dated to the sixth century A.D. in the south.

The reason for suttee is unclear. It was evidently confined mainly to warlike groups, leading some to suggest that it was part of a warrior cultural complex that required a warrior to prevent his possessions from falling into the hands of the enemy. Other interpretations stress the need for grave goods to accompany the deceased into the next life, a desire to control women's sexuality, and a desire to control the purity of the kinship group by preventing a widow from remarrying outside of it.

Suttee also occurred in conjunction with another custom that required a widow to live the remainder of her life in a condition of great austerity. The following poem lists the options available to a Tamil widow in the past:

> O you many great men!
> O you many great men!
> O you many great men
> with your wicked schemes
> to prevent me—
> you say "stop"
> but you will never tell me to go.
> I am no woman to suffer,
> eating as food velai leaves
> cooked in tamarind

with white sesame paste,
and a squeezed out ball of cooked rice,
set down in the middle of a leaf,
untouched by abundant, fragrant ghee.
like seed plucked
from a cucumber striped like a squirrel,
split by a sword.
I am no woman to suffer,
laying down without a mat
to sleep on a bed of stones.
The pyre of black wood kindled in the burning ground
may be frightening to you,
but to me
since my broad-shouldered husband has died
a pond of cool waters
where lotuses loose full petals from buds
and that fire
are the same.

Although suttee has disappeared, many of the austerity restrictions remain among Tamil Brahmins, including shaving the head, eating only bland foods, wearing a single-color sari, a ban on sexual relations, and keeping separate from others at festivals. Other Tamil caste groups have similar, though less restrictive customs.

See also AGGRESSION IN REACTION TO DEATH; SELF-PUNISHMENT; SUICIDE.

Reynolds, Holly B. (1982) *To Keep the Tali Strong: Women's Rituals in Tamil Nadu, India.*

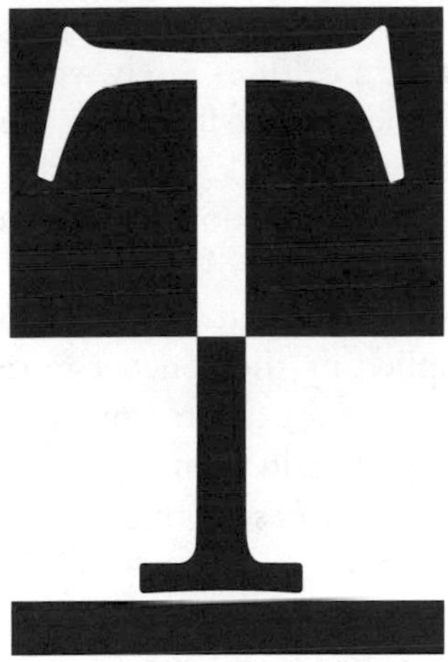

Torturing the Enemy

In the aftermath of combat, the victorious side (or sometimes both sides) is faced with the question of what to do with enemy captives. The captives are usually enemy warriors but may also be noncombatants, including women and children. In most cultures there are set rules that govern the treatment of captives, although the rules may sometimes be broken in special circumstances. For example, a culture that usually releases captives may kill them instead if it believes that the enemy did the same in a previous war or battle.

Cross-culturally, the variety of treatments afforded captives includes releasing them, ransoming them back to their group, selling them to a third group, enslaving them, killing them on the spot, sacrificing them, integrating them into the group through adoption or marriage, and torturing them. There is no general cross-cultural patterning to the treatment of war prisoners. For example, the warlike Iroquois tortured some captives but more commonly they adopted them into the families and kin groups of the community. In the late 1660s, the Seneca (one of five nations of the Iroquois Confederation) had natives of eleven different nations in their communities and the Oneida had more foreign-born residents than native-born Oneidas. On the other hand, the peaceful Papago, when forced to fight to defend themselves, generally killed all enemy warriors and took their scalps; women who were captured were quickly traded to other groups.

Torturing may be done as a prelude to death or done so that the captives survive and are then enslaved or returned to their group. In a sample of 48 cultures, half reportedly tortured captives while the other half did not. In cultures where captives were not tortured, immediate killing or enslavement were the two most likely fates of captives. The most frequent tortures were scalping, beating, burning, cutting off a limb, burying alive, cutting the person into pieces, and, less frequently, raping, starving, spearing, and crippling.

While found in all parts of the world, torturing the enemy is largely a New World custom. Of the 24 societies in the sample of 48 where it is reported as being practiced, 10 are in North America and 6 in South America. The remainder are in Oceania, Asia, and North Africa. Most reports of torture in American Indian cultures date to prereservation times in North America and prepacification times in South America and describe the torture of both Indians from other groups and of whites. While it is probable that torture of the enemy did take place, it is also likely that some of these reports exaggerated both the frequency and cruelty of the torture. Some Indian groups tortured some captives and treated others differently. For example, as noted above, the Iroquois both tortured and adopted other warriors, some of whom might be selected by Iroquois women as husbands. The Mescalero chose between killing, torturing, or enslaving captives.

Torturing the enemy is one component of a complex of related customs centered on waging war and the pursuit of military glory by warriors. Torturing is usually practiced in cultures that wage war frequently, in which warfare is the primary means warriors have of gaining prestige, property, or revenge, and where the goal of war is to gain property, territory, or destroy the enemy. This warfare complex was typical of many American Indian cultures in the past who were under pressure and attack of various kinds from Europeans moving into their traditional territories.

See also Cannibalism; Counting Coup; Head-Hunting; Human Sacrifice; Military Glory; Scalping.

Abler, Thomas S. (1993) "Iroquois: The Tree of Peace and the War Kettle." In *Portraits of Culture: Ethnographic Profiles,* edited by Melvin Ember, Carol R. Ember, and David Levinson.

Patterson, Orlando. (1982) *Slavery and Social Death.*

Underhill, Ruth. (1946) *Papago Indian Religion.*

Total War

Total war and genocide are the two major forms of mass killing that are undertaken by entire societies. Total war—as compared to other forms of war or conflict between societies—is characterized by the use of all available resources in waging war, a high level of destruction and loss of life, and the goal, or real possibility, that one of the warring societies will not survive. Throughout human history total wars have often been religious wars, with the Crusades and the Thirty Years' War as classic examples.

Histories of human warfare have portrayed non-Western cultures as wagers of total war against one another. In fact, the opposite is true, as non-Western cultures rarely waged total war against one another and following Western contact were themselves likely to be the victims of both total war and genocide. One reason that non-Western cultures did not wage total wars with one another is that they rarely had the resources implied by the concept to destroy one another. Perhaps for this reason and for others, a survey of warfare in 50 non-Western cultures indicates that total destruction of the enemy was rarely the primary goal of war. Only 8 percent of the societies surveyed waged war mainly to subjugate the enemy and just 4 percent did so to take enemy land. The remaining 88 percent went to war to plunder the enemy, to seek honor for warriors, for revenge, or in defense. Of these 50 cultures, 60 percent ended war through diplomatic negotiations, suggesting that destroying the enemy was not the primary goal. Additionally, many non-Western cultures raided rather than engaged in fully organized war. In general, raiding required only limited use of available resources for war and was carried out for specific purposes such as taking livestock or slaves. Of the various non-Western cultures that have been described as warlike—such as the Iroquois, Aztec, Plains Indians, and Zulu—none engaged in total war. In the case of the Iroquois, Plains Indians, and Zulu, their frequent involvement in wars and readiness for war were to a large extent the result of Western influence.

Rather than being the perpetrators of total war against each other, non-Western cultures were more often the victims of total war or genocide, especially during the opening decades of colonial expansion into the New World, South Africa, and Australia. The Herero of what is now Botswana, for example, were reduced from a population of 80,000 to about 15,000 by the German military in 1904. In the Caribbean, the native Carib and Arawak tribes who first encountered Columbus and subsequent colonizers were destroyed completely through a

This Soviet rocket displayed in 1965 is the type of weaponry capable of causing mass damage.

combination of genocide, epidemics of European diseases such as smallpox and influenza, and total war. Similarly, in North and South America, the earliest contacts between the Portuguese, Spanish, and English and the indigenous cultures were often attempts by the former to destroy the latter.

See also Feuding; Genocide; Omnicide; Raiding; War.

Bridgman, Jon M. (1981) *The Revolt of the Hereros.*

Carroll, Berenice A. (1968) *Design for Total War: Arms and Economics in the Third Reich.*

Fuller, J.F.C. (1961) *The Conduct of War: 1789–1961.*

Markusen, Eric. (1989) "Genocide and Total War: A Preliminary Comparison." In *Genocide and the Modern Age,* edited by Isidor Wallimann and Michael N. Dobkowski, 97–123.

Otterbein, Keith F. (1989) *The Evolution of War.* 3d edition.

Treatment of War Captives

See Military Glory; Raiding for Slaves; Torturing the Enemy.

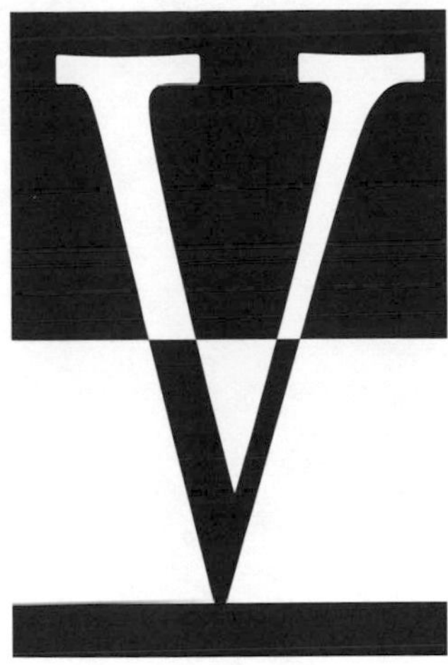

Verbal Aggression

Verbal aggression is behavior designed to cause harm to another person through the use of speech. Verbal aggression can be either overt or covert. In overt verbal aggression the aggressor confronts the other person directly, usually for the purpose of airing the aggressor's grievance, settling the grievance though competition, or publicly embarrassing or shaming the other person. Overt verbal aggression includes song duels, word duels, harangues, sarcastic and derogatory humor, and insults. In covert verbal aggression, the aggressor attempts to harm the other person privately, by gossiping about him or her or by accusing the person of witchcraft or sorcery.

Verbal aggression is a cultural universal; at least some forms, such as arguing, gossiping, insulting, and expressing anger in other ways with words, are found in all cultures. There is some debate as to whether verbal aggression should be seen as a form of aggression or whether it is should be viewed as a form of behavior that is used in place of physical aggression.

Cross-culturally, the use of verbal aggression varies widely. In some cultures, verbal aggression is the major means through which anger and aggression are expressed within the family and community. When used to express anger directly and to resolve a conflict, verbal aggression can be viewed as a powerful social control mechanism that prevents conflicts from becoming violent. However, if such means as accusations of witchcraft or sorcery are used, the result is often retaliation, mistrust, hostility, and violence. In this context, verbal aggression is less a mechanism of social control but rather a component of a culture pattern of conflict resolution through causing harm to others.

In other cultures, verbal aggression is the preferred method of expressing anger, although physical violence might also occur, depending on the cause of the conflict, its severity, and the nature of the relationship between the parties involved. For example, the !Kung use jokes, insults, and mild teasing to express anger or displeasure with someone else, as well as loud screaming arguments. These generally enable individuals to express anger and to air grievances, although they do not always work and are not relevant for all types of grievances, some of which are resolved only through fights and sometimes homicide. In some cultures, the use of verbal aggression to resolve conflicts is highly ritualized, as in song duels, gossiping, and harangues.

See also Gossip; Harangue; Humor; Insults; Joking Relationships; Song Duels; Sorcery; Witchcraft; Word Duels.

Marshall, Lorna. (1961) "Sharing, Talking, and Giving." *Africa* 31: 231–249.

War

While there is no single definition of war that is accepted by all experts, nearly all definitions include most of the following components: (1) warfare is a form of human conflict, (2) it involves the use of organized force, (3) it occurs between politically autonomous communities, (4) it is purposeful, (5) it involves the use of weapons, and (6) it involves the killing of the enemy.

In applying these six criteria to conflict within and between cultures around the world, three types of war can be distinguished: feuding, internal war, and external war. These are defined by anthropologist Keith Otterbein (1968a: 93) as follows:

> **Feuding.** A type of armed combat occurring within a political community during which, if a homicide occurs, the kin of the deceased take revenge through killing the offender or any member of his kin group.
>
> **Internal War.** Warfare between political communities within the same cultural unit.
>
> **External War.** Warfare between culturally different political communities, i.e., political communities that are not members of the same cultural unit. There are two aspects of external war that can be measured separately: political communities of a cultural unit can either attack or be attacked by culturally different political communities.

Central to this conceptualization of warfare is the presence of a political community. A political community is a group of people whose sense of membership in the group is based minimally on common residence and the presence of an official responsible for announcing group decisions. Political communities take a variety of forms, with the most common being bands composed of several families, villages, kinship groups (such as lineages or clans), tribes, nations, and alliances of any of these. As this list suggests, political communities vary widely in size and complexity across cultures. For example, for the Yanomamö, the basic political community is the village, which is composed of about 100 individuals who are often at war with other Yanomamö villages. For the Somali, political communities include the six major Somali clans, each of which is composed of several hundred thousand members, and subclans within each of the six clans, each with tens of thousands of members. And, for the United States during the Civil War, the political communities were the Union (North) and the Confederacy (South), while during World Wars I and II the operative political community was the nation that was at war with other nations. Culturally different political communities—the key element in defining armed combat as external war—are ethnic units whose members mostly live in the same region and who speak a language distinct from neighboring societies. In addition, they usually have a distinct name for their ethnic group and see themselves as being different from other groups.

One of the primary advantages of Otterbein's classification scheme is that it allows us to distinguish among different types of warfare by focusing on the relationship between the groups at war. Perhaps the one limitation of the scheme is that it does not easily allow for the classification of wars of ethnic separatism, the most common type of war in the world today. In these conflicts, such as that between the Tamils and Sinhalese in Sri Lanka or those involving the Kurds in Iraq, Iran, and Turkey or the Basques in Spain, the conflict can be thought of as either internal or external, depending on the point of view of the combatants. For example, from the Sinhalese perspective, the Tamil are a minority group within Sri Lankan society and therefore the conflict is an internal war. From the Tamil perspective, however, they are culturally distinct from the Sinhalese and their goal in fighting is to achieve political autonomy, suggesting that the conflict is more like an external war. This distinction between internal and external war is important in the contemporary world, as other nations or international bodies such as the United Nations are more likely to intervene to end the fighting and negotiate a settlement when the war is external than when the war is internal.

Any discussion of war in non-Western cultures must consider the influence of Western contact on the nature of war in indigenous societies. This influence was exerted by colonial powers such as Germany, Portugal, the Netherlands, France, Spain, and England on the native peoples of the New World, Africa, Oceania, and southeast Asia. In all these places, Western influence eventually led to a reduction in the frequency of, or an end to, war. However, cessation of war was often preceded by other changes in the types of war waged, the frequency of war, the groups people fought with, the reasons for making war, and the manner in which wars were fought. Because Western influence on indigenous warfare was so dramatic, so rapid, and so widespread, we have few firsthand accounts of purely indigenous warfare. Instead, most of our knowledge of native warfare is based on descriptions of traditional patterns modified to some extent by Western contact.

Frequency and Nature of War

A number of surveys have attempted to measure the frequency of warfare in non-Western cultures around the world. Because the different surveys use different definitions of war (for example, some lump feuding with internal war, while others ignore feuding), the survey findings are not in complete agreement; however, they are close enough to give us a general sense of the frequency of war around the world. Internal wars were fought frequently or continually by political communities in about 55 percent of societies and not fought or rarely fought in about 45 percent. External wars were fought frequently (more than once every ten years) by about 60 percent of cultures and fought very frequently (at least once per year) by about 35 percent. About 60 percent of societies frequently attacked other societies while about 55 percent were frequently attacked. The nature of these three types of war—internal, external-attacking, external-attacked—is made clear by the warfare practices of three societies: the Jivaro of Ecuador, who until very recently were regularly embroiled in internal and external wars; the Orokaiva of Melanesia, who mainly attacked other societies; and the Papago of North America, who were often attacked and fought only to defend themselves.

The Jivaro fought both internal and external wars. Internally, a common pattern would involve a man from one village organizing and leading a raid against a man in another village in order to kill that man for revenge. Externally, Jivaro men would raid other societies, such as the Achuara and Aguaruna, to kill and take heads in order to acquire soul power (*arutam*) and to achieve positions of status and power in Jivaro society. While intervillage raids were confined to killing a specific individual, intersocietal raids were usually directed at an entire household, with the men killed and their heads taken and with the women abducted. Occasionally, a warrior was so well-known that he might be hired as a mercenary by a neighboring society to lead a raid against a third society.

For the Jivaro, the possession of *arutam* is vital because a man with an adequate amount of it is impervious to harm by others, while one whose power is depleted or lost is easy prey for a raiding party. Additionally, the Jivaro believe it is the acquisition of new soul power, called *kakarma,* that motivates men to keep killing. Jivaro warriors raid only when they are sure that the intended victim's power has been stolen. Thus warriors engage in preraid rituals to steal the victim's power and look for signs, such as illness, that the victim's power has been stolen. Acquiring the power from the victim not only adds to one's own power but also "locks in" the power of the existing soul.

Closely tied to the goal of acquiring soul power is the goal of achieving status within Jivaro society as a fearless and successful warrior, called a *kakaram,* meaning "powerful" or "the possessor of soul power." For the majority of Jivaro men, warfare is a major activity throughout their lives. A man's military career begins as a participant in intervillage raids for revenge and intertribal raids for heads. If he is successful, he is then expected to lead an intervillage revenge raid. If again successful, his reputation spreads and other men will ask him to organize and lead raids against their enemies. This brings him the status of a *kakaram* and allows him to take a leadership role in the community and an assertive stance in his dealings with others. It also might mean that he is feared by others and that neither he nor his community is likely to be attacked, affording him the higher status of *untä kakaram* (big powerful one). Finally, he reaches the highest status when even his enemies ask for his help in killing their enemies. While *kakaram* status is not passed on from father to son, *kakaram* will often train their sons to be warriors and take them on raids.

The Orokaiva of Melanesia provide an example of a society that mainly waged war by raiding other societies. Prior to pacification, the Orokaiva were frequently at war. While internal wars between clans sometimes took place to exact revenge following a dispute, such wars were infrequent and produced few casualties when compared to the external wars that were waged against other societies. This type of war was called *isoro* and usually took the form of raids to avenge the killing of an Orokaiva. The raids were often surprise massacres in which as many enemy men, women, and children as possible were killed or taken captive to be killed later. Orokaiva raiding to kill or capture members of other groups was motivated by a number of Orokaiva customs. For example, the widow of a man killed by another tribe had to remain in seclusion until a man was captured from that tribe and killed. It is also possible that sometimes the killing of an enemy was required before a couple could marry or a boy or girl could complete their initiation ceremony. It is also reported that enemies were killed for cannibalism, but since reports of cannibalism in non-Western cultures are often wrong or exaggerated, this possible motivation for war needs to be treated skeptically.

Bravery in warfare was considered a virtue and a notable warrior was called a *koropa-embu* (spearman) or an *ivu-embu* (manly man), while a coward was called an *atoha.* While Orokaiva warfare disappeared before the twentieth century, their warfare ethos lived on well into this century in the form of frequent sham battles between armed villagers and visitors from other villages; these sometimes escalated into spear and club fights that needed to be broken up by the village police officer.

The Papago are an example of a society that is attacked by others but does not attack. Papago farming villages in Arizona and northern Mexico were the frequent target of Apache raids for food, horses, women, children, and other plunder. While the Papago did not raid the Apache, the continual threat of attack required that they prepare for war. Beginning at about 12 years of age, boys were taught to be warriors by old men who recounted to them tales of war and by other men who taught them to use a bow and arrow and to protect themselves with a shield. All men were expected to be warriors, although they took the warrior role reluctantly and saw military service as little more than a duty. However, because defense of the village was vital to group survival, bravery was valued and men who did not fight were classified socially as women. Although they were prepared to fight and did not hesitate to fight to defend themselves and their property, the Papago preferred not to be involved with or to discuss war. Therefore, they either avoided the enemy or killed them quickly, rarely taking captives or any plunder from the battlefield because they believed the enemy to be evil and their possessions to be imbued with evil magic. A warrior's only reward was the scalp of an enemy warrior, which was believed to bring the victor the magical power of the slain warrior. Papago dead were left on the battlefield or burned, contrary to their usual custom of burying the dead, and their wounded were ritually purified. Papago warfare and victory ceremonies focused not on war but instead on bringing rain and crops, the central concern for the Papago. Thus, unlike the Jivaro and Orokaiva, warfare was a necessity for the Papago and was devoid of the ritual and social importance associated with it in these two more warlike cultures.

These three examples of war point to a number of central characteristics of what has been called "primitive war" in non-Western cultures. First, both internal and external war often took the form of surprise raids against an enemy village or community in order to kill the enemy, take some type of plunder (most often people), or both. Second, the casualty rates were often high, and in terms of the size of the societies, higher than often occur in modern warfare. Third, warfare rarely involved societies using all their resources in total war against each other. Instead, it was often community against community or one small war party raiding a single household or village. Fourth, warfare was not an isolated activity, but instead was integrated with other beliefs and customs. Fifth, cultures vary in the extent to which they are involved in internal war, external war, or both.

Causes of War

Consideration of the causes of war involves three issues: (1) the reason or reasons a particular society goes to war at a particular point in time; (2) the factors or processes that perhaps explain why war, as a form of human behavior, exists across cultures; and (3) the factors or processes that perhaps explain the frequency, intensity, and type of war engaged in by a culture. The qualifier "perhaps" is used here to indicate that there is no single "best" or "right" explanation for war as a form of human behavior nor any single factor that completely explains variation among cultures in how war is waged.

The primary reasons a society might go to war (sometimes called the "proximate" causes of war) are: (1) to subjugate and collect tribute; (2) to gain access to land for hunting or grazing of livestock or as a source of food or other resources; (3) to take such plunder as women to use as wives, men to trade or sell as slaves, children to adopt into the society, livestock to replenish or expand existing herds, supernatural power possessed by the enemy (a major reason for headhunting), and material wealth; (4) to capture war trophies or earn war honors such as captives for sacrifice, heads, scalps, coup points, etc.; (5) to seek revenge, usually in response to the killing of a kin or the abduction of women; and (6) to defend oneself, family, kin group, community, or society.

Defense is the basic reason for war, as all cultures that engage in war will fight to defend themselves, even if, like the Papago, they fight for no other reasons. However, societies that fight only in defense are quite rare, accounting for just 3 out of 50 societies in one survey; most societies fight for more than just this one reason. The second most common reason for war is for plunder and to take land, with 78 percent of cultures fighting for this reason. The third most frequent reason is for prestige, common to 38 percent of cultures, with all of these also fighting in defense and most also fighting for plunder and land. Finally, wars for political subjugation are found in 18 percent of societies, with most of these cultures also fighting for plunder, land, and in defense. Societies that fight for political purposes are mainly large societies with a professional military and centralized government powerful enough to control internal conflict and organize and direct societal resources against other societies. Societies of this type include the Thai, Lau Fijians, ancient Hawaiians, Egyptians, Javanese, and Mossi.

As war is nearly a cultural universal (almost all societies engage in war at some time), explanations for war tend to emphasize equally universal aspects of the human experience. One such aspect is the possibility that humans are innately aggressive and that warfare is one expression of that aggressive tendency. A second is that warfare is functional in that it is a mechanism that enables groups to adapt to and survive in their social and physical environment.

Biological explanations take a variety of forms. One is the so-called frustration-aggression hypothesis, which in its original form suggests that frustration causes people to act aggressively. This theory, developed in the 1930s, has undergone considerable revision and is now seen as too limited to explain a phenomenon as complex as war. In the 1960s another set of biological explanations became popular. These suggested that human, or at least male, aggression was the product of aggressive or territorial instincts. These ideas have now been discarded as overly broad and simplistic and have been replaced by sociobiological explanations for war that rest on the premise that individual human beings have a genetic predisposition to behave in ways that increase the likelihood that they will reproduce and pass their genes on to future generations. Within this framework, warfare is seen as one possible mechanism individuals may use to achieve this goal. Warfare can be reproductively beneficial by helping men obtain women to reproduce with, by killing off rivals for resources such as food that are necessary to support offspring and kin, and as a way of acquiring these same resources. Warfare can also be reproductively beneficial by providing a warrior with higher status than other men and thereby affording him greater access to societal resources, such as women, food, and wealth, that allow him to produce and raise more children and, in turn, allows them to do the same.

Functional explanations for war are based on the premise that warfare is a mechanism that societies use to adapt to their environment. One of the primary functions of warfare is to enable a society to cope with problems of resource scarcity that threaten the survival of the group or prevent it from expanding. Resource scarcity might result from overpopulation, environmental disasters such as floods or droughts that destroy food sources, environmental constraints that limit the quantity of natural resources a society can manage, or competition with other societies for scarce resources. For example, frequent warfare between groups in New Guinea is often the result of land shortages, while raiding for cattle in East Africa is often the result of cattle shortages. Warfare enables a society to adapt to this situation by reducing the population through battle deaths and acquiring such scarce resources as land, food, water, women, or slave labor. Warfare might also be psychologically adaptive in that it enables individuals to discharge stress resulting from overpopulation and resource shortages by fighting with outsiders.

While both reproductive fitness (which benefits the individual) and environmental adaptation (which benefits the group) may be two major causes of war in general and provide a framework for understanding war, they are too general to account for the considerable variation in the form, frequency, and intensity of war in cultures around the world. Here such considerations as the size of the society, its type of government, kinship organization, methods of conflict resolution, childrearing practices, and values all may be important. Perhaps the two most important are the nature of relations between groups in a society and the level of control exerted by the central government. When the groups that compose a society, such as villages, clans, or bands, regularly engage in various forms of interaction with each other, such as trade, the exchange of women in marriage, and ceremonial obligations, there is little internal war and a greater likelihood of external war. Similarly, when a society is governed by a strong, centralized government that can control internal conflict and coordinate the collection and use of societal resources, it is more likely to engage in external wars, with internal wars being mostly revolts or riots by segments of the population seeking greater power for themselves or greater freedom from the government. Finally, it should be noted that once a community or society is engaged in war, a variety of factors work to perpetuate the war or a pattern of recurring wars. These factors include revenge (this is very common in internal wars, which often begin out of revenge and continue as a series of revenge-motivated raids), a pattern of conflict resolution that favors responding to violence with violence, and the establishment of a professional military that may encourage war.

See also COMBATIVE SPORTS; ETHNIC CONFLICT; FEUDING; GENOCIDE; HEAD-HUNTING; INTERNAL CONFLICT; MILITARISM; MILITARY GLORY; MILITARY SOPHISTICATION; PACIFICATION; PEACE; PEACEMAKING; RAIDING; TORTURING THE ENEMY; TOTAL WAR; TREATMENT OF WAR CAPTIVES; WESTERN INFLUENCE ON INDIGENOUS WARFARE.

Durham, William H. (1976) "Resource Competition and Human Aggression, Part I: A Review of Primitive War." *Quarterly Review of Biology* 51: 385–415.

Ember, Carol R., and Melvin Ember. (1992) "Resource Unpredictability, Mistrust, and War." *Journal of Conflict Resolution* 36: 242–262.

Ember, Carol R., and Melvin Ember. (1992) "Warfare, Aggression, and Resource Problems: Cross-Cultural Codes." *Behavior Science Research* 26: 169–226.

Ferguson, R. Brian, ed. (1984) *Warfare, Culture and Environment.*

Ferguson, R. Brian. (1990) "Blood of the Leviathan: Western Contact and Warfare in Amazonia." *American Ethnologist* 17: 237–257.

Harner, Michael J. (1973) *The Jivaro: People of the Sacred Waterfalls.*

Koch, Klaus-Friedrich. (1983) "Epilogue. Pacification: Perspective from Conflict Theory." In *The Pacification of Melanesia,* edited by Margaret Rodman and Matthew Cooper, 199–207.

Leavitt, Gregory C. (1977) "The Frequency of Warfare: An Evolutionary Perspective." *Sociological Inquiry* 47: 49–58.

Loftin, Colin K. (1971) *Warfare and Societal Complexity: A Cross-Cultural Study of Organized Fighting in Preindustrial Societies.*

Nammour, Valerie W. (1975) *Drums and Guns: A Cross-Cultural Study of the Nature of War.*

Otterbein, Keith F. (1968) "Cross-Cultural Studies of Armed Combat." *Buffalo Studies* 9: 91–109.

Otterbein, Keith F. (1968) "Internal War: A Cross-Cultural Study." *American Anthropologist* 70: 277–289.

Otterbein, Keith F. (1974) "The Anthropology of War." In *Handbook of Social and Cultural Anthropology*, edited by John J. Honigman, 923–958.

Otterbein, Keith F. (1989) *The Evolution of War.* 3rd edition.

Ross, Marc H. (1985) "Internal and External Conflict and Violence." *Journal of Conflict Resolution* 29: 547–579.

Ross, Marc H. (1986) "A Cross-Cultural Theory of Political Conflict and Violence." *Political Psychology* 7: 427–469.

Turney-High, Harry H. (1949) *Primitive War: Its Practice and Concepts.*

Underhill, Ruth M. (1946) *Papago Indian Religion.*

Vayda, Andrew P. (1976) *War in Ecological Perspective.*

Williams, Francis E. (1930) *Orokaiva Society.*

Western Influence on Indigenous Warfare

As pointed out in the entry of war, contact with Western colonial nations, most importantly Spain, Portugal, Germany, England, France, and the Netherlands, had a great influence on war as waged by indigenous peoples. Over time Western contact in all places led to the cessation of wars waged by indigenous peoples against each other. However, in many places, pacification followed what anthropologist R. Brian Ferguson calls, "warrification," an increase in the frequency and intensity of warfare. In response to Western contact, indigenous warfare changed in frequency, in who fought whom, in why they fought, and how they fought. Western contact also led to the development of new modes of fighting without violence and also disrupted alliances and diplomatic relations among native cultures.

The actual changes that resulted from European contact were determined to some extent by the goals of the Europeans. For example, in Middle America and the North American southwest, the Spanish policy was the total conquest of the native cultures. Thus, the Spanish sought to control the flow of guns to native peoples so as to prevent resistance and rebellions. Conversely, in northern North America, the earliest European settlers included individual traders and trading companies, such as the Hudson's Bay Company, who were interested in exploiting the region and the people for furs. These traders quite willingly supplied the Indians with guns and ammunition and any other goods that would increase the flow of furs. The only groups they were reluctant to arm and provision were those aligned with their European competitors. Similarly, in New Guinea, Europeans whose activities were confined to the coast had little interest in controlling raiding and war among groups in the interior highlands until the twentieth century, when control of the interior became politically important.

Perhaps the most predictable consequence of contact between Europeans and native peoples was war between the two. This was nearly always the case when Europeans wanted to settle or control the land occupied by the indigenous people and made war against them to either kill them or drive them off the land. Much of the warfare that took place for this purpose in the New World and Australia falls within the definitions of total war and genocide. But contact with Europeans did not just lead to war between the settlers and native peoples, it also increased the frequency of war among native peoples, both directly and indirectly. Some of these wars were instigated by Europeans who encouraged and paid native groups to fight other groups in order to pacify frontier territories, to acquire slaves, or to weaken native groups allied with their European competitors. In addition, Indian men in North and South America and native men in Africa, Melanesia, and Southeast Asia were often recruited to serve as messengers, translators, scouts, mercenaries, and soldiers in colonial armies. On the eve of the American Revolution, for example, both the British and the American revolutionaries actively courted the Iroquois, who controlled New York State west of the Hudson, in order to win their support or, short of that, their neutrality. To sum up, the usual direct effect of European contact on warfare frequency was more war by involving native peoples in wars with Europeans, by encouraging war between native peoples, and by creating alliances with natives in wars between European nations.

European contact indirectly influenced the frequency of war through the dramatic reduction of the native populations due to deaths from infectious diseases such as smallpox, measles, and influenza, for which native peoples had no natural immunity; migration; and the availability of trade goods, most importantly guns. The decimation of the native population by disease led to both more and less war. Because the groups were now smaller and required less resources and were less able to wage war, some groups who had previously been aggressively warlike were no longer able to wage war. In other places, however, the overwhelming amount of illness and death was attributed by some people to witchcraft or sorcery practiced by their enemies and led to raids and wars of revenge. Additionally, some cultures were forced to begin or increase raiding for girls and women to replace their population losses. Migration also led to more war, as native peoples fleeing from European settlers and armies often crossed or attempted to settle on lands of people living further inland, producing wars between the groups over land. This was especially common in South America, where early European incursions, mainly against groups near the coast, drove those groups inland, where they came into conflict with native groups in the Amazon region.

A final indirect cause of increased warfare was the availability of goods and tools produced by the Europeans and desired by the native peoples. These included steel tools, various foodstuffs, and guns. The desire for these goods led native peoples to raid Europeans and each other for these goods and for heads, scalps, and other items such as furs that could be traded for goods. Guns were the most desirable of all trade goods and access to them led to both more fighting between groups and created a greater reliance on warfare as means of achieving societal goals.

As the above outline of changes in the frequency of fighting suggests, those whom native people fought with was also significantly altered by Western contact. Prior to contact, war was waged mainly with neighboring peoples. After contact, war was waged not only with these groups but also with whites, with groups encountered during migrations, as well as with neighboring peoples with whom relations had been generally friendly. Also, efforts by Europeans to control fighting between groups sometimes created more internal conflict. For example, when the British succeeded in preventing the Turkana of Kenya from raiding other cultures for cattle, the Turkana turned instead to raiding other Turkana communities for cattle. Population reductions, migrations, competition for trade goods, and involvement in wars started by Europeans all played a role in creating a whole new range of enemies for native peoples.

Changes in how often indigenous people fought and whom they fought with were accompanied by, and often motivated by, changes in the reasons why they fought. Prior to European arrival, most wars were fought for rather limited goals, such as to acquire slaves, women for marriage, or prestige for warriors; to revenge a wrong; or to expand hunting territory. European influence changed all this, and the new goals were often political and economic, including the protection of a society's traditional territory and the acquisition of valuable trade goods.

With these new goals and new enemies, the strategy and tactics of warfare changed as well. Although the information is not completely clear, it is likely that before European contact most warfare took the form of either raiding and feuding or of large battles that involved many warriors, although the number of casualties was often low. There were exceptions of course, such as the Caribs in the Caribbean, the Aztec in central Mexico, and the Iroquois in North America (although here European influence may have been important), but most groups mainly raided and feuded. The introduction of horses, guns, and steel tools, along with the new, more ambitious goals of war, meant that war that produced few casualties was replaced in many places by war that resulted in more casualties and deaths and greater destruction of property. This was primarily because the use of guns meant that equipment, rather than the number of warriors, was the most important factor in victory or defeat. In "primitive war," with weapons such as spears, lances, bow and arrow, clubs, and shields used in hand-to-hand or close combat, more warriors usually meant victory. The availability of guns meant that the group with superior firepower had the advantage and that small, well-equipped war parties could defeat large, poorly equipped ones.

European presence also disrupted alliances and patterns of diplomacy that had existed in some places for centuries among the indigenous cultures of the region. In Africa, for example, the ties among western African states, based on diplomacy and involving treaties and foreign emissaries, was disrupted by European colonization. Additionally, relations between groups deteriorated into continual raiding to acquire slaves for the New World slave trade. In North America, the Iroquois Confederacy of Six Nations was broken apart by the American Revolution and the efforts of the British and the Americans to win the support of the Iroquois nations. Unable to decide as a confederacy which side to support, the six groups followed their traditional decision-making practice of making no decision and instead allowed each of the six nations to make its own choice. The Seneca, Mohawk, and Cayuga sided with the British, the Oneida and Tuscarora with the Americans, and the Onondaga sought to remain neutral. The divisions led the groups to raid each others' fields and villages during the war. After the war, the groups were dispersed and the League of the Iroquois disappeared as a political power, with the constituent groups forced to move or placed on reservations in New York, Ontario, Wisconsin, and Oklahoma.

As mentioned above, the ultimate effect of European settlement was the cessation of warfare, both between native peoples and the Europeans and between native groups. In some places war ended because the native peoples were conquered; in others places, such as the interior of New Guinea, pacification efforts ended local conflict without conquest. While conquest generally ended or reduced the frequency of war between groups, colonialism had in some regions the effect of creating a social and political climate that encouraged warfare when the colonizers departed. Today, we see this effect in both the southern Middle East and in African nations such as Rwanda, Kenya, Nigeria, Senegal, Mali, and the Sudan, where ethnic and tribal wars over political power and territory have followed the waning of colonial influence. The same situation exists in eastern Europe and the former Soviet Union, but here ethnic rivalries have reappeared after the collapse of the strong, centralized Communist regimes rather than the demise of colonial powers.

A final effect of Western influence was the development by native peoples of nonviolent ways of fighting. The most elaborate of these are called "fighting with property" and "fighting with food" and involve rival groups attempting to shame and outdo one another by giving away valuable property. For example, the Goodenough Islanders of Melanesia give away vast quantities of yams and pigs to rival groups, while the Kwakiutl on the northwest coast of North American developed a highly elaborate ritual for giving away valuable property. In both cases, fighting with food or property developed after traditional warfare was ended by Europeans and is a way of competing and fighting without using violence.

See also FIGHTING WITH PROPERTY; FEUDING; PACIFICATION; RAIDING; RAIDING FOR SLAVES; WAR.

Dyson-Hudson, Rada, and J. Terrence McCabe. (1985) *South Turkana Nomadism: Coping with an Unpredictably Varying Environment.*

Ferguson, R. Brian. (1990) "Blood of the Leviathan: Western Contact and Warfare in Amazonia." *American Ethnologist* 17: 237–256.

Levinson, David. (1976) "An Explanation for the Oneida-Colonist Alliance in the American Revolution." *Ethnohistory* 23: 265–290.

Lewis, Oscar. (1942) *The Effects of White Contact upon Blackfoot Culture.*

Rodman, Margaret, and Matthew Cooper. (1979) *The Pacification of Melanesia.*

Secoy, Frank R. (1953) *Changing Military Patterns on the Great Plains.*

Smith, Robert. (1973) "Peace and Palaver: International Relations in Pre-Colonial West Africa." *Journal of African History* 14: 599–622.

WIFE BEATING

Wife beating is the physical assault of a woman by her husband and includes pushing, shoving, slapping, hitting, hitting with an object, burning, cutting, shooting, etc. This definition of wife beating can be expanded to include not just husband and wives but any couple involved in an ongoing, intimate relationship, whether or not they are recognized by society as married. This definition encompasses only physical aggression, with other types of nonphysical aggression such as verbal assault, threats, ridicule, etc. not included. Cross-culturally, these nonphysical forms of aggression in marriage have been little studied, mainly because they are difficult for outsiders to observe.

Some social scientists suggest that wife beating is one of four types of physical violence between spouses found around the world. The three other forms are wife battering, wife beating/husband beating, and mutual violence. In this scheme, wife beating is defined as physical aggression by a husband against his wife that is considered acceptable by some members of the culture. Wife battering is a pattern of aggression by husbands against their wives that is often accompanied by nonviolent forms of coercion that some people in the culture consider to be abusive. Wife beating/husband beating is the situation where both occur in a given society, with husband beating often defensive in nature. Mutual violence is a situation characteristic of very few cultures with both husband beating and wife beating, usually independently of each other or with considerable violence. Although this conceptualization of four types of spousal violence has not been explored systematically, it is important to consider because each may have different causes.

Wife beating is the most common type of family violence found around the world. A survey of 90 cultures indicates that at least some wives are beaten by their husbands in 84.5 percent of societies, a percentage that is consistent with findings of other cross-cultural surveys. Wife beating takes place in most if not all households in 19 percent of cultures, in a majority but not nearly all in 30 percent, in a minority of households in 38 percent and in only a few households or none in 15.5 percent. Additionally, beatings serious enough to permanently injure, scar, or kill a wife occur in 47 percent of cultures.

For a phenomenon so widespread, it is not surprising that wife beating takes a number of different forms. Cross-culturally, cultures can be categorized as one of four different types, based on the type of wife beating found there: sexual jealousy, punitive, at will, or alcohol-related. In cultures where wife beating occurs because of sexual jealousy, wives are beaten for actual or suspected adultery but are generally not beaten for any other reason. Such cultures constitute 22 percent of societies with wife beating. In these cultures women experience the most severe beatings and there is little or no effort by others in the community to control or prevent the beatings. Sexual jealousy–beating societies include a number of Native American groups in North and South America prior to the reservation period. Here, as in other sexual jealousy–beating cultures, men were expected and even encouraged to beat wives who had or were suspected of having sexual relations with other men. These beatings were often brutal and the wives might be killed or, among some Plains Indian cultures, facially disfigured so as to be unattractive to other men. Sometimes, but not always, the wife's lover was also beaten and killed.

Punitive-beating cultures are ones where men are permitted to beat their wives for reasons that are condoned by others in the community. Usually the reason has to do with the wife's failure or perceived failure to perform her wifely duties or treat her husband correctly. Twenty percent of cultures fall into this category. Beatings in these cultures tend to be less severe, and others in the community will intervene if beatings occur too often or are too severe.

At will–beating cultures are ones where men can and do beat their wives for any reason the husband deems appropriate. Thus, unlike the first two types, there are no cultural guidelines for wife beating; instead group norms permit the husband to decide how often and for what reasons he will beat his wife. However, others in the community may intervene if beatings occur too often or if they are disruptive to community life. At will cultures constitute 51 percent of cultures with wife beating.

In about 8 percent of cultures with wife beating, beatings take place almost exclusively when the husband is drunk, not uncommonly following a public drinking feast that might also include drunken brawling between men. In these cultures, the beatings are highly stylized, with the husband apologizing and swearing never to beat her again the morning after, the wife forgiving him and excusing his behavior, and the pattern repeated again in the near future.

Since wife beating became a matter of social concern some 20 years ago, numerous social, cultural, economic, political, and psychological explanations have been suggested and tested. It now seems clear that, both cross-culturally and in individual cultures, the basic explanation is that wife beating is a means men use to maintain control over women. Both the beatings themselves and the threat of future beatings enable husbands to control the behavior of their wives. Societies where husbands beat their wives regularly are mostly ones where men are able to obtain more wealth than women and where the husband controls the family income. In these cultures men rather than women inherit family property and wealth, men control the fruits of family labor, and men own the family home. Additionally, it is more difficult for women to obtain a divorce and men are the ultimate authority in family decisions. In cultures where women have economic freedom—and especially freedom to control the income produced through their own work—wife beating is unusual, probably because men are no longer in control of their wives and because women have the economic resources that enable a woman to leave if she is beaten. A second factor that also encourages wife beating is a cultural pattern that favors the use of physical violence to settle disputes. Thus, wife beating occurs most often in cultures where women are economically unequal and where men and women settle disputes by fighting.

Around the world a variety of interventions are used either to prevent a beating from taking place, to end one in progress, or to prevent it from reoccurring. These include: (1) immediate intervention by a relative, neighbor, or mediator; (2) the wife being sheltered by a relative or neighbor; (3) public censure of the husband; (4) the wife divorcing the husband; or (5) any two or more of the above. Interventions occur in nearly all societies, although they are used more often and are most effective in cultures that already have little wife beating. In cultures with much beating the norms that allow or encourage beatings tend also to inhibit the use of interventions.

Bedouin virginity test in Egypt. A concern with control of female sexual behavior is common in societies with much wife beating.

See also BRIDE THEFT AND RAIDING; DRUNKEN BRAWLING; HUSBAND BEATING; MACHOISM; RAPE; SUICIDE; SUTTEE.

Counts, Dorothy Ayers, Judith K. Brown, and Jacquelyn C. Campbell, eds. (1992) *Sanctions and Sanctuary: Cultural Perspectives on the Beating of Wives.*

Daly, Martin, and Margo Wilson. (1988) *Homicide.*

Gelles, Richard J., and Claire P. Cornell, eds. (1983) *International Perspectives on Family Violence.*

Levinson, David. (1989) *Family Violence in Cross-Cultural Perspective.*

WITCHCRAFT

Witchcraft is about jealousy, envy, anger, and getting even. In some societies it is a way that people harm their neighbors. Witchcraft is different from sorcery. A witch (a witch is a female, a male witch is called a warlock) is someone who can cause harm to an individual by simply wishing the harm to take place. A witch has direct access to the supernatural world and can call on the powers of supernatural forces to cause harm to another. Sorcery, on the other hand, requires the use of a sorcerer who through his knowledge of formulae and rituals can direct supernatural power. Sorcerers, unlike witches, cannot simply cause supernatural forces to affect the lives of the living by so wishing. Sorcerers are often used by people to remove the harm caused by witches. Anthropologist Clyde Kluckhohn studied witchcraft among the Navajo and suggests the following function of witchcraft:

> . . . a means of attaining wealth, gaining women, disposing of enemies and "being mean." In short, witchcraft is a potential avenue to supernatural power. Power seems to be an important central theme in Navaho culture of which gaining wealth, disposing of enemies, and even, to some extent, obtaining possession of women are merely particular examples.

Kluckhohn's description applies equally well to many other cultures, as does his conclusion:

> . . . Since most hostile impulses must to greater or lesser extent be suppressed, there is a need in every society for hate satisfaction. But unless there are some forms of hating which are socially acceptable and justified, everyone will remain in an intolerable conflict situation, and neuroticism will be endemic in the population.

Thus, witchcraft serves two purposes: it helps maintain social order by providing an outlet for aggression, and it alleviates individual stress that might result from unexpressed anger.

The attribution of at least some misfortune to witchcraft is found in 58 percent of societies. Witchcraft is often believed to be a cause of illness and death. In a sample of 186 societies, witchcraft was the predominate cause of illness in 4 percent, an important secondary cause in 10 percent, and a minor cause in 14.5 percent. Witchcraft is not distributed evenly around the world; it occurs far more commonly in societies around the Mediterranean Sea, neighboring regions of sub-Saharan Africa, and in communities in the New World formed by descendants of immigrants from the Mediterranean region. It has been suggested that witchcraft beliefs began in Mesopotamia because belief in the evil eye and protective formulae were present among the Babylonians at least as early as 1750 B.C. Witchcraft beliefs were also fairly common in traditional Native American cultures, although unusual elsewhere in the world and virtually absent in East Asia.

Explanations for witchcraft emphasize the presence of "unlegitimized social relationships" among people in societies where witchcraft attribution occurs. These are relationships in which people interact closely and work toward common goals, but they do not necessarily enter into these relationships willingly, and disputes cannot be resolved in commonly agreed upon ways. Unlegitimized relationships tend to occur when any of the following conditions obtain: marriage partners typically come from other communities, there are conflicts between the generations, people are differentiated on the basis of wealth or social status, one group in the community is the conqueror of the other group, individuals owe allegiance to more than one competing group, or there are no duly recognized individuals or councils with the authority to settle disputes. Any of these conditions may produce feelings of jealousy, envy, rivalry and mistrust, which may then lead to anger and feelings of aggression that are manifested in wishes to cause others harm and the expectation that others wish to cause you harm. As the people live close to one another in small communities and must interact peacefully on a daily basis, the expression of anger must be indirect and hidden, as is the case with witchcraft.

Many of the essential features of witchcraft as it exists in contemporary societies are displayed by small-town Mexican-Americans in rural southern Texas. Bewitchment is the most serious of diseases and a matter the people are reluctant to discuss with outsiders. A belief in witchcraft is strongest among low-class and lower-middle class adults and generally dismissed as unimportant or ridiculed by those in the upper class and by children. Believers believe in both male and female witches (*brujo*), with female witches more common. Witches can fly and often take the form of an animal, usually a cat or an owl. The signs that one has been bewitched include a chronic illness, mental illness, insomnia, or misfortune following good fortune. Although many are suspected, a witch is rarely identified and accusations are made only after a person dies or leaves town. A person who is a witch can act directly, while a nonwitch will hire a witch to place a hex. Witches act out of envy (this is why misfortune after good fortune is attributed to witchcraft), sexual jealousy, and to revenge a real or perceived offense. The hex can be removed by identifying the witch and getting her to remove it; by destroying an object thought to cause the hex, such as a dead toad or bat; or more often by retaining a specialist to reverse the hex.

In some cultures, witchcraft also works to control and channel aggression through witchcraft accusation. When something goes wrong in the community, a person is accused of being a witch (often an old woman) and killed, thus relieving tension in the community by transferring community anger to a scapegoat. This was exactly the situation in the Salem, Massachusetts, witchcraft hysteria of 1692, when hundreds were accused and 20 were executed as witches. Community harmony was disrupted by deep disputes about civil versus church authority, morality, and wars with the local Indians, leading to a breakdown of traditional legal procedures and the resulting scapegoating of local citizens. While the accused individuals suffered, the trials provided a needed outlet for stress in the community.

While witches are often tolerated in some cultures, when illness, death, or social disorder becomes threatening to the community, as in Salem, efforts will be made to identify the witch who is responsible. The Turkana of Kenya, for example, have three ways of identifying witches. First, witches are thought to have unusual eyes, although in what way they are unusual is not easily described. Second, by putting one's hand over one's mouth and pulling it away quickly, the name of the witch will be spoken. Third, a diviner can be consulted to discover the name of the witch. Whatever means are used, in most cultures the persons identified as witches are ones who stand out because of some physical feature (they are old, ugly, crippled, etc.) or unusual behavior (they act crazy, socialize with outsiders, etc.) or because they are envied (they are rich, young, beautiful, etc.).

See also EVIL EYE; SORCERY; SUPERNATURAL AGGRESSION.

Gulliver, Philip H. (1951) *A Preliminary Survey of the Turkana. A Report Compiled for the Government of Kenya.*

Kluckhohn, Clyde. (1944) *Navaho Witchcraft.* Papers of the Peabody Museum of American Archaeology and Ethnology, 22, no. 2.

Masden, William, and Andre Guerrero. (1973) *Mexican-Americans of South Texas.*

Murdock, George Peter. (1980) *Theories of Illness: A World Survey.*

Naroll, Raoul, Gary L. Michik, and Frada Naroll. (1976) *Worldwide Theory Testing.*

Swanson, Guy E. (1968) *The Birth of the Gods.*

Whiting, Beatrice B. (1950) *Paiute Sorcery.*

WORD DUELS

Word duels are a form of verbal communication in which individuals engage in a ritualized exchange of insults. Such duels are customary in a number of cultures around the world, including Turkey, the Ona in South America, the Chamula in Mexico, Puerto Rico, southern Italy, and African-Americans in the United States. Other labels used for word duels include ritualized verbal insults, verbal assault, verbal duels, defamation contests, and profanation games. Song duels are a specialized form of word duels in that the insults are in the form of songs prepared before the duel and then sung by the participants.

Although they vary from one culture to another, word duels in different cultures share a number of common characteristics:

1. They include two participants who hurl insults back and forth at one another.
2. The insults are usually obscene and often refer to the participant's female relatives.
3. The duel occurs in public in front of an audience that laughs and cheers.
4. The duel is governed by a set of rules known to the participants and observers. For example, in Chamula, one's response must be in the form of a rhyme and in southern Italy the word duel called *LaLegge* (The Law) takes place only between drunken men.
5. The winner is the participant who hurls the better insults. Better can mean more insulting, more creative, quicker, more in accord with the rules, or simply overwhelming. An individual usually wins when his competitor gives up.
6. The participants are expected to accept the insults without a show of emotion and duels are generally free of violence, although a duel might escalate into a fight if the participants were unfriendly to begin with.
7. The participants are usually adolescent boys (Turkey, Chamula, African Americans) or men (Puerto Rico, southern Italy). Only among the Ona do women regularly engage in word duels, and then the duels are less ritualized and more charged with anger than in other cultures.

The primary cross-cultural variation in word duels is the extent to which they are either a mechanism for directly expressing aggression or more of a game or contest in which the expression of aggression is only one component. For example, among the Ona word duels are mostly about expressing aggression and resolving disputes and are part of broader dueling complex that also includes wrestling, fighting, and arrow duels. Similarly, song duels among Inuit groups in North America occur when one party wants to express a grievance; the duels are generally thought of as a mechanism for discharging aggression that might otherwise result in physical violence. In most other cultures word duels are better described as contests, with the humorous nature of the insults and the rules of the game often as important as the harshness of the insults.

Word duels among African-American adolescent boys (and sometimes girls) in the United States have drawn the most scholarly attention. Traditionally called "Playing the Dozens" or "the Dozens," these duels go by a wide variety of other names, including "joning," "sounding," "burning," "ranking," "dusting," "icing," "putting down," "cutting down," "tearing down," and other regional and local varieties. These duels have also been reported among white adolescents, although they are less complex and less formalized, and the insults are not as rich or as culturally meaningful. It is likely that white adolescent word duels are a cultural borrowing from African-American urban culture.

The Dozens is played mostly by young adolescent boys, although girls will sometimes play the Dozens with other girls and young boys will often imitate the older boys. By the time a teenager reaches late adolescence he will have stopped participating. The Dozens typically involves two boys exchanging ritualized insults in front of an audience who cheer, rate the insults, laugh, and generally encourage the participants.

The insults might be one-liners:

> Your mother play baseball for the U.S. Navy.

Or single and multiverse songs:

> See that man
> aha
> In the white
> aha
> I betcha five dollars your mother smoke a pipe
> A ha ha baby I know.

As these examples suggest, the target of the insults is usually the opponent's mother or some other female relative. As the insults are highly stylized, rarely about the opponent, and the activity is often seen as a game to pass the time, actual violence rarely results. The game ends when the participants or the audience tire of it.

Four different explanations have been suggested for the Dozens. These may be labeled the frustration-aggression, male sex identity formation, peer group socialization, and role modeling explanations. The frustration-aggression explanation suggests that the exchange of insults is a way for African-Americans to release the aggression that results from their being an oppressed group in American society. This explanation is probably too general to explain a custom as restricted as the Dozens and also fails to explain why the insults would be directed at the adolescent participant's female relatives rather than at each other or at whites. The male sex identity formation explanation sees the Dozens as part of the psychosocial process of male identify formation. The basic assumption is that African-American boys are close to and identify with their mothers, a relationship that weakens and grows more ambiguous as boys reach adolescence. Some boys react to this ambiguity and loss of closeness with anger; because they can't strike out at their mothers, they instead insult mothers of their peers. The role modeling explanation is an extension of this explanation, but suggests instead that because adult male and female relations are distant and conflict-ridden, boys play the Dozens to break their ties to their mothers and to begin acting like men in relation to women. The peer group socialization explanation also emphasizes the breaking of ties, but in this formulation the ties broken are those the boys have with their families and the new ties established are with the adolescent peer group.

See also Insults; Song Duels.

Abrahams, Roger D. (1962) "Playing the Dozens." *Journal of American Folklore* 75: 209–220.

Ayoub, Millicent R., and Stephen A. Barnett. (1965) "Ritualized Verbal Insult in White High School Culture." *Journal of American Folklore* 78: 337–344.

Dollard, John. (1939) "The Dozens: Dialectic of Insult." *American Imago* 1: 3–25.

Dundes, Alan, et al. (1970) "The Strategy of Turkish Boys' Verbal Dueling Rhymes." *Journal of American Folklore* 83: 225–249.

Gossen, Gary H. (1976) "Verbal Dueling in Chamula." In *Speech Play,* edited by Barbara Kirshenblatt-Gimblett, 121–146.

Gusinde, Martin. (1931) *The Fireland Indians. Vol. 1: The Selk'nam, On the Life and Thought of a Hunting People of the Great Island of Tierra del Fuego.*

Hannerz, Ulf. (1969) *Soulside: Inquiries into Ghetto Culture and Community.*

Labov, William. (1972) "Rules for Ritual Insults." In *Studies in Social Interaction,* edited by D. Sudnow, 120–169.

Lauria, Anthony Jr. (1964) "'Respeto,' 'Relajo' and Inter-personal Relations in Puerto Rico." *Anthropological Quarterly* 37: 53–67.

Vaillant, Roger. (1959) *The Law.*

Bibliography

Abler, Thomas S. (1993) "Iroquois: The Tree of Peace and the War Kettle." In *Portraits of Culture: Ethnographic Profiles,* edited by Melvin Ember, Carol R. Ember, and David Levinson.

Abrahams, Roger D. (1962) "Playing the Dozens." *Journal of American Folklore* 75: 209–220.

Adams, David. (1983) "Why There Are So Few Women Warriors." *Behavior Science Research* 18: 196–212.

Adriani, N., and A. C. Krutz. (1951) *The Bare'e-Speaking Toradja of Central Celebes (The East Toradja).*

Ahmed, Akbar S. (1980) *Pukhtun Economy and Society: Traditional Structure and Economic Development in a Tribal Society.*

Alford, Richard D. (1988) *Naming and Identity: A Cross-Cultural Study of Personal Naming Practices.*

Alford, Finnegan, and Richard D. Alford. (1981) "A Holo-Cultural Study of Humor." *Ethos* 9: 149–164.

Allen, Martin G. (1972) "A Cross-Cultural Study of Aggression and Crime." *Journal of Cross-Cultural Psychology* 3: 259–271.

Apte, Mahadev L. (1985) *Humor and Laughter: An Anthropological Approach.*

Archer, Dane, and Rosemary Gartner. (1984) *Violence and Crime in Cross-National Perspective.*

Arens, W. (1979) *The Man-Eating Myth: Anthropology and Anthropophagy.*

Axtell, James, and William C. Sturtevant. (1986) "The Unkindest Cut, or Who Invented Scalping?" In *The American Indian Past and Present,* edited by Roger L. Nichols, 47–60.

Ayoub, Millicent R., and Stephen A. Barnett. (1965) "Ritualized Verbal Insult in White High School Culture." *Journal of American Folklore* 78: 337–344.

Ayres, Barbara. (1974) "Bride Theft and Raiding for Wives in Cross-Cultural Perspective." *Anthropological Quarterly* 47: 238–252.

Bacon, Margaret K., Irvin L. Child, and Herbert Barry III. (1963) "A Cross-Cultural Study of the Correlates of Crime." *Journal of Abnormal and Social Psychology* 66: 291–300.

Balikci, Asen. (1970) *The Netsilik Eskimo.*

Barnett, Homer. (1959) "Peace and Progress in New Guinea." *American Anthropologist* 61: 1013–1019.

Barry, Herbert, III, and Alice Schlegel, eds. (1980) *Cross-Cultural Samples and Codes.*

Barry, Herbert, III, et al. (1980) "Agents and Techniques for Child Training: Cross-Cultural Codes 6." In *Cross-Cultural Samples and Codes,* edited by Herbert Barry III and Alice Schlegel, 237–276.

Barry, Herbert, III, et al. (1980) "Traits Inculcated in Childhood: Cross-Cultural Codes 5." In *Cross-Cultural Samples and Codes,* edited by Herbert Barry III and Alice Schlegel, 205–236.

Barton, Roy F. (1919) *Ifugao Law.* California University Publications in American Archaeology and Ethnology 15: 1–187.

———. (1946) *The Religion of the Ifugaos.*

———. (1949) *The Kalingas.*

Basso, Keith H. (1970) "'To Give Up on Words': Silence in Western Apache Culture." *Southwestern Journal of Anthropology* 26: 213–230.

Beals, Ralph L. (1966) *Community in Transition: Nayón—Ecuador.*

Berglund, Axel-Ivar. (1976) *Zulu Thought-Patterns and Symbolism.*

Berndt, Ronald. (1962) *Excess and Restraint.*

Besnier, Niko. (1989) "Information Withholding as a Manipulative and Collusive Strategy in Nukulaelae Gossip." *Language and Society* 18: 315–341.

Best, Eldon. (1924) *The Maori.* 2 vols.

Binder, David, and Barbara Crossette. (1992) "As Ethnic Wars Multiply, U.S. Strives for a Policy." *New York Times* (7 February 1992).

Black, Robert A. (1967) "Hopi Grievance Chants: A Mechanism of Social Control." In *Studies in Southwestern Ethnolinguistics,* edited by Dell Hymes and William E. Bittle, 54–67.

Blok, Anton. (1972) "The Peasant and the Brigand: Social Banditry Reconsidered." *Comparative Studies in Society and History* 14: 494–503.

Bohannan, Paul. (1957) *Justice and Judgment among the Tiv.*

———. (1957) *Tiv Farm and Settlement.*

Bohannan, Paul, and Laura Bohannan. (1958) "Three Sourcebooks in Tiv Ethnography." Unpublished manuscript, Human Relations Area Files.

Bowen, Ralph H., and Pierre Bettez Gravel. (1992) "Peasants and Pirates in the Aegean: An Instance of 'Social Banditry'?" *Studies in Third World Societies* 48, part 2: 159–170.

Brant, Charles S. (1972) "A Preliminary Study of Cross-Sexual Joking Relationships in Primitive Society." *Behavior Science Notes* 7: 313–330.

Bricker, Victoria R. (1973) *Ritual Humor in Highland Chiapas.*

Bridgman, Jon M. (1981) *The Revolt of the Hereros.*

Brison, Karen J. (1992) *Just Talk: Gossip, Meetings, and Power in a Papua New Guinea Village.*

Broude, Gwen, and Sara J. Greene. (1976) "Cross-Cultural Codes on Twenty Sexual Practices." *Ethnology* 15: 409–429.

Brown, Donald E. (1991) *Human Universals.*

Brown, Paula. (1986) "Simbu Aggression and the Drive to Win." *Anthropological Quarterly* 59: 165–170.

Brown, Paula, and Donald Tuzin, eds. (1983) *The Ethnography of Cannibalism.*

Buck, Peter H. (1952) *The Coming of the Maori.* 2nd edition.

Bullock, Charles. (1950) *The Mashona and the Matabele.*

Burbank, Victoria K. (1987) "Female Aggression in Cross-Cultural Perspective." *Behavior Science Research* 21: 70–100.

Calame-Griaule, Genevieve. (1986) *Words and the Dogon World.*

Campbell, Donald T. (1983) "Legal and Primary-Group Social Controls." In *Law, Biology and Culture: The Evolution of Law,* edited by Margaret Gruter and Paul Bohannan, 159–171.

Campbell, J. K. (1964) *Honour, Family, and Patronage: A Study of Institutions and Moral Values in a Greek Mountain Community.*

Carroll, Berenice A. (1968) *Design for Total War: Arms and Economics in the Third Reich.*

Carter, Harold, Jr. (1977) "Military Organization as a Response to Residence and Size of Population: A Cross-Cultural Study." *Behavior Science Research* 12: 271–290.

Caudill, Harry M. (1963) *Night Comes to the Cumberlands.*

Chagnon, Napoleon A. (1968) *Yanomamö: The Fierce People.*

Chaseling, Wilbur S. (1957) *Yulengor: Nomads of Arnhem Land.*

Codere, Helen. (1950) *Fighting with Property.*

Cohen, Yehudi A. (1966) *A Study of Interpersonal Relations in a Jamaican Community.*

Cohen, Alex. (1990) "A Cross-Cultural Study of the Effects of Environmental Unpredictability on Aggression in Folktales." *American Anthropologist* 92: 474–480.

Collier, J., and M. Rosaldo. (1981) "Poltics and Gender in Simple Societies." In *Sexual Meanings,* edited by S. Ortner and H. Whitehead.

Conrad, Barnaby. (1961) *Encyclopedia of Bullfighting.*

Cook, H. B. Kimberley. (1992) "Matrifocality and Female Aggression in Margariteño Society." In *Of Mice and Women: Aspects of Female Aggression,* edited by Kaj Björkqvist and Pirkko Niemelä, 149–162.

Cooper, Roger. (1982) *The Baha'is of Iran.*

Counts, Dorothy A., Judith K. Brown, and Jacquelyn C. Campbell, eds. (1992) *Sanctions and Sanctuary: Cultural Perspectives on the Beating of Wives.*

Cox, Bruce A. (1970) "What Is Hopi Gossip About? Information Management and Hopi Factions." *Man* 5: 88–98.

Crummey, Donald, ed. (1986) *Banditry, Rebellion and Social Protest in Africa.*

D'Andrade, Roy G. (1974) "Sex Differences and Cultural Institutions." In *Culture and Personality: Contemporary Readings,* edited by Robert LeVine.

Daly, Martin, and Margo Wilson. (1988) *Homicide.*

Davis, Shelton H. (1977) *Victims of the Miracle: Development and the Indians of Brazil.*

De Silva, K. M., and S. W. R. de A. Samarasinghe. (1993) *Peace Accords and Ethnic Conflict.*

DeGlopper, Donald R. (1974) *City on the Sands: Social Structure in a Nineteenth-Century Chinese City.*

Dentan, Robert K. (1965) *Some Senoi Semai Dietary Restrictions: A Study of Food Behavior in a Malayan Hill Tribe.*

———. (1968) *The Semai.*

———. (1978) "Notes on Childhood in a Non-Violent Context: The Semai Case." In *Learning Non-Aggression,* edited by Ashley Montagu, 94–143.

Dieterlen, Germaine. (1951) *An Essay on the Religion of the Bambara.*

Dirks, Robert. (1988) "Annual Rituals of Conflict." *American Anthropologist* 90: 856–870.

Dobyns, Henry F. (1966) "Estimating Aboriginal American Population: An Appraisal of Techniques with a New Hemispheric Estimate." *Current Anthropology* 7: 395–416.

Dollard, John. (1939) "The Dozens: Dialectic of Insult." *American Imago* 1: 3–25.

Dow, James.(1995) *The Encyclopedia of World Cultures. Volume 8: Middle America and the Caribbean.*

Dundes, Alan, ed. (1981) *The Evil Eye: A Folklore Casebook.*

Dundes, Alan, et al. (1970) "The Strategy of Turkish Boys' Verbal Dueling Rhymes." *Journal of American Folklore* 83: 225–249.

Durham, William H. (1976) "Resource Competition and Human Aggression. Part 1: A Review of Primitive War." *Quarterly Review of Biology* 51: 385–415.

Dyson-Hudson, Rada, and J. Terrence McCabe. (1985) *South Turkana Nomadism: Coping with an Unpredictably Varying Environment.*

Earle, Timothy. (1982) "The Ecology and Politics of Primitive Valuables." In *Eclectic Perspectives,* edited by John Kennedy and Robert Edgerton, 65–83.

Eckhardt, William. (1973) "Anthropological Correlates of Primitive Militarism." *Peace Research* 5: 5–10.

Eggan, Fred, ed. (1955) *Social Anthropology of North American Tribes.*

Elmer, Glaister A., and Evelyn A. Elmer. (1988) *Ethnic Conflicts Abroad: Clues to America's Future?* AICF Monograph Series, no. 8.

Ember, Carol R. (1978) "Myths about Hunter-Gatherers." *Ethnology* 17: 439–448.

Ember, Carol R., and Melvin Ember. (1992) "Resource Unpredictability, Mistrust, and War." *Journal of Conflict Resolution* 36: 242–262.

———. (1992) "Warfare, Aggression, and Resource Problems: Cross-Cultural Codes." *Behavior Science Research* 26: 169–226.

Ember, Carol R., Melvin Ember, and Bruce M. Russett. (1992) "Peace between Participatory Polities: A Cross-Cultural Test of the 'Democracies Rarely Fight Each Other' Hypothesis." *World Politics* 44: 573–599.

Erickson, Karen P., and Heather Horton. (1992) "'Blood Feuds': Cross-Cultural Variations in Kin Group Vengeance." *Behavior Science Research* 26.

Esposito, John L. (1984) *The Islamic Threat: Myth or Reality?*

Ewers, John C. (1955) *The Horse in Blackfoot Indian Culture with Comparative Material from other Western Tribes.* U.S. Bureau of American Ethnology, Bulletin 159.

———. (1967) "Blackfoot Raiding for Horses and Scalps." In *Law and Warfare: Studies in the Anthropology of Conflict,* edited by Paul Bohannan, 327–344.

Fabbro, D. (1978) "Peaceful Societies: an Introduction." *Journal of Peace Research* 12: 67–84.

Fein, Helen, ed. (1992) *Genocide Watch.*

Ferguson, R. Brian. (1990) "Blood of the Leviathan: Western Contact and Warfare in Amazonia." *American Ethnologist* 17: 237–257.

———. (1990) "Explaining War." In *The Anthropology of War,* edited by Jonathan Haas, 22–55.

Ferguson, R. Brian, ed. (1984) *Warfare, Culture and Environment.*

Firth, Raymond W. (1936) *We, the Tikopia: A Sociological Study of Kinship in Primitive Polynesia.*

———. (1959) *Social Change in Tikopia.*

Forsyth, Thomas. (1912) "An Account of the Manners and Customs of the Sauk and Fox Nations of Indians Tradition." In *The Indian Tribes of the Upper Mississippi Valley and Region of the Great Lakes,* edited by Emma H. Blair, 183–245.

Frayser, Suzanne. (1985) *Varieties of Sexual Experience.*

Fry, Douglas P. (1992) "Female Aggression among the Zapotec of Oaxaca, Mexico." In *Of Mice and Women: Aspects of Female Aggression,* edited by Kaj Björkqvist and Pirkko Niemelä, 187–199.

Fuller, J. F. C. (1961) *The Conduct of War: 1789–1961.*

Gallin, Bernard. (1966) *Hsin Hsing, Taiwan: A Chinese Village in Change.*

Garb, Paula. (1993) "Abkahazians: Growing in Age and Wisdom." In *Portraits of Culture: Ethnographic Profiles,* edited by Melvin Ember, Carol R. Ember, and David Levinson.

Geertz, Clifford. (1973) *The Interpretation of Cultures.*

Geertz, Hildred. (1961) *The Javanese Family.*

Gelles, Richard J., and Claire P. Cornell. (1983) *International Perspectives on Family Violence.*

Gibson, Thomas. (1989) "Symbolic Representations of Tranquility and Aggression among the Buid." In *Societies at Peace: Anthropological Perspectives,* edited by Signe Howell and Roy Willis, 60–78.

Girodet, Jean. (1981) *Dictionnaire du Bon Français.*

Glascock, Anthony P. (1984) "Decreptitude and Death-Hastening: The Nature of Old Age in Third World Societies." *Studies in Third World Societies* 22: 43–67.

Glascock, Anthony P., and Richard A. Wagner. (1986) *HRAF Research Series in Quantitative Cross-Cultural Data. Volume 2: Life Cycle Data.*

Glazer, Ilsa M. (1992) "Interfemale Aggression and Resource Scarcity in a Cross-Cultural Persepctive." In *Of Mice and Women: Aspects of Female Aggression,* edited by Kaj Björkqvist and Pirkko Niemelä, 163–171.

Gluckman, Max. (1954) *Rituals of Rebellion in South-East Africa.*

———. (1963) "Gossip and Scandal." *Current Anthropology* 4: 307–316.

Goldschmidt, Walter. (1986) "Personal Motivation and Institutionalized Conflict." In *Peace and War: Cross-Cultural Perspectives,* edited by Mary LeCron Foster and Robert A. Rubinstein, 3–14.

Gossen, Gary H. (1976) "Verbal Dueling in Chamula." In *Speech Play,* edited by Barbara Kirshenblatt-Gimblett, 121–146.

Grajdanzev, Andrew J. (1944) *Modern Korea.*

Granzberg, Gary. (1973) "The Psychological Integration of Culture: A Cross-Cultural Study of Hopi Type Initiation Rites." *Journal of Social Psychology* 90: 3–7.

———. (1973) "Twin Infanticide—A Cross-Cultural Test of a Materialistic Explanation." *Ethos* 4: 405–412.

Greenhouse, Carol J. (1985) "Mediation: A Comparative Approach." *Man* (new series) 20: 90–114.

Gregerson, Edgar. (1982) *Sexual Practices: The Story of Human Sexuality.*

Griaule, Marcel. (1938) *Dogon Games.*

Grinnell, George B. (1962) *Blackfoot Lodge Tales: The Story of a Prairie People.*

Grünhut, Max. (1972) *Penal Reform: A Comparative Study.*

Guenther, Mathias G. (1979) *The Farm Bushmen of the Ghanzi District, Botswana.*

Gulliver, Philip H. (1951) *A Preliminary Survey of the Turkana. A Report Compiled for the Government of Kenya.*

———. (1979) *Disputes and Negotiations: A Cross-Cultural Perspective.*

Gurr, Ted R. (1993) *Minorities at Risk: A Global View of Ethnopolitical Conflicts.*

Gurr, Ted R., and James R. Scarritt. (1989) "Minority Rights at Risk: A Global Survey." *Human Rights Quarterly* 11: 375–405.

Gusinde, Martin. (1931) *The Fireland Indians. Vol. 1: The Selk'nam, On the Life and Thought of a Hunting People of the Great Island of Tierra del Fuego.*

Gutierrez de Pineda, Virginia. (1950) *Social Organization in La Guajira.*

Gutman, Israel, ed. (1990) *The Encyclopedia of the Holocaust.* 4 vols.

Haas, Jonathan, ed. (1990) *The Anthropology of War.*

Handy, E. S. Craighill. (1923) *The Native Culture of the Marquesas.* Bernice P. Bishop Museum, Bulletin 9.

Hannerz, Ulf. (1969) *Soulside: Inquiries into Ghetto Culture and Community.*

Harner, Michael J. (1972) *The Jivaro: People of the Sacred Waterfalls.*

———. (1977) "The Ecological Basis for Aztec Sacrifice." *American Ethnologist* 4: 117–135.

Harris, Marvin. (1977) *Cannibals and Kings: The Origins of Cultures.*

Hausfater, G., and S. Blaffer Hrdy, eds. (1984) *Infanticide: Comparative and Evolutionary Perspectives.*

Haviland, John B. (1977) *Gossip, Reputation, and Knowledge in Zinacantan.*

Heckwelder, John G. E. (1819) *An Account of the History, Manners, and Customs of the Indian Nations, Who Once Inhabited Pennsylvania and the Neighboring States.*

Henderson, Richard N., and Helen K. Henderson. (1966) *An Outline of Traditional Onitsha Ibo Socialization.*

Hickson, Letitia. (1986) "The Social Contexts of Apology on Dispute Settlement: A Cross-Cultural Study." *Ethnology* 25: 283–294.

Hobsbawm, E. J. (1969) *Bandits.*

Hockings, Paul. (1992) "Thug." In *Encyclopedia of World Cultures. Volume 3. South Asia,* edited by Paul Hockings, p. 294.

Hoebel, A. Adamson. (1960) *The Cheyennes: Indians of the Great Plains.*

———. (1973) *The Law of Primitive Man.*

Horowitz, Donald L. (1985) *Ethnic Groups in Conflict.*

Hosken, Fran. (1982) *The Hosken Report: Genital and Sexual Mutilation of Females.*

Hostetler, John A. (1980) *Amish Society.* 3rd edition.

Howard, Alan. (1990) "Dispute Management in Rotuma." *Journal of Anthropological Research* 46: 263–292.

Howell, P. P. (1954) *A Manual of Nuer Law: Being an Account of Customary Law, its Evolution and Development in the Courts established by the Sudan Government.*

Ingersoll, Jasper C. (1969) *The Priest and the Path: An Analysis of the Priest Role in a Central Thai Village.*

Jaimes, M. Annette, ed. (1992) *The State of Native America: Genocide, Colonization, and Resistance.*

Jenness, Diamond. (1922) *Report of the Canadian Arctic Expedition, 1913–1918,* vol. 12, part A.

Jonassohn, Kurt, and Frank Chalk. (1987) "A Typology of Genocide and Some Implications for the Human Rights Agenda." In *Genocide and the Modern Age,* edited by Isidor Wallimann and Michael N. Dobkowski, 3–20.

Joseph, Alice, Rosamond B. Spicer, and Jane Chesky. (1949) *The Desert People: A Study of the Papago Indians.*

Justinger, Judith M. (1978) *Reaction to Change: A Holocultural Test of Some Theories of Religious Movements.*

Kang, Gay E. (1976) *Solidarity Theory: A Cross-Cultural Test of the Relationships among Exogamy, Cross-Allegiance, Peace, and Survival Value.*

Karsten, Rafael. (1935) *The Head-Hunters of Western Aamazonas: The Life and Culture of the Jibaro Indians of Eastern Ecuador and Peru.*

Kennedy, Raymond. (1942). *The Ageless Indies.*

Kennett, Austin. (1925) *Bedouin Justice: Laws and Customs among the Egyptian Bedouin.*

Kiefer, Thomas M. (1968) "Institutionalized Friendship and Warfare among the Tausug of Jolo." *Ethnology* 7: 225–244.

Kluckhohn, Clyde. (1944) *Navaho Witchcraft.* Papers of the Peabody Museum of American Archaeology and Ethnology, 22, no. 2.

Koch, Klaus-Friedrich. (1983) "Epilogue. Pacification: Perspective From Conflict Theory." In *The Pacification of Melanesia,* edited by Margaret Rodman and Matthew Cooper, 199–207.

Koch, Klaus-Friedrich, John A. Sodergren, and Susan Campbell. (1976) "Political and Psychological Correlates of Conflict Management: A Cross-Cultural Study." *Law and Society Review* 10: 443–466.

Koch, Klaus-Friedrich, Soraya Altorki, Andrew Arno, and Letitia Hickson. (1977) "Ritual Reconciliation and the Obviation of Grievances: A Comparative Study in the Ethnography of Law." *Ethnology* 16: 269–283.

Kuper, Leo. (1985) *The Prevention of Genocide.*

———. (1992) "Genocide." In *Encyclopedia of Sociology,* edited by Edgar Borgatta, 2: 757–761.

Kuschel, Rolf. (1992) "'Women Are Women and Men Are Men': How Bellonese Women Get Even." In *Of Mice and Women: Aspects of Female Aggression,* edited by Kaj Björkqvist and Pirkko Niemelä, 173–185.

Labov, William. (1972) "Rules for Ritual Insults." In *Studies in Social Interaction,* edited by D. Sudnow, 120–169.

Laguna, Frederica de. (1972) *Under Mount Saint Elias: The History and Culture of the Yakutat Tlingit.*

Lancy, David F. (1975) *Work, Play and Learning in a Kpelle Town.*

Lang, Olga. (1946) *Chinese Family and Society.*

Langer, William L. (1974) "Infanticide: A Historical Survey." *History of Childhood Quarterly: The Journal of Psychohistory* 1: 353–365.

Lauria, Anthony, Jr. (1964) "'Respeto,' 'Relajo' and Inter-personal Relations in Puerto Rico." *Anthropological Quarterly* 37: 53–67.

Leavitt, Gregory C. (1977) "The Frequency of Warfare: An Evolutionary Perspective." *Sociological Inquiry* 47: 49–58.

Lebra, Takie S. (1984) "Nonconfrontational Strategies for Management of Interpersonal Conflicts." In *Conflict in Japan,* edited by Ellis S. Krauss, Thomas P. Rohlen, and Patricia G. Steinhoff, 41–60.

Lemkin, Raphael. (1944) *Axis Rule in Occupied Europe.*

Levine, Donald N. (1965) *Wax and Gold: Tradition and Innovation in Ethiopian Culture.*

Levine, Nancy. (1992) "Nyinba." In *Encyclopedia of World Cultures. Volume 3. South Asia,* edited by Paul Hocking, 210–213.

Levinson, David. (1976) "An Explanation for the Oneida-Colonist Alliance in the American Revolution." *Ethnohistory* 23: 265–290.

———. (1989) *Family Violence in Cross-Cultural Perspective.*

———. (1993) "Ethnic Conflict and Refugees." *Refugees* 93 (August 1993): 4–9.

Levinson, David, and Martin J. Malone. (1980) *Toward Explaining Human Culture.*

Levy, Howard S. (1966) *Chinese Footbinding: The History of a Curious Erotic Custom.*

Lewis, Bernard. (1990) "The Roots of Muslim Rage." *Atlantic Monthly* September 1990: 47–60.

Lewis, Ioan M. (1955) *Peoples of the Horn of Africa.*

Lewis, Oscar. (1942) *The Effects of White Contact upon Blackfoot Culture.*

Lifton, Robert J., and Erik Markusen. (1990) *The Genocidal Mentality: Nazi Holocaust and Nuclear Threat.*

Lizarralde, Manuel. (1992) *Index and Map of the Contemporary South American Indigenous Peoples.* Unpublished manuscript, University of California at Berkeley.

Loftin, Colin K. (1971) *Warfare and Societal Complexity: A Cross-Cultural Study of Organized Fighting in Preindustrial Societies.*

McAllester, David P. (1954) *Enemy Way Music: A Study of Social and Esthetic Values as Seen in Navaho Music.*

McLean, Scilla, and Stella Efua Graham, eds. (1983) *Female Circumcision, Excision, and Infibulation: The Facts and Proposals for Change.*

Madsen, William, and Andre Guerrero. (1973) *Mexican-Americans of South Texas.*

Mair, Lucy P. (1934) *An African People in the Twentieth Century.*

Malinowski, Bronislaw. (1926) *Crime and Custom in Savage Society.*

Maloney, Clarence, ed. (1976) *The Evil Eye.*

Man, Edward H. (1932) *On the Aboriginal Inhabitants of the Andaman Islands.*

Markusen, Eric. (1989) "Genocide and Total War: A Preliminary Comparison." In *Genocide and the Modern Age,* edited by Isidor Wallimann and Michael N. Dobkowski, 97–123.

Marshall, Lorna J. (1961) "Sharing, Talking, and Giving." *Africa* 31: 231–249.

———. (1976) *The !Kung of Nyae Nyae.*

Marshall, Mac, ed. (1979) *Beliefs, Behaviors, and Alcoholic Beverages: A Cross-Cultural Survey.*

Masamura, Wilfred T. (1977) "Law and Violence: A Cross-Cultural Study." *Journal of Anthropological Research* 33: 388–399.

———. (1977) "Social Integration and Suicide: A Test of Durkheim's Theory." *Behavior Science Research* 12: 251–269.

Maxwell, Robert J., and Philip Silverman. (1989) "Gerontocide." In *The Contents of Culture: Constants and Variants: Studies in Honor of John M. Roberts,* edited by Ralph Bolton, 511–523.

Mead, Margaret. (1930) *Social Organization of Manua.*

———. (1934) *Kinship in the Admiralty Islands.* Anthropological Papers of the American Museum of Natural History, vol. 34, part 2, pp. 180–358.

Melko, Matthew. (1973) *52 Peaceful Societies.*

Merker, Meritz. (1910) *The Masai: Ethnographic Monograph of an East African Semite People.*

Messina, Anthony M., et al., eds. (1992) *Ethnic and Racial Minorities in Advanced Industrial Democracies.*

Messing, Simon D. (1957) *The Highland-Plateau Amhara of Ethiopia.* Ph.D. Dissertation, University of Pennsylvania.

Miller, Carol. (1975) "American Rom and the Ideology of Defilement." In *Gypsies, Tinkers and Other Travelers,* edited by Franham Rehfisch, 41–54.

Miller, Elmer. (1980) *Harmony and Dissonance in Argentine Toba Society.*

Miller, Judith. (1992) "The Islamic Wave." *New York Times Magazine* 31 May 1992: 22–26, 38, 40, 42.

Minority Rights Group. (1990) *World Directory of Minorities.*

Minturn, Leigh, and Jerry Stashak. (1982) "Infanticide as a Terminal Abortion Procedure." *Behavior Science Research* 17: 70–90.

Mitchell, William E. (1992) "Why Wape Men Don't Beat Their Wives: Constraints Toward Domestic Tranquility." In *Sanctions and Sanctuary: Cultural Perspectives on the Beating of Wives,* edited by Dorothy A. Counts, Judith K. Brown, and Jacquelyn C. Campbell, 89–98.

Montagu, Ashley, ed. (1978) *Learning Non-Aggression.*

Morgan, Lewis H. (1901) *League of the Ho-de-no-sau-nee or Iroquois.* Vol. 2. Edited and annotated by Herbert M. Lloyd.

Moss, David. (1979) "Bandits and Boundaries in Sardinia." *Man* 14: 477–496.

Munroe, Ruth H., and Robert L. Munroe. (1980) "Household Structure and Socialization Practices." *Journal of Social Psychology* 111: 293–294.

Munroe, Ruth H., Robert L. Munroe, and Beatrice B. Whiting. (1981) *Handbook of Cross-Cultural Human Development.*

Murdock, George P. (1949) *Social Structure.*

———. (1980) *Theories of Illness: A World Survey.*

Murdock, George P., et al. (1987) *Outline of Cultural Materials.* 5th edition.

Nachman, Steven R. (1986) "Discomforting Laughter: Schadenfreude among Melanesians." *Journal of Anthropological Research* 42: 53

Nagata, Judith A. (1969) *Continuity and Change among the Old Order Amish of Illinois.*

Nammour, Valerie W. (1975) *Drums and Guns: A Cross-Cultural Study of the Nature of War.*

Naroll, Raoul. (1969) "Cultural Determinants and the Concept of the Sick Society." In *Changing Perspectives in Mental Illness,* edited by Stanley C. Plog and Robert B. Edgerton, 128–155.

Naroll, Raoul, Gary L. Michik, and Frada Naroll. (1976) *Worldwide Theory Testing.*

Naroll, Raoul, Vern L. Bullough, and Frada Naroll. (1974) *Military Deterrence in History.*

Nash, June. (1967) "Death as a Way of Life: The Increasing Resort to Homicide in a Maya Indian Community." *American Anthropologist* 69: 455–470.

Newman, Katherine S. (1983) *Law and Economic Organization: A Comparative Study of Preindustrial Societies.*

Norbeck, Edward. (1954) *Takashima: A Japanese Fishing Community.*

O'Leary, Timothy J., and David Levinson, eds. (1990) *The Encyclopedia of World Cultures. Volume 1. North America.*

O'Malley, Pat. (1979) "Social Banditry, Modern Capitalism and the Traditional Peasantry: A Critique of Hobsbawm." *The Journal of Peasant Studies* 6: 489–501.

O'Nell, Carl W. (1986) "Primary and Secondary Effects of Violence Control among the Nonviolent Zapotec." *Anthropological Quarterly* 59: 184–190.

Opler, Morris E. (1946) "Reaction to Death among the Mescalero Apache." *Southwestern Journal of Anthropology* 2: 454–467.

Ortiz de Montellano, Bernard R. (1978) "Aztec Cannibalism: An Ecological Necessity?" *Science* 200: 611–617.

Otterbein, Keith F. (1968) "Cross-Cultural Studies of Armed Combat." *Buffalo Studies* 9: 91–109.

———. (1968) "Internal War: A Cross-Cultural Study." *American Anthropologist* 70: 277–289.

———. (1974) "The Anthropology of War." In *Handbook of Social and Cultural Anthropology,* edited by John J. Honigman, 923–958.

———. (1979) "A Cross-Cultural Study of Rape." *Aggressive Behavior* 5: 425–435.

———. (1986) *The Ultimate Coercive Sanction: A Cross-Cultural Study of Capital Punishment.*

———. (1989) *The Evolution of War.* 3rd edition.

Otterbein, Keith F., and Charlotte S. Otterbein. (1965) "An Eye for an Eye, a Tooth for a Tooth: A Cross-Cultural Study of Feuding." *American Anthropologist* 67: 1470–1482.

Overing, Joanna. (1989) "Styles of Manhood: An Amazonian Contrast in Tranquility and Violence." In *Societies at Peace: Anthropological Perspectives,* edited by Signe Howell and Roy Willis, 79–99.

Pagès, G. (1933) *A Hamitic Kingdom in the Center of Africa: In Ruanda on the Shores of Lake Kiva (Belgian Congo).*

Paine, Robert. (1967) "What Is Gossip About? An Alternative Hypothesis." *Man* 2: 278–285.

Palmer, Craig. (1989) "Is Rape a Cultural Universal? A Re-Examination of the Ethnographic Data." *Ethnology* 28: 1–16.

Palmer, Stuart. (1965) "Murder and Suicide in Forty Non-Literate Societies." *The Journal of Criminal Law, Criminology, and Police Science* 56: 320–324.

Parsons, Elsie W. C. (1945) *Peguche, Canton of Otavalo, Province of Imbabura: A Study of Andean Indians.*

Patterson, Orlando. (1982) *Slavery and Social Death.*

Paulme, Denise. (1940) *Social Organization of the Dogon.*

Pearson, Keith L. (1985) *Process of Political Development in a Navajo Community.*

Petersen L. R., G. R. Lee, and G. J. Ellis. (1982) "Social Structure, Socialization Values, and Disciplinary Techniques: A Cross-Cultural Analysis." *Journal of Marriage and the Family* 44: 131–142.

Phillips, Herbert P. (1966) *Thai Peasant Personality: The Patterning of Interpersonal Behavior in the Village of Bang Chan.*

Piker, Steven I. (1983) *An Examination of Character and Socialization in a Thai Peasant Community.*

Pitt-Rivers, Julian. (1993) "The Spanish Bull-Fight and Kindred Activities." *Anthropology Today* 9: 11–15.

Podolefsky, Aaron. (1984) "Contemporary Warfare in the New Guinea Highlands." *Ethnology* 23: 73–87.

Pospisil, Leopold. (1958) *Kapauku Papuans and Their Law.*

Price, Barbara J. (1978) "Demystification, Enriddlement, and Aztec Cannibalism: A Materialist Rejoinder to Harner." *American Ethnologist* 5: 98–115.

Pryor, Frederic L. (1977) *The Origins of the Economy.*

Radcliffe-Brown, A. R. (1922) *The Andaman Islanders: A Study in Social Anthropology.*

———. (1965) *Structure and Function in Primitive Society.*

Rasmussen, Knud. (1929) *Intellectual Culture of the Iglulik Eskimos.* Fifth Tule Expedition, Report 7(1).

Rattray, R. S. (1929) *Ashanti Law and Constitution.*

Reynolds, Henry. (1981) *The Other Side of the Frontier.*

Reynolds, Holly B. (1982) *To Keep the Tali Strong: Women's Rituals in Tamil Nadu, India.*

Richards, Audrey, and Adam Kuper. (1971) *Councils in Action.*

Rivera, Generoso F., and Robert T. McMillan. (1952) *The Rural Philippines.*

Robarchek, Clayton A. (1978) *Semai Nonviolence: A Systems Approach to Understanding.*

Roberts, John M. (1967) "Oaths, Autonomic Ordeals, and Power." In *Cross-Cultural Approaches,* edited by Clelland S. Ford, 169–195.

Rodman, Margaret, and Matthew Cooper, eds. (1983) *The Pacification of Melanesia.*

Rohner, Ronald P. (1975) *They Love Me, They Love Me Not.*

———. (1976) "Sex Differences in Aggression: Phylogenetic and Enculturation Perspectives." *Ethos* 4: 57–72.

———. (1986) *The Warmth Dimension.*

Rosaldo, Michelle Z. (1977) "Skulls and Causality." *Man* (new series) 12: 168–169.

Rosenblatt, Paul C., R. Patricia Walsh, and Douglas A. Jackson. (1976) *Grief and Mourning in Cross-Cultural Perspective.*

Rosnow, Ralph L., and Gary A. Fine. (1976) *Rumor and Gossip: The Social Psychology of Hearsay.*

Ross, Marc H. (1983) "Political Decision-Making and Conflict: Additional Cross-Cultural Codes." *Ethnology* 22: 169–192.

———. (1985) "Internal and External Violence and Conflict: Cross-Cultural Evidence and a New Analysis." *Journal of Conflict Resolution* 29:547–579.

———. (1986) "A Cross-Cultural Theory of Political Conflict and Violence." *Political Psychology* 7: 427–469.

Rozée-Koker, Patricia. (1987) "Cross-Cultural Codes on Seven Types of Rape." *Behavior Science Research* 21: 101–117.

Rummel, R. J. (1991) *China's Bloody Century: Genocide and Mass Murder since 1900.*

Rupesinghe, Kumar. (1987) "Theories of Conflict Resolution and Their Applicability to Protracted Ethnic Conflicts." *Bulletin of Peace Proposals* 18: 527–539.

Russell, Elbert W. (1972) "Factors of Human Aggression: A Cross- Cultural Factor Analysis of Characteristics Related to Warfare and Crime." *Behavior Science Notes* 7: 275–312.

———. (1973) "An Additional Warfare Element in Territorial Expansion." *Behavior Science Notes* 8: 201–207.

Ryan, Stephen. (1990) *Ethnic Conflict and International Relations.*

Sahlins, Marshall. (1979) "Cannibalism: An Exchange." *New York Review of Books* 26: 45–47.

Samarasinghe, S. W. R. de A., and Reed Coughlan, eds. (1991) *Economic Dimensions of Ethnic Conflict.*

Sanday, Peggy R. (1981) "The Socio-Cultural Context of Rape: A Cross-Cultural Study." *Journal of Social Issues* 37: 5–27.

———. (1986) *Divine Hunger: Cannibalism as a Cultural System.*

Schaden, Egon. (1962) *Fundamental Aspects of Guarani Culture.*

Schaefer, James M. (1973) *A Hologeistic Study of Family Structure and Sentiment, Supernatural Beliefs, and Drunkenness.*

Schlegel, Alice. (1972) *Male Dominance and Female Autonomy.*

Schwartz, Richard D., and James C. Miller. (1964) "Legal Evolution and Societal Complexity." *American Journal of Sociology* 70: 159–169.

Schweider, Elmer, and Dorothy Schweider. (1975) *A Peculiar People: Iowa's Old Order Amish.*

Secoy, Frank R. (1953) *Changing Military Patterns on the Great Plains.*

Segall, Marshall H., et al. (1990) *Human Behavior in Global Perspective.*

Seymour-Smith, Charlotte. (1986) *Dictionary of Anthropology.*

Shankman, Paul. (1969) "Le Rôti et le Bouilli: Lévi-Strauss' Theory of Cannibalism." *American Anthropologist* 71: 54–69.

Sheils, Dean. (1980) "A Comparative Study of Human Sacrifice." *Behavior Science Research* 15: 245–262.

———. (1986) "Cultural Evolution and Conflict Resolution." *Wisconsin Sociologist* 23: 4–14.

Shostak, Marjorie. (1981) *Nisa: The Life and Words of a !Kung Woman.*

Silberbauer, George B. (1981) *Hunter and Habitat in the Central Kalahari Desert.*

Sipes, Richard G. (1973) "War, Sports and Aggression: An Empirical Test of Two Rival Theories." American Anthropologist 75: 64–86.

Slack, Alison T. (1988) "Female Circumcision: A Critical Appraisal." *Human Rights Quarterly* 10: 437–486.

Smith, David H., and Linda Hackathorn. (1982) "Some Social and Psychological Factors Related to Suicide in Primitive Societies: A Cross-Cultural Comparative Study." *Suicide and Life-Threatening Behavior* 12: 195–211.

Smith, Robert. (1973) "Peace and Palaver: International Relations in Pre-Colonial West Africa." *Journal of African History* 14.

Sokolovsky, Jay, ed. (1990) *Culture, Aging, and Society.*

Soustelle, Jacques. (1962) *Daily Life of the Aztecs.*

Spiro, Melford. (1965) "Religious Systems as Culturally Constituted Defense Mechanism." In *Context and Meaning in Cultural Anthropology,* edited by Melford Spiro.

Stannard, David E. (1992) *American Holocaust: Columbus and the Conquest of the New World.*

Stavenhagen, Rodolfo. (1987) "Ethnic Conflict and Human Rights: Their Interrelationship." *Bulletin of Peace Proposals* 18: 507–514.

Steadman, Lyle B., and Charles F. Merbs. (1982) "Kuru and Cannibalism." *American Anthropologist* 84: 611–627.

Stephens, William, and Roy G. D'Andrade. (1962) "Kin-Avoidance." In *The Oedipus Complex: Cross-Cultural Evidence,* by William N. Stephens, 124–150.

Steward, Julian H., et al. (1956) *The People of Puerto Rico: A Study in Social Anthropology.*

Sutherland, Anne. (1975) *Gypsies: The Hidden Americans.*

Swanson, Guy E. (1968) *The Birth of the Gods.*

Sweet, Louise E. (1965) "Camel Raiding of North Arabian Bedouin: A Mechanism of Ecological Adaptation." *American Anthropologist* 67: 1132–1150.

Tanaka, Jiro. (1980) *The San Hunter-Gatherers of the Kalahari: A Study in Ecological Anthropology.*

Tatje, Terence A., and Francis L. K. Hsu. (1969) "Variations in Ancestor Worship and Their Relation to Kinship." *Southwestern Journal of Anthropology* 25: 153–172.

Tefft, Stanton K., and Douglas Reinhardt. (1974) "Warfare Regulation: A Cross-Cultural Test of Hypotheses among Tribal Peoples." *Behavior Science Research* 9: 151–172.

Teksbury, William J. (1967) "The Ordeal as a Vehicle for Divine Intervention in Medieval Europe." In *Law and Warfare: Studies in the Anthropology of Conflict,* edited by Paul Bohannan, 267–270.

Ternon, Yves. (1981) *The Armenians: History of a Genocide.*

Thompson, Virginia M. (1941) *Thailand: The New Siam.*

Thompson, Laura. (1940) *Fijian Frontier.*

Titiev, Mischa. (1974) "Social Singing among the Mapuche." In *Native South Americans: Ethnology of the Least Known Continent,* edited by Patricia J. Lyon, 208–220.

Tollefson, Kenneth D. (1976) *The Cultural Foundation of Political Revitalization among the Tlingit.*

Tschopik, Harry, Jr. (1951) *The Aymara of Chucuito, Peru. Vol. 1: Magic.* Anthropological Papers of the American Museum of Natural History 44: 133–308.

Turnbull, Colin M. (1965) *Wayward Servants: The Two Worlds of the African Pygmies.*

Turney-High, Harry H. (1949) *Primitive War: Its Practice and Concepts.*

Uchendu, Victor C. (1965) *The Igbo of Southeast Nigeria.*

Underhill, Ruth M. (1936) *Social Organization of the Papago Indians.* Columbia University Contributions to Anthropology 30: 1–280.

———. (1946) *Papago Indian Religion.*

Vaillant, Roger. (1959) *The Law.*

Vayda, Andrew P. (1976) *War in Ecological Perspective.*

Wagley, Charles. (1949) *The Social and Religious Life of a Guatemalan Village.*

Walliman, Isidor, and Michael N. Dobkowski, eds. (1987) *Genocide and the Modern Age.*

Watson, Robert J. (1973) "Investigation into Deindividuation Using a Cross-Cultural

Survey Technique." *Journal of Personality and Social Psychology* 25: 342–345.

Weatherford, Jack. (1991) *Native Roots: How the Indians Enriched America.*

Werblowsky, R. J. Zwi, and Geoffrey Wigoder, eds. (1965) *The Encyclopedia of the Jewish Religion.*

West, Stanley A., and June Macklin, eds. (1979) *The Chicano Experience.*

Westerman, Diedrich H. (1921) *The Kpelle: A Negro Tribe in Liberia.*

Westing, A. (1982) "Warfare as a Human Endeavor: The High Fatality Wars of the Twentieth Century." *Journal of Peace Research* 3: 261–264.

Whiting, Beatrice B. (1950) *Paiute Sorcery.*

———. (1965) "Sex Identity Conflict and Physical Violence: A Comparative Study." *American Anthropologist* 67: 123–140.

Whiting, John W. M. (1967) "Sorcery, Sin and the Superego: A Cross-Cultural Study of Some Mechanisms of Social Control." In *Cross-Cultural Approaches,* edited by Clelland S. Ford, 147–168.

Wiberg, H. (1981) "What Have We Learned about Peace." *Journal of Peace Research* 15: 110–149.

Wilbert, Johannes. (1963) "Los Sanema [The Sanema]." In *Indios de la Región Orinococ-Ventuari,* 11–20, 177–236.

Williams, Francis E. (1930) *Orokaiva Society.*

Wimberly, Howard. (1973) "Legal Evolution: One Further Step." *American Journal of Sociology* 79: 78–83.

Witkowski, Stanley R. (1972) "A Cross-Cultural Test of the Proximity Hypothesis." *Behavior Science Notes* 7: 243–263.

Wolf, Margery. (1972) *Women and the Family in Rural Taiwan.*

Worchel, Stephen. (1974) "Societal Restrictiveness and the Presence of Outlets for the Release of Aggression." *Journal of Cross-Cultural Psychology* 5: 109–123.

Wright, George O. (1954) "Projection and Displacement: A Cross-Cultural Study of Folk-Tale Aggression." *Journal of Abnormal and Social Psychology* 49: 523–528.

Young, Michael. (1971) *Fighting with Food: Leadership, Values and Social Control in a Massim Society.*

Illustration Credits

10	Reuters/Bettmann
20	North Wind Picture Archives
32	ITAR-TASS/Sovfoto
41	American Museum of Natural History, #1562
45	ITAR-TASS/Sovfoto
55	AP
67	American Museum of Natural History, #338431
74	American Museum of Natural History, #332913. Richard A. Gould, photographer.
77	American Museum of Natural History
90	The Bettmann Archive
115	ITAR-TASS/Sovfoto
117	ITAR-TASS/Sovfoto
119	AP
135	David Maybury-Lewis/Anthro-Photo
164	Stuart Smucker/Anthro-Photo
169	Hank Meals
173	The Bettmann Archive
179	ITAR-TASS/Sovfoto
194	Lila AbuLughod/Anthro-Photo

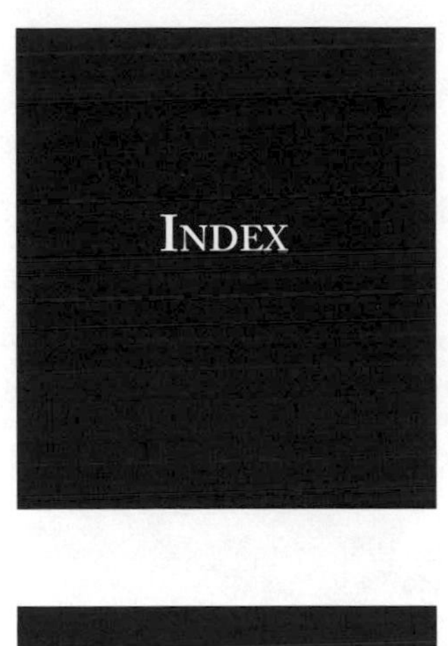

Index